DIARY

Angela McInnes Jan 1915 – Dec 1918

Angela Thirkell Dec 1918 – Jan 1919

The Angela Thirkell Society of North America

Publication's Title:

Diary
Angela McInnes Jan 1915-Dec 1918
Angela Thirkell Dec 1918-Jan 1919

Issued:
September 2022
Authorized Organization's Name and Address:
Angela Thirkell Society of North America

c/o Susan Scanlon
P. O. Box 1376
Southeastern, PA 19399-9002

Thirkellmembership@gmail.com
AngelaThirkellSociety.org
Cover production: Diane Smook
Editors: Susan Verell and Barbara Houlton
Guide and Introduction Copyright 2022
Angela Thirkell Society of North America

Contents

INTRODUCTION

"The Armistice was signed at 5 o'clock this morning and hostilities ceased on all fronts at 11 o'clock which was announced to London by maroons like an air raid. I tried to get into town after lunch but was turned back at Hyde Park Corner. Dined with Val." November 11, 1918

The diary transcription with its guide is a gift to all who love and appreciate Angela Thirkell's work or want to learn more about her and her times. It was contributed to the Angela Thirkell Society by her grandson, Simon McInnes. The contents are provided with his approval and that of the Thirkell Literary Estate. The transcription adheres to the original, and Angela did not write with the idea that anyone would read her words in the future.

Many Angela Thirkell readers know the details of 1915-1918 in her life (preceded by her 1911 marriage to James McInnes). Her eventual divorce and her marriage to George Thirkell are followed by her move to Australia due to her remarriage. When the diary began, she had two small children, Graham, age 3, and the baby, Colin. Her third baby, Mary, was born before the divorce was filed in 1917 and died in early 1918. During the war, Angela volunteered regularly and participated in fund-raising efforts to help the troops. James McInnes and George Thirkell both served in the military, as did many of Angela's friends.

The guide following the diary is provided to enrich the experience of reading Angela's original words. The research was done from various sources (see the bibliography) to provide context and information about the wide variety of people Angela interacted with each day, as well as to provide background on the places, music, and theater in her life. A detailed index is also

i

provided for the names that fill the pages. The reader may review the guide while reading the diary, may prefer to refer to the index and guide as needed, and may decide to use it for future research.

The guide is organized into categories because Angela's life often involved seeing groups of people connected by their interests, families, and relationships with Angela's family's multi-generational members. The alphabetized index provides additional referencing.

Footnotes are not frequently used because added information had multiple sources for a single item. Single-source data is footnoted. The Bibliography provides these sources.

"Oh, Angela!" one wanted to cry out across the more than a hundred years since she wrote these diaries, "Tell us more!" But she was mostly silent about her thoughts and feelings. Her diary from 1915 through 1918 was also a daily planner for the singing business and performance schedule of her husband, James McInnes. World War I was devastating to England when the diary began, but she only told of the daily events – an air raid, volunteer duties, or "Jim had duty 12-3."

Many strangers are referenced; the guide will help the reader feel they are familiar. Mysteries remain regarding some of Angela's friends and acquaintances, although the pleasure of reading about them is undiminished. So many people appear that the diary may have served the purpose of keeping track of them for her. If a first name was written, only Angela knew for sure whom she meant.

One benefit of reading the diary is the ability to feel a closer association with the woman who went on to write the Barsetshire novels. She had not yet published anything original, although she had a hand in some translations. As far as is known, she had not expressed a desire to become a writer: Barsetshire was still in the future when the year of her 25th birthday opened the diary.

Entries in the guide provide information about names, places, music, and people when they are known. They are intended to be consulted when reading Angela's account of her life from January 1, 1915, through January 1, 1919.

The diary contains some recognizable historical figures and some names that reappear in the Barsetshire books –Amy and Everard, Mrs Middleton. The diary and the book *Three Houses*[1] are the only autobiographical record of Angela's early life.

For everything the reader will learn about Angela McInnes and then Angela Thirkell, interesting questions remain. How could she leave London life for life in Australia? And why on earth did her father send her to cooking school? Was it to help her mother, so that she could be hired as a cook (which seems an ill-fated idea), or so that she would be prepared to live as a housewife?

Angela talked about food only a few times (one of those was a description of food poisoning), and her mention of places was often vague. Why did she choose George Thirkell and not Major Roos? Or did she have that choice? The diary reflects a way of life seen again in Barsetshire.

The purpose of the Angela Thirkell Society is to encourage the studies of Angela Thirkell's writing, in addition to honoring the memory of Angela Thirkell as a writer. The purpose of this publication is not only to provide the author's words about herself, but to encourage further study and analysis of her life and

---

[1] Thirkell, Angela, *Three Houses,* Wakefield, RI: Moyer Bell, 1998.

works. This rare glimpse was as close as one comes to an autobiography of Angela Thirkell in 1915-1918, ending January 1, 1919, when she ends it with "In all day." The diary provides tantalizing information in Angela's true voice.

JUST AS ANGELA WROTE

The diaries are transcribed exactly, although the editors used page headings for the years and months for clarity. The punctuation is her own, as she experiments with styles of punctuation and presentation.

Plain notebooks were used, about this book's size with handwritten dates and content. Although her words and punctuation were reproduced as in the original, these are sometimes subject to interpretation, written with a fountain pen filled with ink and becoming pale, until they darkened with the refilling of the pen from the bottle of blue ink. At best, the spelling of unknown names can be subject to argument; if possible, the spellings from other documents were used to validate them.

In addition, punctuation and some spellings were not identical to those used now, but one cannot imagine Angela being ungrammatical. If she wrote "clarionet," the reader will see that instead of clarinet. Standards change over the years, and Angela's writing reflected a time when punctuation was not as fixed as it is now. A girl was first taught by a governess and was not expected to continue her education later.

People were thrifty with paper, and Angela separated lists of names with periods or colons on the same line instead of using a separate line for each. People who arrived together at an event were usually joined by ampersands or separated by periods or semicolons between groups.

The only slightly different format from the original are titles of plays, music pieces, and lectures italicized for clarity. Angela often did not capitalize the words in song titles. Her use of quotation marks from the diary are reproduced.

Time was written 10.30 instead of 10:30, although sometimes 10. or 10 o'clock. Commas were seldom used and occasionally not where they would be used today. "Mr" and "Mrs" are not followed by periods. Acronyms are written with periods, for example, "W.H.S.D." as in the original.

Angela commented on grammar herself, and the reader will see that she used apostrophes to designate names ending in "s": the Hills', not common today. She describes this usage in *O, These Men, These Men!* and Mrs Lester delights in becoming Mrs Lester instead of her previous name of Mrs Harris, "getting away from those horrible apostrophes." [2]

Angela did not always use sentences, but her meanings were usually comprehensible, although sometimes vague about the locations. She wrote the diary for herself, and having a modern audience would have astonished her.

Over the years, she did not always use the same form. Sometimes the restaurants are named Trocadero or Demaria and sometimes Trocadero's or Demaria's.

Names create their own puzzle. Angela called relatives with titles by their first names, Di, not Lady Diana. There was a bewildering mix of Mr and Mrs, Lord and Lady. She seldom used titles, even when they were known. People who knew each other as children only used first names.

---

[2]Hall, Anne. *Angela Thirkell: A Writer's Life*. London, UK: Unicorn Publishing Group, 2021.

Text the editors added to the diary or in phrases from the diary are in italics and enclosed in brackets. The rest is a verbatim facsimile of what she wrote, including strikeouts. The pictures are not all from the 1915-1919 era.

ABBREVIATIONS AND ACRONYMS

Abbreviations occur throughout the diary, primarily names of volunteer groups supporting the World War I effort, although some are abbreviated.

Angela uses standard abbreviations as well as her own. P. G. refers to the home of Angela's parents in Pembroke Gardens. Other abbreviations had to do with World War I life in London. Angela volunteered during the war at W.H.S.D. This abbreviation refers to the War Hospital Supply Depot. Some volunteers worked at Burlington House, but other groups gathered in private homes to make supplies needed by the troops. The volunteer effort involved many people known by Angela and her family, and many people in England participated. Angela mentioned giving her time at W.H.S.D. over sixty times in the diary. The A.S.A.D. (with Depot, sometimes written out) represented the Anglo South American Depot. Located in Kensington in London, this was a reception area for service members from Chile and other South American countries who came to serve in World War I.

Abbreviation/Acronym List

4et	Quartet
A&N	Army and Navy Stores.
A.S.A.D.	Anglo South American Depot. A reception center, sometimes called A.S.A. Depot, for soldiers from Chile who were fighting in the

war. Dame Clarissa Reid organized it in Kensington.

A.S.C. "Jim wore his A.S.C. Uniform" Army Service Corps.

Ba Grandfather (Angela called her grandfather, Edward Burne-Jones, by the name Ba). In the diary, the one time she referenced Ba, she was referring to her father, James Mackail, as he was attending the funeral of Angela's daughter Mary.

B'Mouth Bournemouth

E.B.J. Edward Burne-Jones

L.S.Q. London String Quartet.

L.S.O. London Symphony Orchestra.

Ma'am/Maam Grandmother

P.C.S. P.C.S. appeared only once when Angela and Jim went to Greenwich for a P.C.S. The meaning remains unknown.

P. G. Pembroke Gardens.

R.A. Royal Academy.

R.AC. The Royal Automobile Club was founded in 1897. It was a private social and athletic club located on Pall Mall in London. Club members volunteered during the war. The large club contains restaurants, bedrooms, banqueting rooms, and sports facilities. Major Roos,

Winston Thirkell, and George Thirkell took Angela here to dine.

R.A.F.	The Royal Air Force was formed in April of 1918. It merged the Royal Flying Corps and the Royal Naval Air Service, controlled by the Air Ministry of the British government. Angela went to the R.A.F. office at the Cecil Hotel when she was trying to get support for her children from James McInnes.
R.F.C.	Royal Flying Corps
R'Dean	Rottingdean
S.E.S.	This appears only once. Unknown.
S. Ken.	South Kensington
W.H.S.D.	War Hospital Supply Depots. Volunteers met a private homes and Burlington House to make items needed for World War I.

DIARY 1915

[Editors' note: Angela Mackail is reportedly happily married to the singer James McInnes when the diary opens. Until their marriage in 1911, Angela had always lived with her parents. Jim was identified as a singer of unusual talent when he was a child. His music education in London had been funded by two well-to-do women in Scotland and London. When Angela and Jim met, he lived with his benefactor and lover, the wealthy composer Graham Peel. Upon their marriage, Graham moved back to his home in Bournemouth. Less than enthusiastic about the wedding, he remained cordial to the new family and became the godfather of Graham McInnes. The McInnes family lived near Angela's family (Mother and Papa and her siblings Denis and Clare).

Georgiana Burne-Jones, the widow of the painter Sir Edward Burne-Jones, lived at Rottingdean and is Angela's grandmother. Angela refers to her as Ma'am or Maam. There were two siblings in the family, Margaret (Angela's mother) and Philip (Uncle Phil), who is also close to Angela and Jim, who frequently dine with Uncle Phil. Other relatives are called Uncle Edward, etc., even though they are Margaret's relatives. John Mackail pays for the nurse, cook, and housemaid for the McInnes family, possibly from the estate of Sir Edward Burne-Jones, of which Mackail was an executor. The diary frequently reports dining out and attending country weekends at lavish estates first visited by the grandparents. The young couple was still enjoying their traditional lifestyle, but the effects of World War I started to be felt in Jim's singing career. Prominent families who lost their young sons in the war were not inclined toward the German leider of his repertoire, and his concerts were beginning to lose popularity in England as the diary begins.]

ANGELA MARGARET MCINNES

1915

January

Friday 1st

We went to Carlisle by the 10.0 and were met by a taxi which took us to Highhead Castle, 8 miles out whence the Eustace Hills had asked us. Mr and Mrs Merriman there: he is history professor at Harvard and she is a niece of ex. President Eliot.

Saturday 2nd

We walked morning and afternoon and played hide and seek after tea.

Sunday 3rd

We walked in the morning, except Mrs Hills and Mr Merriman who went to church. We all went to the chapel in the afternoon for the Intercession service. Jim sang before tea and the little girls recited.

Monday 4th

It rained nearly all day, but we got a little walk. Mr Hills and Mr Merriman shot. We played hide and seek after tea.

Tuesday 5th

Mr Hills, the Merrimans (who branched off at Rugby for Oxford), and we, all came up. I found a note from Mother to tell me that the cook had had a man in the house while I was away.

Wednesday 6th

Sacked the cook and house parlourmaid. Left Graham at P. G. for lunch and went to registry offices. Tea at P. G. and brought Graham home. Dined Netta.

Thursday 7th
Hilda Cook to tea. In with the babies.

Friday 8th
Jim, Graham, and I to lunch at P. G. Sylvia Jennell came to tea. The Gillicks dined with us and then also came Mother and Papa, Hay, Hilda and a sister-in-law, Mrs Limond, Mr Hills, Miss Anderson and a niece, Ers and Eric, Mrs Hopkins and Gerry, Mr & Mrs Llewellyn, Mr Beigel, Harold, Dicky C-S and his wife, Mary Fletcher, Mrs and Miss Lamb, Riette.

Saturday 9th
Mr Jennings to tea. We dined with the Passmores.

Sunday 10th
Jim to R'dean for the day. Colin took his first outing since December 10th. In with the babies.

Monday 11th
To tea with Aunt Marion and Sylvia. Jim on duty 12-3.

Tuesday 12th
Did sale-time shopping. Riette to tea.

Wednesday 13th
We lunched with Aunt Marion and Sylvia at the Albemarle Club. Jim on duty 12-3.

Thursday 14th
Shopped. In with the babies. Jim dined with Hay.

Friday 15th
The babies to lunch at P. G. Lyal to tea. Hay dined with us and afterward came Hilda Cook, with Mr and Mrs Ashbridge, Miss Christison, Mr and Miss Irvine, 3 Mackails, Marie Lewis, Frank Carter, George Reeves, Mr Shakespeare, Miss Anderson, Miss

Lasker, Miss Passmore, Miss Davey, Mr Hills, Mrs Craies, Sissie, Mr and Mrs Ranalow.

Saturday 16th
We lunched with Marie and she drove me home, calling at Portland Place. Jim on duty 12-3.

Sunday 17th
We lunched with Uncle Phil and then to tea with Mrs Fletcher. Jim on duty 12-3.

Monday 18th
Graham unwell and I had to have Dr Mills. Dined with the Millars.

Tuesday 19th
Graham in bed. We lunched with Lady Lewis. I dined with the Ritchies and Clare and Peggy acted. Jim was called up on duty for an air raid but was home again at 12.30.

Wednesday 20th
Graham still in bed. Mother came to see him. I went to bed early.

Thursday 21st
Shopped. Graham up after lunch. Barbara McLaren and Hilda Cook to tea. Jim out to S.E.S.

Friday 22nd
Lyal sent the car and Jim and I lunched at Kingston. It was the snowiest, coldest day for years; then fog and slush. I went to tea with Nina Hills. We tried to put people off on account of the weather, but there came Mr and Mrs Birch-Reynardson. Miss Paget with a Miss Brocklehurst, Ambrose, Mr Gleadowe, and Clare. I had to accompany.

Saturday 23rd

Very dark and slushy. I shopped. We lunched ~~with~~ at P. G. Henry there. Jim and Clare for a walk. Jim and I dined at Treviglio and then met Henry and went to the pit of *Potash and Perlmutter*.

Sunday 24th

Sewed and wrote. Jim for a walk with Clare. Graham to lunch at P. G. Dolly and Mr Gibson called. In with the babies.

Monday 25th

Called on Mrs Morris. Jim and I dined at Treviglio and went to the L.S.O. Mrs Morris drove us home.

Tuesday 26th

Went to see Mother in bed. Mr Reeves came to dinner and rehearsal.

Wednesday 27th

Jim sang for Mr Cook at Stratford.

Thursday 28th

I called on Mother. Jim dined with Henry.

Friday 29th

Shopped. To tea with Mrs Lamb. Mr Reeves dined here and we had Hilda Cook and Mrs Bob Cook, Nina and Mr Hills, Lady Whitelegge, Mrs Eric Maclagan, Miss Olivier, Miss Sparrow, Mrs Frank Dawes, Mr Bird, Mr Beigel, Zoe and Mr Manuel. Miss Stevenson, and Mrs Ronald Carter, Henry, Dorothy and Peter Warren, Papa.

Saturday 30th

My twenty-fifth birthday. We lunched with Uncle Phil, and then had tea at P. G. with a birthday cake. Papa, Jim and I went to Morley College to hear the *Magnificat* under Mr von Holst as Clare and Peggy Ritchie take part.

Sunday 31th

We lunched with the Morrises and came home to tea. Dined with Maria and the Aranyis and Suggia played afterwards.

Denis Mackail and Angela with their grandfather, Sir Edward Burne-Jones.

Monday, Feb. 1ˢᵗ

I called on Mrs Mounsey and to tea with Sibyl.

Tuesday 2ⁿᵈ

Jim and I went for a walk and it poured. Nina brought the little girls to tea. Dined with the Gillicks.

Wednesday 3ʳᵈ

Shopped.

Thursday 4ᵗʰ

Called on Mother. We lunched at S. Ken. with the MacLagans, and M Verhaeren and Miss Lawley. Shopped. In with babies.

Friday 5ᵗʰ

Took some music to the Cripples to be bound. Tea with Stella Speyer and looked in at P. G. Lyal came to dine and spend the night. To dinner also Hilda Cook, Miss and Mr Passmore and Miss Davey. Afterwards & Miss Edens, Miss Anderson. Uncle Phil and Mr Ward, Mrs Patullo, Mr Gleadowe. Clare and Papa. Miss Eady, Miss Winn, Major Swinburne and Margot, Dr Moon, Susan and Aurelian, Miss Broome.

Saturday 6ᵗʰ

Jim and I looked at the silly Rodins at S. Ken. Dined with the Hills'.

Sunday 7ᵗʰ

Sewed and wrote. In with the babies.

Monday 8ᵗʰ

Jim to stay with Miss Lushington and sing. I called on Mother. Mrs Morris drove me to and from the L.S.O. where there was a fine César Franck symphony.

Tuesday 9th
I and the babies to lunch at P. G. Mlle Rücker to tea.

Wednesday 10th
I took Nanny and the babies to R'dean by the 10.5. Ma'am was downstairs and fairly well. I walked out with them after lunch.

Thursday 11th
I came up by the 11.0. Called at P. G. for tea. Jim back from Kingsley and we dined with the Colliers.

Friday 12th
Very foggy. I went to a foul Belgian party given by the Doustes at the Grafton Galleries. Papa, Clare, Mr Walron, Mr Denroche-Smith and Hilda to dinner. Jim was singing for Belgians with Hay at 7.30 and came back rather tired to sing. There came Mr Marillier, Christabel and Rosalind: Nancy & Eva Batry Pain: Ers and Eric: Miss Dora Cook: Alice MacPherson and a Miss Easton: Mr and Mrs Birch-Reynardson & a Miss Stuot: Pamela and Oswald Horsley, Mrs Craig Sellar, Mr Stewart Gemmell and Marjorie: Mrs Craies and Sissie: Miss Reeves: Mrs Little & Dora: Mrs Morris and Arthur: Jekylls late.

Saturday 13th
Shopped. Called at P. G. Mr Reeves to tea.

Sunday 14th
We had tea and supper at P. G.

Monday 15th
Jim and I to Manchester by the 10. He had a rehearsal with Hay and orchestra for the Gentlemen's Concert. Then we walked about and saw the Art Gallery. The concert was successful and they liked Graham's *Requiem* and *In Youth is Pleasure*. We had supper with Hay afterwards.

Tuesday 16th

Came up with Hay on the breakfast train. I sewed all afternoon. Hay dined here and we went to the College to hear *Verdi's Requiem*. Also the Franck *Symphonic Variations*.

Wednesday 17th

Shopped. The new cook Sally Jackson came.

Thursday 18th

Sewed. Mr Reeves to high tea and we went to Chislehurst for Mr Allen's concert.

Friday 19th

Shopped. Wrote programmes. To dine came Nina and Mr Hills Mr Beigel and Mr Reeves. Afterwards Hilda & Mrs Warren: Mrs Lamb and a Miss?: Mrs Dawes & Miss Timothy and Mrs Robertson: Mrs Fletcher, Dorothy and Miss Richmond: Mr & Mrs Harry Fletcher: Henschel: Mr James and Lord Coke: Mother, Papa, Clare and Miss Radcliffe: Dolly and Mr Gibson: Miss Anderson: Miss Sparrow: Mr & Mrs Walter Ford Mrs & Miss Ritchie: Miss Reeves & Miss Howarth: Lily Severn & Miss Blagden.

Saturday 20st

Jim and I lunched with Mrs Warren and Hilda Cook at Dysart's Hotel and I went down to Woodford with them and Jim went to Bournemouth by the 4.50. We stopped to have some tea with Mrs Ashbridge and they came down to dinner. Mr and Mrs Bob Cook were the only others staying.

Sunday 21st

It was Mrs Cook's birthday and she had flowers. Mr Leonard Cook came. Hilda, I and Mr Ashbridge went for a walk in the forest. We read and slept till tea-time and played games a little afterwards.

Monday 22ⁿᵈ

I came up by the 2.41 with Mrs Bob Cook. Lyal came in to tea. Jim back about 5 o'clock. We dined with Netta.

Tuesday 23ʳᵈ

Shopped. Mr Shakespeare to dinner.

Wednesday 24ᵗʰ

I went to tea with Mrs Morse. Mr Reeves to dinner. I went round to P. G. where they had a little party.

Thursday 25ᵗʰ

I went to a little show of clothes got up by Mel to help poor dressmakers. To tea with Nina who wasn't well and is now in bed for three weeks. We dined chez Treviglio and went to the *Tales of Hoffman*.

Friday 26ᵗʰ

Mr Hills and Mr Reeves dined. Afterwards we had the Morrises, Lord and Lady Coke, Mr James. Miss Reeves. Mr von Holst. Mrs Gibson and Mrs Patullo.

Saturday 27ᵗʰ

Jim to Canterbury for the night to sing to soldiers for Mr Passmore. I went to a stupid party at the Professional Classes Relief thing. Graham and Colin came back from Rottingdean.

Sunday 28ᵗʰ

Jim back. In with the babies.

Monday March 1st

To see Mother after lunch. We dined at the Pall Mall Restaurant with Aunt Marion and Sylvia and Mrs la Tharque and went to *David Copperfield.*

Tuesday 2nd

Netta to tea. We dined with the MacPhersons.

Wednesday 3rd

I called on Nina who is still in bed.

Thursday 4th

I took Graham to lunch with Netta. I met Alice at Bradleys and saw hideous clothes on mannequins. Hilda to tea. In with babies. Mr von Holst dined here and talked business with Jim.

Friday 5th

Mrs Morris and Joyce Crawshay-Williams to tea. Miss Sparrow and Mr Reeves to dinner. Afterwards came Aunt Marion & Sylvia; Lady Lewis and Katie; Maisie & Mr Woolner; Mrs Debanham & Marjorie; Mrs Saffery; Mr W P Ker; Sir Frederick and Lady Macmillan; Mrs and Miss White; Stella & Mr Speyer; Clare; Hilda & Captain Cook; Mr & Mrs Binyon; Miss Anderson.

Saturday 6th

I had lunch at P. G. and then called on Mrs Dicky Cobden-Sanderson. Jim for a walk with Clare.

Sunday 7th

Jim rehearsed with Miss Twisleton. I went to P. G. to see Mrs Gaskell. In all afternoon.

Monday 8th

Very cold. Mrs Gibson to tea and Peggy McInnes and Sissie.

Tuesday 9th
I went to see Nina in bed. To tea with Mollie and saw Hugh and Uncle Edward. Denis came in after lunch.

Wednesday 10th
Mrs Gillick, Hilda, Mr & Mrs de Morgan and Madame Haas came to tea. We went to P. G. after dinner.

Thursday 11th
Marie took us in the motor to Englefield Green where Jim sang the *Winterreise* at Miss Weisse's school. Jim dined with Henry.

Friday 12th
Miss Spring Rice to tea. After dinner came Mrs Middleton and Peggy, Ers & Eric, Hilda and Miss Cook, Mr Spender, Mr Micholls, Miss Reeves, the Colvins, Mr Strachey and Jack.

Saturday 13th
We lunched with Uncle Phil. In with babies.

Sunday 14th
Denis to lunch. Jim to Dorking for the day to see Mr Cassels-Brown. In with babies.

Monday 15th
Called at P. G. I had tea with Aunt Marion and Sylvia.

Tuesday 16th
Jim out with Clare all day. Denis to lunch. Marjorie Sellar came to tea and Mrs Somerville called. I dined at P. G. and Jim picked me up.

Wednesday 17th
I went to tea with Nina. We dined with the Middletons.

Thursday 18th

In with the babies. After dinner, Pamela brought Sir Edward Grey to have some music, and Papa came in too. Jim sang the *Purcell Hymns*: *Star Vicino* and *Vittoria*: *Where'er you walk* and *si tra i ceppi*: *Silent Noon* and *Bredon*: *The People that walked* and *Nasce al bosco*: *Feldeinsamkeit; Honor and arms*.

Friday 19th

Mrs Ranalow brought Sheila to tea. After dinner we had Nina & Mr Hills: Hilda and Mrs Bob Cook: Ers & Eric: Marjorie Sellar and Mrs Drew: Miss Sparrow: Clare.

Saturday 20th

Jim and I to the Cooks to lunch and then for a walk with Hilda.

Sunday 21st

Finished writing and stamping circulars. Rehearsal of *Bavar. Cantata* at St Paul's Girls' School at 3. Tea at P. G. Denis to supper.

Monday 22nd

It rained most of the day. Miss Trollope to tea.

Tuesday 23rd

I called on Mrs John Somerville and enquired after Mrs Ronaldson. Hilda to tea. Jim to Bournemouth for one of Graham's concerts. Dined P. G.

Wednesday 24th

Mrs Denroche-Smith to tea.

Thursday 25th

Jim back from B'Mouth. I took the babies out. To a rehearsal of the *Matthew Passion* in the Abbey at 4 and then tea at Rumplemeyer's.

13

Friday 26th

We dined with the Hills and went to the *Passion* at the Abbey. Mrs Andrew Lang was there: she had never been inflicted on me before.

Saturday 27th

Jim and I lunched at the Albemarle Club to which he has just been elected. I went to P. G. and then to see Harold's pictures and to a party at the Whitelegges for Christopher and Miss Brice. Jim sang in the *Bavar. Cantata* at Morley College for Mr von Holst.

Sunday 28th

In with the babies.

Monday 29th

We dined with Netta. I had a bad cold, got in the Abbey.

Tuesday 30th

Shopped and packed. Hilda to tea. Jim dined at P. G.

Wednesday 31st

Jim and I and Nanny and the babies to Bournemouth by the 2 o'clock. I took the babies straight up to Marden Ash and found Mrs Peel and Graham waiting, while Jim came on with the luggage.

Thursday, April 1st
We walked in the morning and afternoon.

Friday 2nd
We walked about the town and on the cliffs.

Saturday 3rd
Graham and Jim and I to Lyndhurst where G. visited Mr Acton while we went on to Romsey and had tea and looked at the Abbey.

Sunday 4th
A brilliant day. We went up to tea with Mrs Dixon. Graham's sister.

Monday 5th
We went a short walk. Mr Graham came down in time for lunch and he walked with us afterwards. Mr and Mrs Dixon to dinner.

Tuesday 6th
Rained hard. We drove over to Poole Harbour before tea. Mr Graham went.

Wednesday 7th
We came up by the 2.0 which was very late & I took the babies back from Vauxhall. We dined at the Hyde Park Grill Room.

Thursday 8th
Jim and I walked to the club and had tea there. In with the babies.

Friday 9th
We dined at P. G.

Saturday 10th
Nanny went away for her holiday and Hilda came to stay and help me with the babies.

Sunday 11th
We left Graham at P. G. for lunch. Jim and I to supper at the Hopkins' to see Gerry.

Monday 12th - Friday 16th
Walked with babies morning and afternoon.

Saturday 17th
Took babies to tea with Mrs Ranalow.

Sunday 18th
Out with babies. Graham naughtier than usual.

Monday 19th
Out with babies. George Reeves to supper.

Tuesday 20th
Out with babies.

Wednesday 21st
Took Graham to P. G. to be photographed with Maam, Mother and me.

Thursday 22nd
Took Colin to see Maam. Hilda to Bow.

Friday 23rd
Graham to lunch at P. G. Henry came to lunch here and he and Jim helped us to clean the perambulator.

Saturday 24th
Colin had rather a frightening screaming fit after lunch and I gave him a warm bath and put him to bed and he was quite happy. Nanny got back at 6.30 and Jim and I dined at the Pall Mall Restaurant and went to *Oliver Twist*.

Sunday 25th

We went to Cholsey by the 10.20 and spent the day with the Hills'. It was very wet but we got flowers and brought back cowslips, cherry blossom, and daffodils.

Monday 26th

I left cards on babies all afternoon. Mr Reeves to supper.

Tuesday 27th

I lunched at P. G. Called on Lady Wood and to tea with Joan at the Colliers. Dined with the Gibsons.

Wednesday 28th

A lovely spring day. Hilda came to tea. We went round to P. G. after dinner.

Thursday 29th

We went to Oxford Street where I had some shopping to do and then to lunch with Graham who was up for a night at the Café Royal. Graham came in to tea and to see little Graham. Jim's recital at the Aeolian Hall went very well and we made nearly £100.

Friday, April 30th

We went to the Academy Private View and lunched at the club. Dined at P. G.

Saturday, May 1st

Lady Speyer took Jim and me to Clare's hospital at Balham. Where they played and sang to the soldiers. Dined with Cherry and Ambrose.

Sunday 2nd

Took the babies in afternoon.

Monday 3rd

Had my hair washed. Sewed. Henry to dinner.

Tuesday 4th

We had tea at P. G. and Jim sang to Maam.

Wednesday 5th

Our fourth wedding day. We lunched at the club. I had tea with Mrs Noble. We dined at P. G. and went to a dreadful concert of the ex. Magpies whom Mr Walter Ford is conducting.

Thursday 6th

In with babies. ~~Moth~~

Friday 7th

We went down to the Cooks for lunch. Tennis in afternoon.

Saturday 8th

Mrs Cook, Mrs Ashbridge, Hilda, Jim and I to a motor drive. Tennis in afternoon.

Sunday 9th

Hilda and I walked in the forest. We also went to tea with Mr and Mrs Bob Cook.

Monday 10th

We came up very early. Tea at P. G.

Tuesday 11th
Jim sang at a charity concert at the Duchess of Somerset's.

Wednesday 12th
We met Wig and Mrs Bob Cook by appointment in the Gardens and the little boys played together. I went to the Memorial Service for Major Costeker. Jim and I for a walk. Hilda to tea.

Thursday 13th
Very wet. I had lunch at P. G. In with babies.

Friday 14th
Jim and I lunched at the Club and went round the Academy. After tea at the club we went to a lecture of Colvin's as Past President of the English Association at the Burlington Gardens Theatre. It was on *Condensation and Suggestions in Poetry* and would have been more interesting if the quotations of which the lecture was almost entirely made up had been at all audible.

Saturday 15th
To the Cooks for the day.

Sunday 16th
To Oxford with Jim and we stayed at Balliol. For a walk with the Master before lunch. Jim to Dr Walker to rehearse and I had tea with the Murrays. Jim sang in the evening in hall including the *Ernste Gesänge*.

Monday 17th
Back early. Graham looked in after lunch. Jim went to dine with Sir Herbert Thompson.

[Editors' note: Dates misaligned May 18th through 23rd, as 23rd listed twice].

Tuesday 19th

Jim and Graham to lunch at the club. In with the babies. We dined with the Hornbys and Jim sang in a very mixed programme.

Wednesday 20th

We had a letter from Douglas which I took to Baileys Hotel to show Graham. To tea at P. G. Nina and Mrs Hills dined here.

Thursday 21st

I went to the Chelsea Flower Show with Nina. We lunched at the Albemarle Club with Cherry, Ambrose, and Mr Lucas.

Friday 22nd

Jim and I to Crowborough to the Beacon Hotel.

Saturday 23rd

We had a walk and lazed about.

[Editors' note: Information a part of Sunday below was not readable because of a spill on the page. Dates inconsistent following.]

Sunday

We motored over to Shere; had lunch at the Surrey Trust. Jim and I called on Mr Beaumont.

Monday 24th

A heavenly day. We motored over to Burwash to see the Kiplings.

Tuesday 25th

We went over to Buckhurst for lunch and found just Mrs Benson there. After lunch we walked in the garden and then went on to Old Buckhurst and spent the night with the Colefaxes.

Wednesday 26th

Back to town. I went to tea at Belgrave Square to settle about Charford which Mrs Guy is lending to us for a fortnight. Aunt Madeline there and Dorothy and then Leroy Ellis and Olivia and Gussie. We dined at P. G.

Thursday 27th

In with the babies. Hilda to tea.

Friday 28th

We lunched at the Club with Laurence. Then Alma-Tadema to talk about the Polish Victims Concert. Lucy to tea. Henry came to dinner.

Saturday 29th

To the Cooks for tennis. We dined with Mr St John Lucas at the Quadrant in Fleet Street and then went back to his rooms. Mr Dawkins of the British School in Athens was there.

Sunday 30th

In with the babies.

Monday 31st

I left cards on Rosalind (Toynbee) and Mrs Hornby and Mrs Playfair. We dined at Belgrave Square only Aunt Madeline and Dorothy and had a delicious evening of letters and photographs.

Tuesday, June 1st

Jim and I to a concert at Mrs Cazalet's in Grosvenor Square where he sang for Mrs Norman Salmond. Jim dined out.

Wednesday 2nd

I spent the afternoon with Clare at Balham and we went over to Merton Abbey and saw the indigo lotus and picked yellow irises by the Wandle. Hilda dined here.

Thursday 3rd

I went to P. G. directly after lunch to pick up Graham and take him to Dr Mills to ask about his ankles but Dr M. is quite pleased with them. Mother had a birthday tea party and I stayed with the babies till 5.30. Shaky to dinner.

Friday 4th

I took the babies to tea with Sissie. There were also the two younger Ritchie boys whom Graham bullied horribly. Con's little boy. Younger than Graham and a dull little girl Bridget Selincourt with a dull mother. Dined with Netta.

Saturday 5th

I had rather a fright in a bus accident and though not hurt or bruised felt shaken and ill. Jim put off going to Bournemouth till the 4.50 to be with me. Sheila and Patrick to tea with the children. Mrs Ranalow fetched them and Mother looked in.

Sunday 9th

I stayed in bed still feeling the shock. To lunch at P. G. and stayed on to tea. Jim back.

Monday 7th

To see Anna Pearce and her new baby.

Tuesday 8th
Graham went to spend the day with Lyal. Jim fetched us. Jim and I dined at the Hyde Park Grill Room and called later at P. G.

Wednesday 9th
I packed and took some books back to Belgrave Square. The babies and I to lunch at P. G. Took Graham to buy a hat.

Thursday 10th
I took Nanny and the babies down to Charford which the Guy Wyndhams have lent us. It was a lovely evening and I went on the river after tea. Jim at Petersfield.

Friday 11th
Jim was on a jury all today. Mrs Wyndham came over to tea.

Saturday 12th
Jim came down by the first train and was here to breakfast. We were in the garden all day.

Sunday 13th
Very warm. Mrs Peel, Graham and Daphne came to tea. Jim and I for a walk later.

Monday 14th
Jim to town by the 3.20. I drove into Bournemouth with him.

Tuesday 15th
I had a drive after lunch.

Wednesday 16th
Mrs Wyndham and Olivia to lunch.

Thursday, 17th
Drove round by Downton and Breamore.

Friday 18th

Drove to the edge of the New Forest through Downton. Mother, Papa and Hilda came.

Saturday 19th

Hilda and I went into Salisbury to meet Jim. We had lunch at the Red Lion and looked at the cathedral and St Martin's. Jim & Hilda played tennis.

Sunday 20th

We worked hard at flowers all morning. A big party to tea. From Clouds came Mr and Mrs Guy, Olivia, Aunt Madeline, Lady Wemyss and Mr Miles, the agent. From Newlands came and Lettice Fowler, Mrs Guy's grand-daughter. Colonel & Mrs Cornwallis-West, the Duchess of Westminster and Lady Ursula Grosvenor, and two ladies unknown.

Monday 21st

Mother and Papa to London early. After lunch walked into Downton and back by the fields. Jim and Hilda played tennis.

Tuesday 22nd

Jim and I walked up to Miz-Maze which is the labyrinth in Chartres, cut on the turf on the top of a hill. Jim to London after lunch.

Wednesday 23rd

I went over to Clouds for the day. Just Aunt Madeline, Mrs Guy, "Pamela Preston" and Mrs Fowler. Just as I was going Guy came back to London. I drove out from Salisbury.

Thursday 24th

I took Hilda to Miz-Maze. Mrs Guy came over to tea and Jim came back.

Friday 25th

Jim and Hilda played tennis. I practiced transposing some Polish songs.

Saturday 26th

Jim practiced a little. Mr Krauze, the Pole supplied by Laurence came down for the night. We walked up to Miz-Maze. Jim and Mr Krauze worked after dinner.

Saturday 27th

Jim worked with Mr Krauze. Graham came over from Bournemouth to tea and Hilda and Mr Krauze left. There was a bad thunderstorm.

Monday 28th

We all came up by the 12.27.

Tuesday 29th

I went to tea at Jim on duty 8-12.

Wednesday 30th

To tea at P. G. for Clare's birthday party. We stayed on to supper. Also Lady Jekyll, Antonia Somervell and Laurence Tadema. Jim went through his Polish songs after supper.

Thursday July 1st

To a Private View of Mr Collier's pictures at the Leicester Galleries. In with the babies. Hilda to supper. Jim duty 12-3-8-6.

Friday July 2nd

Had tea with Alice MacPherson. Dined with the Hills' and read *Eothen* aloud. In the morning/ works at Mel's slipper factory in Lexham Gardens.

Saturday, 3rd

We went down to stay with the Dixons, parents of a pupil near Milford. A heavenly day.

Sunday 4th

Another fine but heavy day. Mrs Ernest Richards came over to tea with her three children. We had a little drive before supper and came up to town late. Jim on duty 12-3.

[Editors' note: Monday should read the 5th. This deviation corrects itself on Saturday, July 10th, as the day before is not labeled. Although days are skipped later in the month, the days of the week are aligned.]

Monday 6th

I went to tea with Mrs Woods and met Mr Lucas in Pump Court on the way. The tea party was Mrs Cuthbert Baynes, Mr & Mrs Ezra Pound, Mr Pearsall Smith, a Mr _____. I came back to look in on Sibell Shuttleworth and found Nina there and Madeline staying with Sibell.

Tuesday 7th

Jim and I walked and fetched a collecting box from Laurence. I sold programs at her Polish Victim's Relief Fund Concert and Jim sang in Polish which the Poles loved.

Wednesday 8th
Very wet. We dined at P. G. and went on to a party at Mrs Reynolds'. Netta came to tea.

Thursday 9th
In with babies. Hills dined.

Friday
Jim and I went to see the Prehistoric Statues. We had lunch at the club and then back - I to Mel, Jim to lessons. We dined with the Poynters and Hugh came back to dinner in his A.S.C. clothes. He is stationed at Deptford. Jim sang a little.

Saturday 10th
We went to the Cooks for the day with Henry.

Sunday 11th
Colin had a temperature and I kept him in. Graham fell off a ladder at P. G. and sprained his ankle.

Monday 12th
Dr Mills to see Graham and said he was not really hurt. I went to tea with Mrs Morris. Dined Netta.

Tuesday 13th
Graham in bed still. Jim and I for a walk and to tea at P. G. Jim on duty 8-12.

Wednesday 14th
Mother took the babies down to R'dean. I called on Mrs Felix Warre (Marjorie Hamilton), Mrs Ralph Hawtrey (Hortense von Aranyi) Anna Pearce. All out, and then to tea with Dolly Gibson. Mrs Eddison called on me. Mr Alfred Hale to dinner.

Thursday 15th

We went to the Cooks for a fortnight, and I forgot to keep my diary.

Thursday 29th

We came up to London, dined with Uncle Phil and went to "*Quinneys*" for which ~~Uncle Phil had~~ Mr Ainley had given Jim seats for the second time.

Friday 30th

I went to the dentist at 10.30 and was turned away. Lunched at P G., back to dentist at 2.30. Back to tea and dinner at P. G. Jim on duty 8-12.

Saturday 31st

To Milford to stay with the Dixons.

Sunday, August 1st

A cloudy day, but lovely in the evening and we motored round the Devil's Jumps and back by Tilford and Elsted. A good deal of Music.

Monday 2nd

Jim, Rachel Dixon and I walked over to Sand Hills and saw Jessie. Music off and on.

Tuesday 3rd

Jim gave Rachel a lesson and we came up by the 1.45. Took Hilda to dine at Treviglio.

Wednesday 4th

Jim to the Cooks for the day. I went to tea at P. G. and Charlie Hallé came.

Thursday 5th

Children back from R'dean. I had Dr Brooke to overhaul Graham's legs and he said that a lump on one of them would go down eventually.

Friday 6th

We lunched with Eustace Hills on Fleet Street. Jim to the Cooks and Eustace out to the Stores to buy waterproof capes for him and Jim.

Saturday 7th

To the dentist. Jim and I walked to the Fletchers who were away. So we had tea in the gardens.

Sunday 8th

Jim and I walked in the gardens and had tea. Called at P. G.

Monday 9th

Went to the dentist. Jim picked me and we walked home.

Tuesday 10th
Dentist. Jim on duty 8-12.

Wednesday 11th
Called on Uncle Phil who had the Couderts with him. He asked Jim and me to lunch with them all at the Bath Club. After lunch Jim helped Mr Coudert with some War Office business. We dined with the Couderts at Pagani and went to a very stupid meeting about cotton being contraband.

Thursday 12th
We went to tea at Egerton Terrace, the babies having called there in the morning. Jim and Uncle Phil went for a walk and then he and Mrs Coudert and we two dined at the Rembrandt.

Friday 13th
The babies to lunch at P. G. Jim and I walked into town and had tea. Dined at P. G.

Saturday 14th
Jim to B'Mouth. Hilda came for the weekend. Nanny out.

Sunday 15th
In with babies.

Monday 16th
Hilda left. To dentist. Jim back and away the same evening to Stockwells. He started next day for a week's walk with Eustace Hills among the Berks and Wilts Downs.

Tuesday 17th
To Mel's slipper room all day.

Wednesday 18th
Took the children to Woodford.

August 19th to September 3rd

We were at Woodford. I came up on the 24th and met Jim at Paddington. We dined at Treviglio, and next morning went to Jim's sister's wedding to Dr Heatley Spencer. Then Jim came down with me to Woodford and we were there till Sept 3rd when we came up with the children and we all dined at P. G.

Lucy Broadwood at home with
James Campbell McInnes (early twentieth century)
(SHC ref 2185/LEB/9/113)

Saturday 4th

Tidied things. We went down to lunch with Aunt Marion and Sylvia who are temporarily in a little house at Sanderstead.

Sunday 5th

In with babies.

Monday 6th

We lunched with Uncle Phil at the Bath Club. Cousin Stan and Oliver came too.

Tuesday 7th

To Mel's slipper room. We walked into town and had tea at the club. Jim to Mr Bucy for dinner.

Wednesday 8th

Jim and I for a long bus ride to Kingston and back by Richmond and Barnes. We had tea at the club. Beastly Zeppelin raid near us.

Thursday 9th

In with babies. Slippers.

Friday 10th

To slipper room to cut out. Tea with Sibell Shuttleworth and fetched the children from Mrs Ranalow.

Saturday 11th

Jim and I to Woodford for the day.

Sunday 12th

Jim and I to tea with the Craies'. Cakes at P. G. and Mother and Papa came back to supper.

Monday 13th

W.H.S.D. Nanny out.

Tuesday 14th
Jim and I to Woodford for the day to help with a soldiers' tea-party.

Wednesday 15th
Children to lunch at P. G. Colin suddenly walked. I went to Sissie's where the children came for tea and then on to P. G. to see Maam. Peggy and Dr Spencer to dinner.

Thursday 16th
W.H.S.D. Bought Graham a winter coat.

Friday 17th
We gave Peggy and Dr Spencer lunch at the Albemarle. Mrs Drew & Miss Gladstone to tea.

Saturday 18th
We lunched at the club. Tea with Netta. Jim sang *Ich will den Kreuzstab* at Morley College.

Sunday 19th
In with babies. Took them to lunch at P. G.

Monday 20th
The children and I to tea with Mrs Drew. Henry to dinner. 3 D.

Tuesday 21st
Jim and I helped Sissie at a depot of the Serbian Relief Fund.

Wednesday 22nd
Jim and I to P. G. for tea. W.H.S.D. Jim on duty 3-6.

Tuesday 23rd
In with babies. Jim out. W.H.S.D.

Friday 24th

In all morning at housework. Lyal to tea. Jim 12-3.

Saturday 25th

We lunched with the Woods and walked back across Richmond Park. Dined at P. G. Children to tea with Zoe Manuel. ~~Jim 12-3.~~

Sunday 26th

Clare came to be shown some music. We called on Uncle Edward (away) and had tea at P. G. Supper with Lucy. Jim 12-3.

Monday 27th

Worked and served. W.H.S.D.

Tuesday 28th

Bought shoes for children W.H.S.D. Jim and I to lunch at the club. Bought shoes for myself. We went into the New Gallery Cinema.

Wednesday 29th

W.H.S.D. I went to Adila von Aranyi's wedding to Mr Fachiri.

Thursday 30th

We lunched with Uncle Phil. In with babies.

Friday, October 1ˢᵗ
W.H.S.D. Took Graham to tea with Miss Passmore.

Saturday 2ⁿᵈ
Shopped. We lunched with Uncle Phil. Graham came up from Bournemouth.

Sunday 3ʳᵈ
Jim Graham and I walked before lunch. I had the babies all afternoon. Graham gave us dinner at the Hyde Park Grill Room.

Monday 4ᵗʰ
Graham left us. Sewed and tidied. George Reeves after dinner.

Tuesday 5ᵗʰ
We spent the day at Chorley Wood with Aunt Marion and Sylvia.

Wednesday 6ᵗʰ
Stella came to tea. Hilda to supper.

Thursday 7ᵗʰ
I had tea with Mrs Morris. In with babies.

Friday 8ᵗʰ
We gave Uncle Phil lunch at the club. Hilda here.

Saturday 9ᵗʰ
Jim and Clare to R'dean walking. Mrs Hopkins gave me lunch at Drivers, 3 dozen oysters. The children came round to Mrs Hopkins for tea. I went on to P. G. and Jim and Clare came back and we had supper there. Very busy all this week with concert letters.

Sunday 10ᵗʰ
We called on the Fletchers. Jim on duty 8-12.

Monday 11th

Worked in house, Mr Reeves in evening.

Tuesday 12th

W.H.S.D. We dined with Netta. Jim sang.

Wednesday 13th

W. H. S. D. We lunched at the AlbemarleClub with Mr Reeves and then to the Aeolian Hall where Jim sang the *House of Life* and a Scotch Group at the first Classical Concert, Mr Borwick playing. We gave Hilda tea at the club afterwards and then dined at Treviglio. Another beastly raid.

Thursday 14th

W.H.S.D. To Mrs Morris working party. Mrs Wood and Lyal to tea. Mother to see the babies.

Friday 15th

In house. Mrs Noble to tea. After dinner we had a rehearsal of *Ich will den Kreuzstab* with Miss Ratcliff playing the violin and Mother, Papa, Clare, Mr and Mrs Hopkins came.

Saturday 16th

Jim in bed with a cold. I and the children to tea with Nina and her family.

Sunday 17th

Jim better. In with babies.

Monday 18th

W.H.S.D. Took Graham to tea with Peggy.

Tuesday 19th

W.H.S.D. in afternoon. Took Mr Reeves to Holly Lodge to try the piano.

Wednesday 20th

Jim and I went to a very dull lecture by Mr Nesbitt on Ballads. Agnes dined.

[Editors' note: No entry for October 21st.]

Friday 22nd

To W.H.S.D. I had lunch with Jim at the club. To tea with Gwynedd Meinertzhagen. Jim sang *Ich will den Kreuzstab* in my translation with Miss Ratcliff to do the obbligato. Audience Mother, Clare, Mrs Ritchie & Peggy, Nina and Eustace Hills, Mr & Mrs Jack Talbot, Lady Lewis, Frank Carter, Mrs Fletcher, Dorothy and her newly engaged Bobby Longman, and Hilda who spent the night. Also he sang

La Procession	César Franck
Le Joli tambour	Graham Peel
D'une prison	Reynaldo Hahn

Saturday 23rd

~~Jim and~~ I saw the children off to R'dean by the 11.0. We lunched at the club.

[Editors' note: No entry for October 24th.]

Monday 25th

W.H.S.D.

Tuesday 26th

W.H.S.D. We gave Mr Cassels-Brown lunch at the club. I had tea with Anna Pearce in her new house.

Wednesday 27th

Jim to Knutsford to sing. W.H.S.D. I was back to lunch at P. G. and spent the day in bed.

Thursday 28th

I didn't get up until after lunch when I went to Kensington to shop. Jim back from singing at Nuneaton after dinner and fetched me home.

Friday 29th

Jim and I to Hindhead by the 3.45.

Saturday 30th

We walked to Thursley Pride of-the-Valley round to Hindhead again. A heavenly morning. After lunch we went beyond Grayshott and back.

Saturday 31st

Raining nearly all day. but we walked morning and afternoon.

Monday Nov. 1st
Rained again. But we walked.

Tuesday, 2nd
We walked over to Sandhills and had lunch with Jessie and Graham Robertson.

Wednesday 3rd
Came home. Lunched at the club. I went to the Valley to tea with Sibell at Princes Grill. A little christening party for her baby. We walked with Margaret Costeker.

Thursday 4th
W.H.S.D. To Mrs Morris' working party.

Friday 5th
Mr Reeves to lunch. We had tea with Uncle Phil. We had a little music after dinner. The Hawtreys came with Jelly, and Gerry Hopkins and Hilda who stopped the night.

Saturday 6th
W.H.S.D. We had tea at P. G. Hay came in after dinner to rehearse.

Sunday 7th
We lunched at the club. Jim sang at the Palladium.

Monday 8th
W.H.S.D. We lunched at the club. Uncle Phil met us there and we all went to the International. We had tea with Uncle Phil and then dinner.

Tuesday 9th
Sewed all morning. To tea with the Blagdens. We dined with the Hopkins'.

Wednesday 10th
W.H.S.D. Shopped. Tea at P. G.

Thursday 11th
To R'dean by the 11. where we found Maam very well and Graham and Colin in excellent spirits. We stayed to tea and back by the 9.45.

Friday, 12th
Very wet. I wrote Shelley House about a concert. Hilda to dine and sleep and the Gillicks came in.

Saturday 13th
W.H.S.D. We went to Eton by the 3.45. I had tea with Dolly Binton while Jim rehearsed. The concert was at 6. Jim and Irene Schanter soloists. We had dinner with the Bintons and came up with a Mr Baddeley by the 9.45.

Sunday 14th
Jim sang for the Craies'. Tea at P. G.

Monday 15th
To Shelley House to see chairs being brought in. Riette came here at ~ ¼ to 4 and we all went to tea with the Hornbys and Jim sang a little program and lots of people came. We looked in on Uncle Phil and dined at the Hyde Park Grill Room.

Tuesday 16th
W.H.S.D. We walked to the club and had tea. Dined with the Hills.

Wednesday 17th
To Debenham's for a fitting.

Thursday 18th

W.H.S.D. We went to Chiselhurst and dined with Mr Allen. Jim and Mr Borwick sang & played at the concert.

Friday 19th

W.H.S.D. We lunched at the club. Jim sang at the Hyde Park Hotel for Mrs Clare Brookes. We went to Mrs Dawes after dinner, and heard music.

Saturday 20th

W.H.S.D. We lunched with Uncle Phil and Mrs Claude Beddington ~~and~~ at the Wellington Club. I heard Clara Butt at the Albert Hall from the Duchess of Wellington's box. We went to Greenwich for a P.C.S.

Sunday 21st

Jim sang for the Craies' again. Supper at P. G.

Monday 22nd

W.H.S.D. Graham came up and we dined with him at the Hyde Park Grill Room.

Tuesday 23rd

W.H.S.D. I met Jim and Graham at the club and we had lunch and went to *Romance* for which Mr Nares had given Jim a box. We dined at the Café Royal.

Wednesday 24th

W.H.S.D. Jim to Canterbury to sing to Eric's soldiers (and a hasty concert it was). I went to P. G. and Mother, Clare and I joined Papa at Treviglio where we dined and went to *More* at the Ambassadors. Slept at P. G.

Thursday 25th

I stayed at P. G. till about 10. Had my hair washed. Jim back. I called on Mrs Page.

Friday 26th

W.H.S.D. I lunched with Jim at the club. Called to enquire after Mel who was ill, and Mother came in from Lady Richmond's funeral and we walked back together.

Saturday 27th

[Editors' note: No entry.]

Sunday 28th

We gave Uncle Phil lunch at the Albemarle Club. He and Jim went to a lecture on Russian music and I came back to P. G.

Monday 29th

To Holly Lodge to arrange chairs etc. We had a crowded audience in the afternoon. Uncle Phil took us to dinner at the Hyde Park Grill Room.

Tuesday 30th

W.H.S.D. To Debenham for a fitting. Called to see Buff and found him alone with Mrs Stillman. She and I came back together.

Wednesday, December 1st

Jim and I to Bath for his and Mr Reeves' recital. It was very empty and a horrid day.

Thursday 2nd

W.H.S.D. We lunched at the club. Jim wants me to try some lessons with Beigel so went for my first but didn't enjoy it. To P. G. after dinner when Jim sang the *Kreuzstab* with Miss Ratcliff's quartet.

Friday 3rd

We had lunch with Uncle Phil and Mother at the Gobelins and all went to *L'Enfant Prodigue*. Jim had to go and sing at a beastly matinee. Uncle Phil gave Mother and me tea at the Bath Club. Jim and I dined with the Whitelegges.

Saturday 4th

Ran about servant hunting. Tea with the Craies' and on to P. G.

Sunday 5th

To visit Mrs Guy Wyndham in her nursing home. Lunched at club with Jim, and to P. G. for tea.

Monday 6th

Very wet. Miss Symonds and Miss Wingates to tea.

Tuesday 7th

To Sargent at 11.0 to sit for a charcoal drawing. Jim fetched me and we lunched at the club then to a stupid charity concert at Southridge. Princess Louise was very nice to us both.

Wednesday 8th

To Bristol. The Warrens sent their car to meet us. I went to rehearsal with Jim. There was a very good performance of

R.V.W.'s *Carols* under Mr Arnold Barter — also *Elijah Part II*. Spent the night with the Warrens.

Thursday 9th
Up by the 12. The babies were home. Both pink and well.

Friday 10th
To Beigel at 12.0. Lunched with Jim at the club. Hilda to dine and sleep. Mr James called. Miss Smith to dine and afterwards she and Mr O'Connor-Morris played the César Franck violin sonata and some Bach. Audience were Nina and Eustace, Mrs Drew & Mrs Wickham, Mrs Lamb & Winifred, Mrs O'Connor-Morris Mr Jenkins, Mrs Fowler, Mrs Fisher-Rowe.

Sunday 11th
To sit to ~~Collier~~ Sargent. Mrs Newmarch to dinner.

Sunday 12th
In with children. Mr Denroche-Smith to tea.

Monday 13th
To 34 Queen Anne's Gate to arrange chairs etc. We lunched at the club. Home to dress and pick up Riette. We had another concert at 5 and heaps of people. Mr Reeves to dinner.

Tuesday 14th
I lunched with Sibyl and found Ethel Dilke, Ella Johns, Mrs Hornby, a Miss Carter and Mrs Adrian Pollock.

Wednesday 15th
To rehearsal for Classical Concert in morning. We gave Mother lunch at the club. The concert was at 6 o'clock and Jim sang very well *Ich will den Kreuzstab* in my translation. We had some supper at the Café Royal and called at P. G.

Thursday 16th
With Jim to Hayes where he made some gramophone records. In with babies. Hilda to supper.

[Editors' note: No entry for December 17th].

Friday 18th
To Beigel at 11.0. I had tea with Barbara McLaren. ~~Hilda stopped to supper.~~

Saturday 18th
 We had dinner with Uncle Phil and Mr Haselden at the Hyde Park Grill Room. Back to Uncle Phil afterwards and Mr Benson came in.

Sunday 19th
We lunched at the club with Uncle Phil, Aunt Marion, and Sylvia. Called on Mudie-Cookes and then to tea with Sissie who is to have an operation for appendicitis on Tuesday. Dined Treviglio.

Monday 20th
I called on Margaret Costeker and Miss Douglas

Tuesday 21st
[Editors' note: No entry.]

Wednesday 22nd
Jim and I lunched at the club. Uncle Phil had a little Christmas tree for the babies.

Thursday 23rd
To Beigel at 12.30. We gave Papa lunch at Treviglio. Walked back with him to office. We dined at the Trocadero.

Christmas Eve

Nanny went home. I took Graham to P. G. and left him there. In with Colin.

Christmas Day

Took Colin to lunch and tea at P. G.

Boxing day

With Colin all day.

Monday 27th

Took Colin to tea at Mrs Hopkins'. Graham met us there and we had a Christmas tree.

Tuesday 28th

With Colin all day.

Wednesday 29th

Nanny home. I went to Wimbledon to get some Swedish songs translated by a friend of the Craies'. We dined at the Trocadero.

Thursday 30th

I went to tea with Dolly Gibson. We went to one of the Hawtreys At Homes after dinner.

Friday 31st

To Beigel. I did a good deal of shopping after lunch.

*January
1916*

DIARY 1916

[Editors' note: The beginning of the year 1916 was the lull before Angela's life took a stormier turn. Angela does not refer to the turbulency in her life. She continued to stay busy with her home life and childcare as well as with her deep involvement in Jim's career.

The toll of World War I became greater. The British had joined the war on August 4, 2014. Patriotism set the tone for the country. Unlike today, services and medical treatment for soldiers were provided by volunteers, not the government, and the diary demonstrates a constant schedule of these volunteer activities, along with benefit concerts and other ways of supporting the war effort from home.

The diary stops from mid-June until mid-September in 1916. During this period, Angela learns that she is pregnant with her third child, and Jim's drinking begins to affect their marriage, although she says in her summary of the skipped entries that she and Jim were very happy in Edinburgh. The biography tells a different story of this trip to Edinburgh, but Angela recorded the one she wanted to remember, or at least the one she wanted to document. There are shorter entries to record activities as Angela and Jim dealt with their own and their country's changing circumstances.]

January
1916

Saturday 1st

Jim and I went to the submarine motion pictures at the Philharmonic Hall. The wind rose to a violent gale in the afternoon, and as we came in, it slammed the gate behind us and broke out one of the upper panels made of cast iron.

Sunday 2nd

To South Place. Jim sang *Ich will den Kreuzstab*. Back to tea at P. G.

Monday 3rd

We went with the O'Connor-Morris after dinner. Jim sang, and Miss Smith, Mrs Salmond, and our host played.

Tuesday 4th

I took my translations to Mrs Newmarch at her club. Mrs Wood and Lyal to tea. We dined with the Perrins.

Wednesday 5th

To inspect a gymnasium class for Graham. Took Graham to tea with Mrs Eddison. Dined with Jim at the club.

Thursday 6th

To Beigel. In with children.

Friday 7th

Children to P. G. Jim and I to Bournemouth.

Saturday 8th

Jim and I for drive in the car. After lunch, all went to Graham's second Winter Gardens concert, where Mr Borwick played, and Jim sang. Mr Graham came down and Mrs Bob Peel.

Sunday 9th

Mr Graham, Jim, and I for a drive. Jim and Graham had a walk. We had some gramophone after dinner, and Mrs Bob played.

Monday 10th

Jim and I up by the 9.52. Children came home. Jim to dine with Douglas.

Tuesday 11th

The Stillmans called to see the Sargent portrait. Faraday sent to put the proper light over it. I and the children went to a little tea-party at Barbara McLaren's.

Wednesday 12th

I took Graham to his first gymnasium class at the place where old MacPherson's used to be. To tea with the Middletons to say goodbye to Peggy, who is going to Grantham to nurse. Lucy to dinner.

Thursday 13th

Netta came to tea. After dinner Pamela and Sir Edward Grey came, and Jim sang. *I long to sing The Siege of Troy! Who is Sylvia? Wandrers Nachtlied.* Then *wherever you walk, Largo* (twice). *Ruddier than the cherry.* Then *The People that Walked. Why do the nations?* Then the *Purcell Hymns.* They stayed till nearly 12 o'clock talking.

Friday 14th

To Beigel. Lunch with Uncle Phil. Tea at P. G.

Saturday 15th

Jim and I dined with Margaret Costeker. Graham's gym

Sunday 16th

Jim in bed all day. Gerry came in after tea.

Monday 17th

Jim and I walked in the rain.

Tuesday 18th

We dined with Netta.

Wednesday 19th

Peggy and Dr Spencer called in the morning. I took Graham to gym. Hilda to supper.

Thursday 20th

To Beigel. Jim lunched with Lucy. We both went to tea with Pamela, and David sang to us. Dr Spencer came to dinner.

Friday 21st

Jim to Worthing for a concert.

Saturday 22nd

Graham to gym. Jim came to fetch us. We dined with the Whites.

Sunday 23rd

Jim's 42nd birthday. He sang at the People's Palace. I was in with babies.

Monday 24th

Mrs Ranalow and Sheila to tea.

Tuesday 25th

Took Graham to have his hair cut.

Wednesday 26th

To the Hornby's to arrange the room. I watched a concert there at 5 o'clock.

Thursday 27th

Nanny to the dentist, but he hadn't got a doctor to give her gas. So she went to another dentist and had teeth out.

Friday 28th

Nanny in bed all day. We dined at Demaria's with Mother and Papa.

Saturday 29th

To Wilmslow with Jim. Mrs Mellor sent to meet us and brought us to Knutsford. We went for a walk with Mr Mellor. Jim sang at one of the Bowdon chamber concerts. Mr Mangeot staying in the house.

Sunday 30th

My 26th birthday – not much remembered. We went over with a Mrs Hamilton to see the John Peels, in their house which they have turned into a hospital. Mr and Mrs Moseley to supper.

Monday 31st

Mrs Mellor and I to lunch with the Bob Peels who were having a shooting party at their new house, Gawsworth. Mr and Mrs Conybeare to dinner and some other people.

Tuesday February 1st
After lunch we went over to Mrs Moseley. She had a dinner party including Mr Hayward, once sub critic of *The Times* under Fuller Maitland, now at the Manchester Art Gallery.

Wednesday 2nd
Jim woke up with a throat. However, he managed to get through the Gentleman's Concert at Manchester.

Thursday 3rd
We went to the Elwes. Jim's cold getting worse.

Friday 4th
Jim in bed all day. Lord Grenfell took Lady Winefride and me to lunch with a Mr and Mrs Carlile. One of the Elwes boys came down to tea.

Saturday 5th
We walked in the garden and came up after lunch. I put Jim straight to bed.

Sunday 6th
Jim in bed all day. I am with children.

Monday 7th
Jim up but not well.

Tuesday 8th
We lunched at the club, and Jim rehearsed with the London String Quartet. Dined at Hyde Park.

Wednesday 9th
Jim and I to Aeolian Hall, where he rehearsed again. We met Peggy and took her to lunch at Treviglio. I met Graham at gym.

L.S.Q. concert in the evening. Jim did very well, considering his cold.

Thursday 10th
Jim's cold worse. In with children.

Friday 11th
Jim in bed all day. I had a lesson with Beigel. Sissie and Mrs Craies to tea.

Saturday 12th
Jim in bed. I lunched at P. G. and went with Mother and Papa to the most delicious puppet show at the Powells in Hampstead. Back to find Jim with violent neuralgia, and we had Dr Baldock.

Sunday 13th
Jim up. We lunched with Denis at the Berkeley and walked home together. Supper with Douglas at the Hyde Park.

Monday 14th
Jim gave lessons all day, but not well. Nina and Eustace came to dinner.

Tuesday 15th
I called on Miss Cory and Lady Slade. To tea with Sissie. Mrs Reeves after supper.

Wednesday 16th
Jim to Kentsford. I took Graham to gym and then on to a L.S.Q. concert. Back with Mother to tea and supper at P. G.

Thursday 17th
In with babies. Naomi came back as temporary.

Friday 18th

Graham's 4th birthday. To Beigel. To tea came Mrs Ranalow with Sheila and Patrick, Netta with Rhona, Peggie and Mother. Mrs Craies and Sissie looked in before tea. Dined with Mother and Papa at Demaria's.

Saturday 19th

Jim back. Children to P. G. Jim and I to Hindhead.

Sunday 20th

We walked about.

Monday 21st

Walked.

Tuesday 22nd

Walked to Sandhills and had lunch with Jessie and Graham Robertson. They walked partway back with us, and it was beginning to snow.

Wednesday 23rd

Snowing hard. We went out for a little.

Thursday 24th

Snowing and beastly.

Friday 25th

Came up by the 10.9. Colin had a cold, so Mother kept the children. I went to see them for tea.

Saturday 26th

Children home in a cab. Douglas to dinner.

Sunday 27th

In with children.

Monday 28th

Snow and horrible. We dined with Mr Beigel.

Leap Day

Jim and I lunch at the club. I had tea with Mrs Fox. We dined with the Hills.

Sir Philip Burne-Jones.

March 1ˢᵗ

Took Graham to gym and then to tea with Mrs Playfair where Colin met us. Diner with Uncle Phil.

Thursday 2ⁿᵈ

In with children.

Friday 3ʳᵈ

To Beigel. Mother to lunch, and we went to Henry James's memorial service in Chelsea Church. Sissie, Clare, and Mr Denroche-Smith to dinner.

Saturday 4ᵗʰ

Lunched with the Perrins. Met Jim, and we walked. Dined at Treviglio's and to the Scala war pictures.

Sunday 5ᵗʰ

We lunched with the Morrises. Called on Mrs Rawlinson and Mrs Morse and P. G.

Monday 6ᵗʰ

Jim to Kettering to sing. Stella Beech's little boy to tea.

Tuesday 7ᵗʰ

Jim and I to Apsley House, where the Duchess of Wellington was giving a party for wounded soldiers. Jim sang, and then we had tea in the sitting room. Jim and I with the Duke and Duchess, Queen Alexandra, Princess Victoria, and the other performers separately.

Wednesday 8ᵗʰ

For a walk with Jim. Mrs Morse and Mrs Warwick-Evans to tea. Hilda for the night.

Thursday 9th

We took Margaret Costeker to lunch at the club, and afterwards to see the Pennell drawings.

Friday 10th

To Beigel. Mrs Morris, Aunt Cissie, and Di to tea. We dined at Demaria with Mother and Papa.

Saturday 11th

Jim and I lunch at club. Douglas to supper.

Sunday 12th

In with children.

Monday 13th

W.H.S.D. We lunched with the Lewises, who sent us home in the car. Talked to Madame Mangeot. Tea with Margaret and then Sibyl.

Tuesday 14th

W.H.S.D. For a walk with Jim.

Wednesday 15th

W.H.S.D. Took Graham out as Colin had a cold. Papa to dinner.

Thursday 16th

Colin in bed all day.

Friday 17th

To Beigel. Graham to P. G. Colin got up after lunch. Mrs Mazails and Mrs Hopkins to tea. Dined with Lord and Lady Coke.

Saturday 18th
W.H.S.D. Lunched with the Leafs. Nanny home for the weekend.

Sunday 19th
Jim to Woods for the day. I took children to P. G.

Monday 20th
Took children to P. G. I rushed out to lunch with Stella. Nanny back after tea. O'Connor-Morris' and Alice to tea. Dined with Margaret.

Tuesday 21st
W.H.S.D. In bed till evening when we dined with Netta.

Wednesday 22nd
Mrs Page to tea. Duchess of Wellington, Aunt Madeline, and Mother.

Thursday 23rd
Sewed. We gave Mrs Cook and Hilda lunch at the club. I went to see Nina, who has been ill.

Friday 24th
To Beigel. I lunched with Jim at the club. Lady Lewis and Katie to tea. To dinner Eustace Hills, Ray Lankester, Mrs Newmarch and Riette Massé.

Saturday 25th
W.H.S.D. To see pictures at the Speeds and to a puppet show at the Powells. We dined at P. G.

Sunday 26th
Jim sang at Toynbee Hall. We gave Hilda tea at the club and then to South Place, where he did the *Senons Songs*.

Monday 27th

W.H.S.D. Stella to tea.

Tuesday 28th

W.H.S.D. I went to tea with Clare. An appalling blizzard blew a big plane tree all across our garden.

Wednesday 29th

W.H.S.D. I took the children to tea at Mrs Henry Gladstone's, then on to call on Nellie Romily, and then to tea with Aunt Madeline, where Jim met me. Picked up children and took them home.

Thursday 30th

W.H.S.D. In with children.

Friday 31st

To Beigel. Lunch with Jim at the club. He sang at the Star and Garter concert. Miss Douglas to tea. We dined with Hilda at Treviglio.

April

Saturday 1st
Took Graham to Uncle Edward's and on to the Craies'.

Sunday 2nd
In with children.

Monday 3rd
W.H.S.D. Children to P. G. I went there to tea and dined with Douglas.

Tuesday 4th
W.H.S.D. We gave Douglas lunch at the club. To P. G. Dined with the Hills.

Wednesday 5th
Sent a servant away and cleaned the house. Lunch with Netta. Cleaned again. We gave the Colliers and the Hopkins dinner at the B & K Electric place. Back here for coffee and talk.

Thursday 6th
We lunched with Mrs Cazalet. Mrs Ford and Katie Scott came from Wickford, sent by Pamela. Graham came for the night. I took him round to P. G. to see the children.

Friday 7th
Graham back by the 2.30. Jim and I lunched at the club. Dined with Margaret.

Saturday 8th

Walked. We wanted to go to Kew, but the trains were too full, so we had tea in Kensington Gardens.

Sunday 9th
We lunched with Ray Lankester, Jacomb-Hoods, Miss Lankester, and a Miss Lake. Tea with Uncle Phil.

Monday 10th
To a pupils' concert at Graham Street. We dined at the Gobelins with Mrs Hopkins, Gerry and Mr Allen and went to *More* at the Ambassadors.

Tuesday 11th
We went to Queen's Hall at 11 for rehearsal with Mr Kelly and the Oxford House Choir. We gave Mr Kelly lunch at the club and he took us to the Zoological Gardens, and we had tea there. Concert in evening.

Wednesday 12th
I took the children to tea with Maisie and on the way back looked in at a concert that Mrs Hutchinson had got up at Miss Theodora Hess' house. Jim singing for her. Dined at P. G.

Thursday 13th
Jim and I to Seaton. Devonshire in the afternoon.

Friday 14th
We walked and sat about. Graham came down in time for dinner.

Saturday 15th
We walked all day and found cowslips.

Sunday 16th
We motored to Exeter and came up to London. Jim to sing at a party in the evening and dined at P. G.

Monday 17th

Mrs Mellor came to tea with me, and the children went to Sheila's birthday party. We dined at the Trocadero.

Tuesday 18th

Writing letters for a concert on May 19th all yesterday and today.

Wednesday 19th

Finished concert letters. Interviewed maids. Speyers and Pearces to dinner.

Thursday 20th

We had lunch at the club.

Friday 21st

To P. G. to see Clare. In with children.

Saturday 22nd

Walked with Jim. We had tea at Rumplemayer's

Sunday 23rd

Jim and I to Kingston to lunch with the Woods. We walked over Wimbledon Common to them, and they took us back in the car.

Monday 24th

We gardened and tidied things. Dined at Treviglio.

Tuesday 25th

We went to Guildford by the 11.10 and had lunch at the Lion. Walked out to Shore and had tea with Mr Beaumont and some nieces and back by Gomshall.

Wednesday 26th

Graham in bed all day.

Thursday 27th
Graham in bed.

Friday 28th
Graham up. To R.A. Private View. Jim to Reigate. I dined at P. G. Tea with Dolly Gibson.

Saturday 29th
To the Dixons for the weekend.

Sunday 30th
Did nothing all day.

Monday May 1st
Back to lunch. Nanny away for her holiday. The temporary Nanny came at tea time. Dined out.

Tuesday 2nd
To tea with Mrs Mellor. Dined at Hyde Park.

Wednesday 3rd
We gave Hilda tea at the club and went on to hear Papa's lecture on Shakespeare at the British Academy. Dined at the club.

Thursday 4th
Children to lunch at P. G. We made bread and baked it. Dr Spencer came in after dinner.

Friday 5th
Our wedding day. We had lunch at the club. Dined at P. G.

Saturday 6th
Uncle Phil fetched us in a motor and took us to Ciro's, picking up his friend Mrs de Grey Warter on the way. We dined and spent the evening there.

Sunday 7th
We went to tea with Mrs de Grey Warter. Jim to sing at a hospital for Miss Arkwright.

Monday 8th
It rained all day. Baked.

Tuesday 9th
I went to Audrey Gotch's wedding at St Margaret's Westminster. Clare and I went to the Academy to kill time, and then I went on to lunch with Mrs Foster also Katie, Miss Braithwaite and Mrs

Hambourg. To tea with Nina. We went round to P. G. after tea to see the nursery.

Wednesday 10th
Cooked and cleaned. To P. G. to sit with Denis, who had had a wisdom tooth out. We dined at the Trocadero.

Thursday 11th
In all day. Hilda to supper.

Friday 12th
Jim and I to a lecture of Mr Ker at Bedford College. Dined with Hills.

Saturday 13th
I had tea at the Morses. Dined with the Hopkins and found Gerry straight back from Ireland.

Sunday 14th
Baked bread. Tea at P. G. and lunch.

Monday 15th
We had tea with Uncle Phil. Dined with him at the Berkeley and went to the Alhambra.

Tuesday 16th
Nurse Forster went. Took children to tea at P. G.

Wednesday 17th
Had children all day.

Thursday 18th
Nanny back. We lunch at the club and went to lecture on plants by Ray Lankester. Jim sang at the Henry Bird Memorial concert.

Friday 19th

We had tea with Uncle Phil. Jim had a very good concert at Aeolian Hall, and Uncle Phil gave us food afterwards.

Saturday 20th

Jim to Guildford to sing. I went to P. G. We dined at Hyde Park.

Sunday 21st

Music at P. G. Dined at Café Royal.

Monday 22nd

Cooked. We dined with Margaret.

Tuesday 23rd

Cooked. Called on Mrs Hornby. Tea with Nina and children too to meet all the Shuttleworth babies.

Wednesday 24th

Cooked and baked. Shopped. Jim to Cooks.

Thursday 25th

I lunched with Mrs Jennings. Jim to Portsmouth. The children to tea with Sissie. I joined them there and then on to tea with Miss Margials, and then to the Temple to see Denis' new rooms. Uncle Phil was there and drove me home. Sibell Shuttleworth and Uncle Phil to dinner.

Friday 26th

Took the children to Victoria and saw them off to Rottingdean. Margaret to tea, later Cousin Stan, Miss Broome and a friend. We dined at Treviglio.

Saturday 27th

Cooked. Jim and I lunched at the club and then walked to Hampstead to see the Powells' puppet show.

Sunday 28th

Uncle Phil gave us lunch at the Carlton and took us out to Richmond and Hampton Court. We had supper with him.

Monday 29th

I had tea with Margaret. Jim and I to the last Symphony Concert supped at Pagani.

Tuesday 30th

To tea at P. G. We dined with the Morrises.

Wednesday 31st

We lunched with Aunt Madeline. To tea came Mr James, Mrs de Morgan, Ray and Fay Lankester, Miss Locke, Mrs Anran, Gertie Buney, 2 Miss Beaumonts. We went down to Harrow with Hay and Agnes to sing at a School concert and had supper with Mr and Mrs Graham afterward.

Thursday June 1ˢᵗ

Lunched at P. G. Jim sang at Kent House for Enid Morse. Dined Hyde Park.

Friday 2ⁿᵈ

Jim and I to Portrait Painters Private View of the Grafton where my Sargent is. Lunched at the club. To tea Mrs Fox, Sissie, Sibyl, Lady Charnwood, Miss Cory, Mrs Campbell. Dined with Sibell Shuttleworth and sister-in-law.

Saturday 3ʳᵈ

Jim to Cooks. I had lunch and tea at P. G.

Sunday 4ᵗʰ

We lunch with Uncle Phil at the Carlton. Called on A. Baldwins and Charnwoods. Dined with Uncle Phil and Mr Haselden.

Monday 5ᵗʰ

I lunched with the Lewises to see Katie after her operation. Mrs Morse, Mrs Lamb, and Mrs Jennings to tea.

Tuesday 6ᵗʰ

We dined with Netta.

Wednesday 7ᵗʰ

Lunch at P. G. To tea Mrs Huxley and Anne, Mrs Gillick, Mrs Hopkins, Mrs Jacomb-Hood, Henry, Olive Heseltine, Lyal. We dined with the Baldwins.

Thursday 8ᵗʰ

I lunched with Mrs Hopkins. To tea Mrs Halsey, Mrs Harvey, Mrs Hamilton, Iris Lindsay. Dined at P. G. and music afterwards.

Friday 9th

To Cooks for the weekend.

Saturday 10th

We walked in the morning. It began to rain and set in to be stormy.

Sunday 11th

Walked to Theydon. Walked in the rain after tea.

Monday 12th

Raining hard. Mrs Cook, Don, Hilda, Mrs Ashbridge, Jim and I to lunch at Treviglio and to the Coliseum.

Tuesday 13th

Home early. Mrs Reeves to lunch. Tea at P. G.

Wednesday 14th

To tea Mrs Fletcher, Dorothy and Bobby Longman, Mrs and Miss Hutchinson, Mrs Lawrence Kay-Shuttleworth. Dined P. G.

Thursday 15th

We had lunch with Uncle Phil at the Wellington Club and then to the Grafton Galleries. Jim sang at Sunderland House. Dined with Margaret.

Friday 16th

We walked to Uncle Phil's and then to the British Museum (where we saw Denis) and round Lincoln's Inn Fields and the purlieus. We had lunch at Treviglio with Uncle Phil and Denis and Oliver. To tea Christabel and Betty Marillier, Alice MacPherson, Mrs Eddison, Zoe Manuel, Joyce Ilbert, Mrs May Daires, Molly Muir, Aroley Dunhill and later Mrs Halsey.

Saturday 17th

We dined with Uncle Phil and Denis at the Bath Club.

Sunday 18th

We went to lunch with the Woods at Kingston. Dined with Douglas and a Mr and Mrs Morrison.

Monday 19th

We had lunch at the B and K restaurant. To tea Madame Haas, Mrs Monce, Mrs Meinertzhagen, Lady Macmillan, Lady Pollock.

Tuesday 20th

Jim to sing at Grosvenor House. I had tea with Mrs Gillick. Hilda dined with us, and Jim and I went to a recital of Suggia's.

Wednesday 21st

I lunch with Mrs Mond. To tea Mrs Middleton, Miss Margials, Mrs Mills, Mr Nichols.

Thursday 22nd

I lunched with Lady Macmillan, and we drove to the Leicester Galleries to see Italian war cartoons and then to Macmillan's to see some Sandy's drawings. I called on Miss Lindsay and then on to Clare. Dined at P. G. Jim at Woodford for tennis.

Friday 23rd

Rained. Gwenny and Margaret Palgrave and Mrs Patullo to tea. We dined with the Mounseys.

Saturday 24th

To Woodford for the day.

Sunday 25th

Lunch with the Jacomb-Hoods. Miss Symonds and Miss _____to tea. Oliver called. Supper at P. G.

Monday 26th

Jim lunched with Uncle Phil. Mrs Thicknesse, Mrs Strachey, Miss Richmond, Miss Robinson and Netta to tea. Jim to sing for Mrs Fletcher.

Tuesday 27th

We went to a rehearsal and found it put off. Had tea at the club. Dined with Mr Hudson in Queen Anne's Gate; a birthday party for Suggia who played. also Tertis, Defaun, Samuel: Cammaerts recited and Jim sang.

Wednesday 28th

I lunch with Mrs Blagden. Mrs Maclean and the Ranee of Sarawak to tea. Dined with Eustace and the little girls. Nina away.

Thursday 29th

The Ranee called for us after lunch, and we went to the Chelsea Fair in the Royal Hospital Grounds, where she conducted Romberg's *Toy Symphony*, in a room in the Governor's House. Jim playing the quail. She and I went on to an exhibition at the Tate Gallery of early Rossetti 's. E.B.J.'s Whistler and a Blake. We dined at P. G., and Jim sang.

Friday 30th

We lunched at the Carlton. Tennis at the Mounseys. Uncle Phil gave us dinner at the Carlton Grill Room, and we joined the Baldwins at *Fishpingle*, a dull play. We went to say good evening to Marion Terry and Mr Ainley afterwards.

JULY
Saturday 1st
We went to the Woods for the day. Mr Wood drove us home. Dined at the Hopkins. Bernard Partridges there.

Sunday 2nd
We lunch with the Macleans. Tea with the Partridges. Supper at P. G.

Monday 3rd
We lunched with Netta. Had tea with Margaret. Dined with the Morris'.

Tuesday 4th
I went down to R'dean by the 1.55, taking Katie Scott.

Wednesday 5th
On the beach and with the children. Nanny out.

Thursday 6th
On the beach ok.

Friday 7th
The same.

Saturday 8th
Children to Mrs Packer's sports and Graham ran in the children's race. I went to see Mrs Stanford.

Sunday 9th
I had tea with Maisie at the Grange. The Mark Hambourgs and a Sir Charles and Lady Lawrence there.

Monday 10th

Georgie Lewis and a little boy from the Dene came to tea with the children.

Tuesday 11th

Denis came down at lunch time to convalesce here. Jim came down by the 1.55. Miss Moens to tea.

Wednesday 12th

Jim back to town. I had tea with Miss Moens.

Thursday 13th

I had tea with Mrs Hambourg. Jim down to dinner.

Friday 14th

Jim and I walked to Lewes for lunch and back.

Saturday 15th

Denis not so well again. I had Lishman in.

Sunday 16th

Lishman to see Denis.

[Editors' note: The diary stops here, with the note below to explain the absence of entries. It resumes in September.].

I was in Rottingdean till August 21st when we went up to London for two nights. On Wednesday 23rd we went up to Westmoreland to stay with the Hills at Terry Bank, near Kirby Lonsdale. We stayed there till Thursday August 31st when we went to Edinburgh for the night and on next day to Boat of Garden on the Spey above Grantown where Graham joined us on September 6th. We had long walks and were very happy. We came to Edinburgh on Sept 14th and next day Graham went to Bath and we to London.

SEPTEMBER

Saturday 16th

We lunched with Uncle Phil and had tea at P. G. Dined at the Pall Mall and to see Oscar Asche's dull play *Chu Chin Chow*.

Sunday 17th

We lunched at P. G. Jim to see the Woods. I stopped to tea at P. G.

Monday 18th

I met the children at Victoria and took them to P. G. after lunch.

Tuesday 19th

Shopped with Graham, winter raincoat and hat. Sissie to lunch and helped me with a cloak. We dined at P. G.

Wednesday 20th

Sewed.

Thursday 21st

W.H.S.D. Bought things for children.

Friday 22nd

W.H.S.D. Jim and I to Wimbledon to sing to soldiers for Mr O'Connor-Morris.

Saturday 23rd

To Slough for the day to see Aunt Marion and Sylvia.

Sunday 24th

At P. G. all afternoon with children.

Monday 25th

W.H.S.D. Dined with Netta.

Tuesday 26th

W.H.S.D. Mr and Mrs Chatham to tea, and Margaret with Miss Carve. Children to Sissie.

Wednesday 27th

W.H.S.D. To tea at P. G. Dined at Treviglio.

Thursday 28th

W.H.S.D. Jim and I lunched at the club.

Friday 29th

Jim and I to dreadful party at Mrs Mudie-Cooke's where he sang. Henry to dinner.

Saturday 30th

In with children in morning. Jim to a cinema with Henry.

Sunday Oct. 1st

To enquire for Dorothy Longman and her baby. Tea at club. Looked in at P. G. Clare in bed overworked from Balham. Jim to Victoria with Papa to meet Denis, who is ill.

Monday 2nd

W.H.S.D. Margaret to tea.

Tuesday 3rd

Took children to Paddington and saw them off to Astley. In bed with a cold after W.H.S.D.

Wednesday 4th

To dentist had a tooth out. Mrs Hopkins gave me oysters at Mrs Drivers. Clare to tea.

Thursday 5th

W.H.S.D. We dined with the Hopkins'.

Friday 6th

We gave Mr Taparell and his Miss Dickson lunch at the club. Dined with Margaret.

Saturday 7th

To the Cooks for weekend. To bed early.

Sunday 8th

Stayed in bed till lunch. Walked a little.

Monday 9th

Home early.

Tuesday 10th

To dentist. Lunch at Treviglio. To Bine's Memorial service at St Margaret's. To bed with a tooth ache.

Wednesday 11th

To Astley by the 1.40. Joined children very well.

Thursday 12th

About with children.

Friday 13th

To Stanway where I found Lady Wemyss, Mary, Bibs, and Grace Lady Wemyss. We walked a little. Lady Elcho, Jim, Lord Wemyss, and the Walter Rubens down to dinner.

Saturday 14th

We walked a little. After lunch a concert at 3. Mr Reeves and a Mr Wood having come and another concert at 6.

Sunday 15th

Wrote and walked. Mr Reeves and Mr Wood went. Lady Elcho went after tea.

Monday 16th

The Rubens went. We drove to Tewkesbury before tea.

Tuesday 17th

We came up after lunch. Margaret to tea.

Wednesday 18th

Dentist. I had to go to bed and had a bad rheumatic chill and couldn't go out for a fortnight.

[Editors' note: The diary stops here until October 31, 1916.]

Tuesday 31ˢᵗ
I had a drive to Richmond Park.

Painting by Sir Philip-Burne Jones, Rottingdean Church.

Wednesday, November 1st

I walked a little.

Thursday 2nd

I walked again and had no pain.

Friday 3rd

We went to Stanway by the late train. Lady Elcho, Guy and his wife, and Lord Wemyss came down with us. We found Aunt Madeline, Lady Wemyss, Mary and Bibs there.

Saturday 4th

Jim out with the shooters and played tennis after lunch. He sang about 40 songs after tea.

Sunday 5th

We had singing again. We came up with Lord Wemyss and Lady Elcho in the evening.

Monday 6th

Sent out more concert notices. To tea with Mrs Simonds to see Mrs Mellor.

Tuesday 7th

Jim, Graham and I to lunch at P. G. Took Graham to tea with Zoe Manuel. Hills and Mr Ker to dinner.

Wednesday 8th

To Queen Anne's Gate to arrange daisies etc. Lunched at the club. Concert at 5 o'clock went very well. Dined at Hyde Park.

Thursday 9th

To the dentist. In with children.

Friday 10th

Shopped. Lunch with Uncle Phil at Rendezvous. Dined with Mrs Morris. Another play and Jim sang.

Saturday 11th
Jim had a rehearsal of quartet for Bach cantata at 3. Dined with Walter Fords.

Sunday 12th
We went to tea at P. G.

Monday 13th
Thick fog. Jim missed a train to Leeds and had to come home. Graham's first visit to dentist.

Tuesday 14th
Jim to Leeds. I lunched with Nina and had tea with Margaret.

Wednesday 15th
Took Graham to dentist. He had four stoppings altogether and enjoyed it very much. Susan brought Esther to tea. Papa to dinner.

Thursday 16th
Jim back with a chill and went to bed. In with children.

Friday 17th
W.H.S.D. Very cold.

Saturday 18th
We lunched with Uncle Phil. Jim rehearsal for next Wednesday. Snow and sleet.

Sunday 19th
In with children.

Monday 20th
W.H.S.D.

Tuesday 21st

A Mrs Micholls came to see the pictures. Tea at P. G. James children to tea in the nursery. Dined with Mr Hudson and Jim sang.

Wednesday 22nd

To Holly Lodge for rehearsal. Concert at 5 o'clock with a full room. Dined at Hyde Park.

Thursday 23rd

Jim to Northampton to sing. In with children.

Friday 24th

Dolly Hambourg to tea.

Saturday 25th

We gave lunch to Bob Cooks at the club. I fetched the children from Mrs Hopkins after tea.

Sunday 26th

We went to tea at P. G. Very cold.

Monday 27th

W.H.S.D.

Tuesday 28th

W.H.S.D. I went to tea with Mrs James to fetch the children.

Wednesday 29th

W.H.S.D. We had lunch out. Tea at P. G.

Thursday 30th

W.H.S.D. To tea with Miss Carter and Mrs Beir.

Friday Dec. 1ˢᵗ

I lunched with Mrs Micholls. Hopkinses, Netta, and Mr Beigel to dinner.

Saturday 2ⁿᵈ

We lunched at Treviglio. Mrs Elverson to tea. Mr James and Mrs Reeves to dinner and afterwards Henry and his sister Mrs Hayman(?). Jim sang late with *den Kreuzstab* and a few songs.

Sunday 3ʳᵈ

In with children.

Monday 4ᵗʰ

W.H.S.D. We dined with Mangeot.

Tuesday 5ᵗʰ

W.H.S.D. Lunched with the Hambourgs. Jim began a cold. Colin in bed.

Wednesday 6ᵗʰ

Jim had to sing at his own recital at Miss Cazalet's with a bad cold.

Thursday 7ᵗʰ

Graham in bed with a chill.

Friday 8ᵗʰ

Graham still in bed. Mr Hudson, Ethel Dilke, Colin, and Marjory Huxley to dinner.

Saturday 9ᵗʰ

Jim in bed all day. Graham in bed.

Sunday 10ᵗʰ

Children and Jim in bed.

Monday 11th

Children and Jim in bed.

Tuesday 12th

Jim up. Children in bed.

Wednesday 13th

Children in bed.

Thursday 14th

Jim teaching again. Children in bed.

Friday 15th

Children in bed. Jim up.

Saturday 16th

Very bad fog.

Sunday 17th

Graham up to tea.

Monday 18th

Graham up. Jim teaching.

Tuesday 19th

Jim and I out to lunch. Children out.

Wednesday 20th

We called on Uncle Phil. Jim sang at his last recital at the Hornbys. Uncle Phil gave us dinner at the Hyde Park Grill Room.

Thursday 21st

Nanny away for her holiday. Temporary Nurse Edwards came.

Friday 22nd
Mr Morris lent me the car to take the children to the Hambourgs Christmas Tree party which they enjoyed frightfully.

Saturday 23rd
Jim and I to the bank, which was shut. We lunched at the Café Royal and bought some books.

Sunday 24th
I took the children to P. G. and left Graham there.

Monday Christmas Day
We all had lunch at P. G. Jim and I stayed to supper.

Tuesday 26th
Rather foggy. Jim's cold worse.

Wednesday 27th
Bad fog. We went to a party at the Hopkins'.

Thursday 28th
Bought books for children from Graham.

Friday 29th
Jim to R'dean. Tea with Sylvia Monsell and picked children from Netta's. Bed early.

Saturday 30th
Lunched at P. G. Jim back. Not very well.

Sunday 31st
Took children for a walk. Mother, Papa and Clare to lunch.

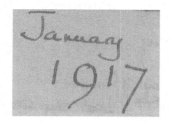

DIARY 1917

[Editors' note: The year 1917 opens with a reference in January that might be missed in the entries of all of Angela's many activities. The reference is uncommon, as Angela doesn't often comment on the hiring and firing of servants. On January 15, under-nursery-maid Lily Cowley began her work at their family home. As recorded in Thirkell's biographies, Lily testified against James McInnes in Angela's divorce trial.

The financial problems for the couple continued, although never mentioned. The entries become irregular and brief. During this time, Mary is born, marital troubles continue, and Angela moves to live with her parents in Pembroke Gardens (P. G.) along with her children. The time spans with no daily entries are summarized as Angela stays at Stanway, Clouds, and visits Lady Lewis. She began to recover and returned to living with her parents in P. G. During this time, Angela met her future husband, George Thirkell, at a house party when she was staying with Lady Elcho and other members of the Wemyss family. On November 17, 1917, her divorce was granted in court.

By this time, other families were devastated by the deaths of their young sons in the war. Although still supporting the war effort, the enthusiasm of 1914 had disappeared. Angela herself did not say much. Dealing with her own problems, she fails to comment in detail on her volunteer activities or other events around her.]

January

1917

Monday 1st
[Editors' note: No entry.]

Tuesday 2nd
Jim to sing at Princess Galleries. Colin flushed and feverish. Mother took Graham home with her.

Wednesday 3rd
Colin better. We dined with Netta.

Thursday 4th
Graham down with influenza at P. G. Miss Sparrow to tea. Cousin Stan dined here.

Friday 5th
In bed with sore throat. Jim rehearsed *"I bear my cross"* with Mr Saunders' 4et.

Saturday 6th
In bed with cold and cough – influenza probably. Children both better.

Sunday 7th
In bed. Jim sang *"I bear my cross"* at South Place.

Monday 8th
I got up to tea in the nursery. Found Colin coughing again. Jim sang for Mrs Wickham.

Tuesday 9th
In bed all day again.

Wednesday 10th
Up to tea. Colin out for the first time.

Thursday 11th
Nanny came back after tea.

Friday 12th
Graham came home very thin and pale.

Saturday 13th
Shopped for nursery.

Sunday 14th
In all day. Jim to P. G.

Monday 15th
Shopped for nursery. The new under nursey Lily Cowley came.
Mrs Douglas Scott to tea.

Tuesday 16th
Children out. Jim to Knutsford.

Wednesday 17th
More nursery shopping.

Thursday 18th
Jim back from Knutsford to breakfast after a 4-hour journey.

Friday 19th
We had lunch at the club. Jim to Shakespeare exhibition at
Grafton Galleries.

Saturday 20th
Jim to memorial service for Mr de Morgan. We lunched at the
Hyde Park Grill Room.

Sunday 21st

In all day.

Monday 22nd

Brought handkerchiefs for Jim.

Tuesday 23rd

Jim's 43rd birthday. He went to Northampton for the day to teach.

Wednesday 24th

Jim to lunch with the Woods.

Thursday 25th

Very cold and getting colder.

Friday 26th

Bitter cold and wind. We dined with the Hills.

Saturday 27th

Very cold again. We lunched at the B & K. I went to bed early with a cold.

Sunday 28th

To tea at P. G. Cousin Stan there.

Monday 29th

Still very cold.

Tuesday 30th

My 27th birthday. Jim to Northampton. I had lunch with Papa at the Pall Mall, and we went to the black and white exhibition at the Academy. Stella Speyer to tea.

Wednesday 31st

Very cold.

Thursday Feb 1st
To inspect perambulator. To registry office.

Friday 2nd
To registry office. Lunch at Hyde Park.

Saturday 3rd
For a walk with Jim. Children went skating on the Round Pond.

Sunday 4th
To P. G. for tea.

Monday 5th
Jim out to supper.

Tuesday 6th
Jim to Northampton. Mrs Micholls took me to Christie's to see the Dowdeswell pictures.

Wednesday 7th
We had tea at P. G. Miss Fanny Davies there. Jim sang for Miss Gwynne Kimpton at the Bechstein Hall.

Thursday 8th
Slight sign of thaw.

Friday 9th
Jim and I to tea with Mrs Fletcher who is leaving Stanhope Street. Jim sang to Clare's soldiers.

Saturday 10th
Jim had a throat. I went to tea with Susan. Mr James here. Henry to supper.

Sunday 11th
Tea at P. G.

Monday 12th

A new pupil a Mr Raymond Peta.

Tuesday 13th

Jim to Northampton. I had lunch at P. G.

Wednesday 14th

Put up a draught stop in my sitting room.

Thursday 15th

[Editors' note: No entry.]

Friday 16th

Jim to Bradford. Mother and Mrs Wood to tea.

Saturday 17th

Graham's birthday party. Reduced by colds to 2 Jameses and 2 Parishes, Mother, Papa, Sissie and we had the magic lantern.

Sunday 18th

Graham's fifth birthday. Children to lunch at P. G. and we went to tea.

Monday 19th

We dined with Margaret Costeker.

Tuesday 20th

Jim to Northampton. I lunched at P. G.

Wednesday 21st

Children to tea at the Baldwins.

Thursday 22nd

Dentist.

Friday 23rd

Graham up for the day. We had lunch with him and gave him tea. Jim sang at Aubrey House for Clare's shell shocked officers.

Saturday 24th

To Eastcote to stay with Douglas for the night.

Sunday 25th

The Gillicks came down to lunch. We left about 3.30. Jim to see Guy Wyndham.

Monday 26th

To the dentist. I had a very bad tooth and had to get it pulled out by a man in Gloucester Road.

Tuesday 27th

Jim to Northampton. Lunched with Hilda at the Bishopsgate Institute.

Wednesday 28th

To Kensington to shop. Lunched at Café Brice.

Thursday March 1st

Henry to supper.

Friday 2nd
[Editors' note: No entry.]

Saturday 3rd

We lunched at the Woods. Tea at P. G.

Sunday 4th

Jim to sing at St Martin in the Fields. Tea with the Austen Cartmells.

Monday 5th

Rachel Dixon to tea.

Tuesday 6th

Jim to Northampton. Mother to tea.

Wednesday 7th
[Editors' note: No entry.]

Thursday 8th

Hilda to tea. Jim to rehearse at St. Martins.

Friday 9th

To St Ermins about National Service. Lunch at the Carlton.

Saturday 10th

Jim to St Ermins again. Tea at P. G. Miss Davies and Miss Pinwell to supper & rehearse the *Kreuzstab*.

Sunday 11th

Jim sang at St Martins.

Monday 12th
Pupils all day.

Tuesday 13th
Jim wouldn't go to Northampton.

Wednesday 14th
Jim to ~~Bize~~ Repton for recital. I lunched at P. G.

Thursday 15th
Jim back. Henry in evening.

Friday 16th
Jim & I lunched at Scotts.

[Editors' note: Saturday date is off.]

Saturday 18th
Children to P. G. I had my hair washed.

Sunday 19th
Rehearsal with Miss Davies. Tea at P. G.

Monday 20th
Mr Dixon and Rachel to supper.

Tuesday 21st
Jim to Northampton. Lunched at P. G. Queenie came.

Wednesday 22nd

[Editors' note: There were no daily entries from March 21 until August 10. No information was entered for March 22. Angela's summary below appeared next in the diary. Two entries appeared for August, followed by another gap.]

March-August

Mary was born on March 30th. On May 1 I came to Pembroke Gardens and have never seen Jim again. I was at Clouds for the last fortnight in May and then in London. Then I went to Rottingdean for two nights and brought Graham up to P. G. with me and June 13th took him to Stanway where we spent a very happy month, with Lady Wemyss there sometimes and glimpses of Grace Lady Wemyss Cynthia and Mary. On July 11th Lady Wemyss took Graham to London and on July 14th I went to Broadway to spend 10 days with Lady Lewis. On July 23rd I came back to P. G. On August 8th the children came up from Rottingdean and Nanny took Mary straight on to her home the same day, while Graham and Colin stayed here at P. G.

Friday August 10th

To the Grove with the children to tidy and bring back some things. Clare to the Howards for the week end.

Another gap owing to laziness. I must write regularly.

Saturday 18th

To the Grove to show a Norwegian Commander Rachlew over it.

[Editors' note: There was another long gap, but an explanation was given. See the next page.]

[Editor's note: No date.]

Another long gap. We all went to Wilsford on August 20th. I came up for a few days to arrange about letting the Grove to a Mrs Wright Boycott for several months at 6 guineas a week. We had to stay at Wilsford. Myra Hess, Winnie Smith, Ruth Howard and her two eldest brothers. I stayed alone for some time with the children. We saw a good many Australians. A Mr Thirkell who we met at the Lombards came over a good deal and brought friends. We came up on Saturday Oct 13th and settled in at Pembroke Gardens. Now I must try again to keep my diary regularly. All Saturday afternoon I spent in tidying and arranging. Audrey Hobson and her husband came to tea.

[Editor's note: Next entry is October 14.]

OCTOBER
Sunday 14th
I called on Miss MacColl, hoping to see Molly Pitts, but she was out. Called on Audrey Hobson to see her baby. Tidied.

Monday 15th
Shopped and did some tidying at the Grove for Mrs Wright Boycott. Mrs Hopkins came in after tea. Sewed.

Tuesday 16th
To Head's to buy wool for children's jersey. Sewed.

Wednesday 17th
I lunched with Lucy.

Thursday 18th
Took the boys out, and we met Sheila in the gardens. Lunched with Mrs Micholls, who took me home. Hopkinses after supper.

Friday 19th
Took Graham to Blackfriars station, we looked at the river and the outside of St Paul's. To see George Lewis and then took Graham on to the dentist. Raid at night.

Saturday 20th
Children to tea with Mrs Hopkins. Lady Lewis, Katie, and Susan Ridsdale called.

Sunday 21st
Had the children all day. I took them to the river in the morning and Addison Road afternoon. Nina and Eustace to tea and Mr Elton.

Monday 22nd
To Myra to fit her dress. Lunched with Margaret Costeker.

Tuesday 23rd
Lunch with Mrs Fletcher. Diana to tea with children.

Wednesday 24th
Aunt Cissie came to lunch here. Went to see Dr Mills about bad neuralgia.

Thursday 25th
I lunched with Nina. To Myra to fetch her dress to alter.

Friday 26th
To dentist and had a wisdom tooth out. To Myra with her dress. Took children to lunch with Susan Ridsdale. To L.S.Q. concert to see and hear Myra. To Uncle Phil, who was having a party for Canadian officers. He had a fly for Mother and me, and we dropped Diana and Mrs Taylor.

Saturday 27th
Sissie came to lunch. Mrs Ritchie to tea.

Sunday 28th
Lunched with Mrs Saffery. Uncle Phil and Mel here to tea came Gladys Holman Hunt. Myra.

Monday 29th
I had lunch with Lady Wemyss at this little restaurant in Sloane Square. To the Berkeley to pick up Uncle Phil, and he and I and Lady Markham went to Debenhams and chose a coat for Mother.

Tuesday 30th
To dentist. To A&N and sold a hideous gold Burmese bracelet and hideous chain for £2.17.6. Lay down all afternoon. Lady Ritchie called. Henry came in after supper and we had a long talk.

Wednesday 31st
I had lunch with Mrs Leaf. Sylvia Thompson to tea. Raid.

Sir Philip Burne-Jones as a child.

Thursday Nov. 1st
To lunch with Ella. To Ers after dinner.

Friday 2nd
Took children out.

Saturday 3rd
Took a parcel to Diana from Mother. Dolly Carr to tea. Hopkins' after dinner.

Sunday 4th
Took Graham to Hammersmith to look at the river. Denis and Diana to tea.

Monday 5th
To see the new Walpole Street House. Lunched with Mrs Fletcher and Dorothy Longman.

Tuesday 6th
Shopped. Sheila and Patrick to tea and Mrs Ranalow to fetch them. Mr Matheson to supper.

Wednesday 7th
Mother to R'dean. Netta after tea.

Thursday 8th
To Henrietta Street to enquire for Douglas who had had an operation – took the children. Took Graham to lunch with the Woods at Putney.

Friday 9th
Lunched with Lady Ritchie. Mrs Warre-Cornish there. I walked by Lady Ritchie's bath chair to Miss Ritchie's new rooms in Radcliffe Gardens and then Miss Ritchie and I went on to the von Glehn's where there was music. Mr Bradley's birthday ode to Mr von Glehn sang by Miss Sichel and played by Mrs Tor (?) Mr

and Mrs Williams and Miss Fanny Davies. Miss Davies also played alone and in a Bach thing for piano and two violins. Fuller Maitland was there.

Saturday 10th
Lunched with the Colvins.

Sunday 11th
Took Graham to see Maisie. Uncle Phil to lunch. Mr Guedalla to tea. Mrs Ramsden to supper.

Monday 12th
Mrs Bowman called. To tea with Lady Whitelegge.

Tuesday 13th
Took Graham to lunch at the Lewises and then to see Douglas in his nursing home. The Hopkins' came in after dinner with Gerry, just back for a fortnight's leave.

Wednesday 14th
Clare and I dined with the Hopkins, Gerry Mr Allen and his brother.

Thursday 15th
I took Diana to the Garden Studio in Bourlet's van to see about getting "Aurora" which she and Denis are borrowing. Clare and I dined with Speeds.

Friday 16th
Out with children. Henry came in after dinner. Lucy to tea.

Saturday 17th
Mother and I and Lily Cowley went to the Law Courts. My case was heard before Mr Justice Hill. I gave evidence first, then Nurse Campbell. Dr Mills, another doctor, Lily, and Sally

Jackson. Cruelty and adultery were proved and a decree nisi given with custody of the children.

Sunday 18th
Took Graham to call on Buff. Peggy to supper.

Monday 19th
I lunched with Mrs Micholls. Aunt Winnie to tea.

Tuesday 20th
To lunch with Diana. Mr Lucas to tea. We had a party for Gerry: 3 Hopkins' Mrs. Somervell with Antonia and Kitty, Audrey, Ers and Veronica, Mr Gleadowe, Mr Birnstingl, Mrs Ritchie and Peggy, Reine Ormond, Ers, Theodora Hess. We acted and played games till about 12 o'clock.

Wednesday 21st
I lunched with Mrs Halsey.

Thursday 22nd
Mother and I lunched at Belgrave Square with Aunt Madeline, Aunt Minnie, and Guy.

Friday 23rd
I took Graham to Kings Cross to meet Nanny and Mary. Lily went. I lunched with Mrs Bowman and Dolly.

Saturday 24th
Took boys out. Dr Mills to see Mary. She has bad glands and some kind of adenoids. Lunched with Aunt Cissie at her club. Mr and Mrs Micholls to tea.

Sunday 25th
Graham and I to Westminster Cathedral and to call on Lucy. We were caught in a sudden snowstorm coming back.

Monday 26th

Took little boys out.

Tuesday 27th

Out with boys. I lunched with Mrs Morris and Margaret. Mrs Morse to tea.

Wednesday 28th

Out with Mary and boys. Lunched with Barrie.

Thursday 29th

Sewed. Had children all afternoon.

Friday 30th

Out with boys, we left a note for Captain Thirkell and then watched cavalry in Hyde Park. Lunched with Alice. Mrs Stillman called.

Saturday, Dec 1st

Out with boys. To a concert at the Craies'.

Sunday Dec 2nd

Took Graham in a bus to Charing Cross. We walked down Whitehall and met the Newbolts near the Abbey and then along the Embankment to Vauxhall Bridge, where we took a tram to Victoria and home by train. I lunched with Mrs de Morgan and her sister and brother-in-law the Stirlings (?). Mrs Millar called and Harry Birnstingl and Captain Thirkell came to tea and supper and a friend of his called Mr Elsum.

Monday 3rd

Took boys out. I lunched with Anna Pearce. Took the boys to tea with Henry.

Tuesday 4th

Took boys out. Lunched with Mrs Morse. Captain Thirkell called for me and we picked up Mr Elsum and a Miss Lanch and dined at the Australian Officers' Club in Piccadilly and went to *Chu Chin Chow*. Captain Thirkell brought me back. He goes back to the Plain and then to France.

Wednesday 5th

Took boys out. Lunched with Winnie Brooke at Marshall's. Mother to R'dean. Air raid at 5 next morning.

Thursday 6th

Shopped. Nanny out and I was with the children.

Friday 7th

Took boys out and in afternoon to tea at the Ritchies. Peggy came back to supper.

Saturday 8th

Took boys out. Mother back from R'dean.

Sunday 9th

In with children.

Monday 10th

To Oxford Street to do some shopping.

Tuesday 11th Wednesday 12th

Took boys out. I don't know what else.

Thursday 13th

In with children in afternoon.

Friday 14th

To lunch with Pamela McKenna. Pamela Glenconner came tea with Stephen.

Saturday 15th

Took boys out. Captain Thirkell rang up to say he was still in England and came to supper.

Sunday 16th

Took Graham to the Cobden-Sandersons. Mrs Ramsden to lunch. Aurelian and Susan called. Then the Toynbees and Oliver Gotch.

Monday 17th

The children and I met Captain Thirkell in the gardens, and he came home with us and then took me to lunch at the Australian Club. Children to tea with Henry. Captain Thirkell came about 6 and stayed to supper. Eustace and Nina came to supper too.

Tuesday 18th

Tube to Waterloo and spent about an hour there with Captain Thirkell and saw him off to Southampton. To Southampton Road after lunch to see about some photographs for him. Rain.

Wednesday 19th

To the Craies' for some music.

Thursday 20th

In with children.

Friday 21st

Took boys out and then to tea with Netta. Ruth to lunch.

Saturday 22nd

Shopped. Took boys to lunch with Mr Leaf.

Sunday 23rd

Graham and I to St James' Park by Underground and walked up through the parks to Piccadilly and home in a bus. In with children.

Monday 24th

Took boys out. Lunched with Mrs Mellor at St James Court. On to the Ranalows to a Christmas Tree and came back with the children.

Tuesday 25th

Christmas Day. The boys brought their stockings down and opened them on my bed. Nanny out all day.

Wednesday 26th

Took boys out. Ronnie Somervell helped us to fly Graham's new aeroplane. Papa, Clare, and I to tea and games at the Ritchies.

Thursday 27th

Took boys out.

Friday 28th

Shopped. Graham in doors not very well. Lunched at Craies'.

Saturday 29th

Shopped. Graham in bed all day. Colin had a temperature.

Sunday 30th

Graham in bed. Antonia came in the morning. Cousin Stan to lunch. Denis and Diana to tea and Mrs de Morgan. Guillaume Ormond to supper.

Monday 31st

Graham in bed. Shopped. To a dance at Australian Club.

ANGELA MARGARET MCINNES

DIARY 1918

[This was a challenging year in the beginning. Angela's father became responsible for the support of Angela and her children. Baby Mary died in February. Angela wrote that she worked as a parlourmaid at a club, as a volunteer or employee is unknown. She celebrated her 28th birthday quietly, and her war comments were cryptic: air raid. By May, her spirits were lifted by a trip away from London, and on June 3, 1918, her divorce was final. The war ended in 1918, and Angela's descriptions of her new friends, the Thirkell brothers, indicate that her life was about to change.]

January 1st Tuesday

Children still in. I went to the Australian Club and did my first lunch as a parlourmaid.

Wednesday 2nd

Children in. To the Club for tea.

Thursday 3rd

Children in. Nanny out.

Friday 4th

Shopped. Children in. Nurse Campbell to tea.

Saturday 5th

Shopped. Children in. To the Club for lunch, tea, dinner & dance.

Sunday 6th

In with children.

Monday 7th

Children in. I went to the Ideal Studios, Oxford Street, and got photographed. Took Mother after lunch to the Leicester Galleries to see *Australia at War* by Will Dyson. We looked in at Belgrave Square where Mr Alexander Fisher was having a foul show of enamels, but only saw Guy. I called on Mrs Steuart Wilson and went to see Diana who was in bed with a throat.

Tuesday 8th

To the Club for lunch. Tea with Sylvia Morom. Amy here to spend two nights while house-moving.

Wednesday 9th

Children still all indoors. To the Club for tea.

Thursday 10th

In with children.

Friday 11th

Lunched with Mrs Micholls, who took me to the Imperial War Exhibition. Bought an evening frock.

Saturday 12th

At the Club all day.

Sunday 13th

At the Club for lunch and tea.

Monday 14th

Out with boys. Rested all afternoon.

Tuesday 15th

To the Club for lunch. Major Brown invited the children to tea there and brought us back.

Wednesday 16th

Did some shopping. To the Club for tea.

Thursday 17th

In with children.

Friday 18th

Took Graham to the Baldwin's Box for the Drury Lane pantomime, *Aladdin*. We only stopped for two acts and he enjoyed it very much.

Saturday 19th

At the Club all day and stopped for the dance.

Sunday 20th

Took Graham to see Uncle Phil. In with children. Major Brown to supper.

Monday 21st

Out with boys.

Tuesday 22nd

To the Club for lunch. We had 23 at three tables and were hard worked. Riette called. Dined with Uncle Phil.

Wednesday 23rd

To the Club for tea, but found I wasn't wanted. So Miss Lund came back to tea with me.

Thursday 24th

In with children.

Friday 25th

Out with boys. To town to do some shopping.

Saturday 26th

To Club for lunch. Mother took Mary to a specialist who says her glands are to be operated on. Picked up Miss Lund at her hotel and went to the Club. I came away very soon and went on to the Baldwins' dance which was very nice and Clare who had been dining with Uncle Phil was there and we came home in a bus provided by him.

Sunday 27th

Took Graham to Hyde Park. Lunched with Uncle Phil and a party at the Berkeley.

Monday 28th

Took boys out. Shopped. Tea with Sibyl. Air-raid.

Tuesday 29th

Took boys out. To the Club for lunch. Tea with Marjorie Miles at 28 Young Street. Air raid.

Wednesday 30th

My 28th birthday. Lunched with Lady Markham. Very foggy. Uncle Phil, Diana, Amy and Sissie to tea and we had 28 candles and the children came down. Olive and Michael to dinner and Mr Benson came in afterwards.

Sunday 31st

Very foggy again. To a dance at Lady Markham's Canadian Club in Prince's Gardens in the afternoon with Uncle Phil. Mr Russell whom I had met at Lady Markham's the day before took me home in the blacker fog I can remember.

February

Friday Feb. 1st

Took boys out and then to lunch with Dolly Hambourg. Stella to tea.

Saturday 2nd

Took boys out. To the Club for lunch. Tea with Mrs Lynn at the Canadian Club & Norfolk House. To a dance at the Club.

Sunday 3rd

In with the children all day. We called on Sissie in the morning.

Monday 4th

Out with boys. Lorna to tea. Dined with Uncle Phil.

Tuesday 5th

Out with boys. To the Club for lunch. A Mr Kerr took me to a dance that Mrs Barton had got up and brought me back after tea.

Wednesday 6th

Out with boys. Mrs Lynn after tea. Dined with Uncle Phil. Captain Butler. Mr Plank an American artist and Miss Dickenson there. We went to a dance at the Canadian Club except Mr Plank.

Thursday 7th

Shopped. In with children.

Friday 8th

Took Mary to a hospital to be examined.

Saturday 9th

To the Club for lunch. To a hideously dull party at the Perkins and to a dance at the St John Hornbys where I met a very interesting Major Roos, a Boer, who was Lumits' private secretary for two years and has just been through the campaigns in German SW and German E. Africa. We talked for about an hour and a half and then he walked home with me.

Sunday 10th

To Club for lunch. Mr Guedalla to tea.

Monday 11th

Lunch with Mrs Lynn at her Club. To Lady Collier who took me on to tea at the Burlington Fine Arts Club with Collier and a Major Locker-Lampson. Dined with Uncle Phil who took me and Captain Butler to a dance at Mr Cunard's.

Tuesday 12th

To Club for lunch. Tea with Baldwins and the little boys who Lorna had brought.

Wednesday 13th

Lunched with Major Roos at the R.A.C. and he came back to tea.

Thursday 14th

To Uncle Phil to fetch some pheasant. Little boys in with temperatures. In with children. Major Roos and Mr Murray to dinner.

Friday 15th

Tea with Cicely Hornby.

Saturday 16th

To the Club for lunch. Back for Graham's party – Sonia and Nadine Hambourg, Mrs Sullivan and Moira, Susan and Esther, and Mel. Mr Nielson, a New Zealander in the R.F.C. Hopkinses came to tea and stopped to supper. We went to the dance at the Club together and he brought me home. There was a raid.

Sunday 17th

In with children. Dined with Major Roos at the R.A.C., and there was a raid so we had to stay till 12 o'clock and walk home.

[Editors' note: Dates February 18-28 are not included. The baby Mary died on Sunday February 24.]

Friday March 1st

Club for lunch. Major Roos took me out to tea and we dined at the R.A.C.

Saturday 2nd

Club for lunch. Mother, Ba and Nanny to Rottingdean to bury Mary's ashes. Amy spent night here. Clare to Oxford.

Sunday 3rd

In with children all day. Amy stopped and played with them. Nanny back to tea also Clare after supper.

Monday 4th

Mother and Papa back.

Tuesday 5th

To Club for lunch. Diana to tea. Club for dinner.

Wednesday 6th

Major Roos took me to tea at the South African Officers' Club. To the Club for dinner. Major Roos fetched me and gave me dinner at the R.A.C.

Thursday 7th

To Club for lunch. In with children. To a dance at the Club. I danced all evening with a very good dancer I didn't know. Major Roos came. There was an air raid and he took me home afterwards.

Friday 8th

To Club for lunch and tea.

Saturday 9th

To Club for lunch. Met Mr and Mrs Norton, one of Captain Thirkell's men and took him to tea at Uncle Phil's, where were

Lady Markham, Joy, Miss Leigh, a Canadian, a strange man, and girl and Kitty Somervell. To the Club for dinner.

Sunday 10th
Took Graham to see Sissie. To Club for lunch. Then Mr & Mrs Holmes who took me back.

Monday 11th
Took the boys to be photographed at the Ideal Studios and on to lunch with Maisie. Nanny fetched them and I stayed to tea.

Tuesday 12th
Club for lunch. Had tea at Belgrave Square with Aunt Madeline. Guy and Aunt Minnie and Olivia came in and Dick back on leave.

Wednesday 13th
To see Marjorie Miles. Lunched with Mrs John Bailey and then to Lady Markham's Canadian Club for a dance. Club for dinner and Major Norman brought me home.

Thursday 14th
Club for lunch. In with children. Dined with Colonel Clogstoun at the Berkeley and took him to a dance at the Club and he brought me home.

Friday 15th
To Club for lunch and tea. Ranalow children here to tea.

Saturday 16th
Lunched with Colonel and Mrs Clogstoun at Jules. Kitty Somervell to tea.

Sunday 17th

Took Graham by bus to the Temple and we walked down to the river and along the Embankment and home by train. In with children. Oliver Gotch to tea.

Monday 18th

Took children to Oxford Street to get the proofs of my photographs. Stella Beech and Pat to tea. Mother and I to one of Adrian Boult's Symphony Concerts and heard the *Scherzo* from Oliver's Symphony.

Tuesday 19th

To the Club for lunch. Miss Vassall came back to tea with me and brought her Pat – a little girl just younger than Graham.

Wednesday 20th

I lunched with Mrs Morris and Margaret at Harrods and Margaret told me she was engaged to a General Poole, an old friend of her husband's. I rested a little at Uncle Phil's (he had gone to R'Dean) and then went to a little afternoon dance at Lady Markham's. To the Club for dinner.

Thursday 21st

Met Winnie Brooke at Marshall's and had a talk. To the Club for lunch. In with children, playing in the garden. Mrs Lynn came to tea.

Friday 22nd

Lunched with Sibell Shuttleworth after sitting back in the Park. With Mother to the *Matthew Passion* at the Abbey. Peggie Ritchie back for the night.

Saturday 23rd

To Club for lunch. Children to tea with Lorna. I dined with Margaret Costeker and looked in at the Club for a little.

Sunday 24th

To Sissie with Graham in morning. To Club for lunch. Mother, Papa, Kitty, Clare, Reine, Peggie, Miss Green and I to South Place to hear Myra.

Monday 25th

In nearly all day. Cold and windy.

Tuesday 26th

To Club for lunch. Mrs Bailey to tea. To see Clara and on to Club for dinner.

Wednesday 27th

Lunched with Mrs Micholls. To the Club for dinner.

Thursday 28th

To the Club for lunch. Took the children to Kitty to tea and went to Lady Markham's dance at the Canadian Club. Fetched children from Somervells and Mr Edwards, a Canadian walked home with us. To the Club for a dance. Mr Lipscombe took Miss Vassall and me home.

Friday 29th

Took Graham to tea with Stella Beech. In the morning I went down to Horseferry Road to enquire about casualties and met Captain Algie who took me home in a taxi.

Saturday 30th

To Club for lunch. Captain Hogg dropped me at Horseferry Road where I enquired again. To see Harold's pictures.

Sunday 31st

Took Graham to Horseferry Road and we walked up to Hyde Park Corner and home in a bus.

Monday, April 1st

I lunched with Mrs White.

Tuesday 2nd

To Club for lunch. Tea Auntie Stella.

Wednesday 3rd

I lunched with Mrs Micholls. Major Roos fetched me and we went for a walk in Kensington Gardens and home to tea. He dropped me at the Club and picked me up after I had done my work and gave me dinner at the R.A.C. He had just heard that his brother had been killed at Gauche Wood. We walked back along the Embankment as far as Tice Street and then came back in a taxi.

Thursday 4th

Club for lunch. In with children.

Friday 5th

To Club after lunch for the commemoration of the 1st anniversary. Captain W. Thirkell came about a quarter to six and I went to Waterloo with him and he gave me news of Thirk. Came back by tube. To a dance at the Club. Major Roos fetched me and we walked home.

Saturday 6th

To Club for lunch. Cousin Stan to supper.

Sunday 7th

To see Sissie in morning. To Club for lunch. Took Graham to call on the Somervells.

Monday 8th

I lunched with Mrs Micholls and she began a drawing of me. To tea with Lilian Ranalow with the children. Dined with Uncle Phil.

Tuesday 9th

Club lunch. To tea with Mrs John Hamilton. Supper with Gwen Vassall.

Wednesday 10th

Took both boys to the dentist. Colin had nothing to be done just yet. Graham had two stoppings and is to go again. I had two stoppings. Called on Mrs Harvey and Diana. To part of Myra's recital and on to the Nursery for dinner. Christine Ratcliff for the night.

Thursday 11th

Went with Gwen Vassall to Cox's and then to the Club for lunch. Took children to tea at Lady Markham's Club. Gwen to supper. Christine left. Mother to R'dean.

Friday 12th

To House agents all morning. Lunch with Auntie Stella and we went on to tea with Diana. Christine for night again.

Saturday 13th

To Club for lunch.

Sunday 14th

Took Graham to call on Sissie. Graham and Papa to Brampton Cemetery after lunch. Ers to call and Sister Anderson to tea. Mother back.

Monday 15th

Lunched with Mrs Micholls and took her to see the Speeds.

Tuesday 16th

Club for lunch. Gerry Howard to spend the night and he and Mother and Papa and Clare went to *The 13th Chair* to see Auntie Stella act. I went to Ers after supper.

Wednesday 17th

Took Graham to dentist. Lunched with Aunt Sissie. To London Library and back to tea with Aunt Madeline. To Mrs Noble's to collect tickets for Suggia at her first recital. Mr Borwick was playing with her. I had to leave before the end to go on to dinner at the nursery.

Thursday 18th

To Anglo South American Depot. To the Club for lunch. In with children.

Friday 19th

To A.S.A. Depot. Dined with Uncle Phil.

Saturday 20th

Club for lunch. Children to tea with Amy.

Sunday 21st

Club for lunch.

Monday 22nd

Lunch with Mrs Halsey. A.S.A. depot in afternoon.

Tuesday 23rd

Club for lunch. Pat Beech to tea. Stella fetched him and Aunt Stella came.

Wednesday 24th

A.S.A. Depot. Lunched with the Heseltines. Tea with Stella Speyer and collected tickets at Suggias 2nd concert. Club dinner.

Thursday 25th

Club for lunch. Took children to Lady Markham's dance.

APRIL   *1918*

Friday 26th
A.S.A.D. Sewed and rested.

Saturday 27th
Club for lunch. To see Molly Wells at Sapphire Lodge. Adele Saffery to tea.

Sunday 28th
In with children.

Monday 29th
Took boys out. Lunch with Mrs Micholls. A.S.A.D.

Tuesday, April 30th
Club for lunch. A.S.A.D. To tea with Mrs White to talk to Australian soldiers. Dined with Uncle Phil.

121

Wednesday, May 1st
A.S.A.D. Lunch Mrs Micholls. To tea with Margaret Costeker. To Suggia's third recital at Kent House. Club for dinner.

Thursday 2nd
Club for lunch. Took children to tea with Gwen.

Friday 3rd
To Academy Private View. Met Captain Thirkell at Waterloo and we arrived and met Miss Carr to whom he is engaged. He was so late by that time that we had to have tea and eggs at a Lyons. Went back to the Academy.

Saturday 4th
Club for lunch. To tea with Auntie Stella and read some translations of Bernstein's *L'Élévation* to her. George came in and took us to dine at Simpson's. Back on the top of a bus.

Sunday 5th
To Club for lunch and dinner.

Monday 6th
Took children out. Lunched with Ruth at her Land Workers Club in Upper Baker Street. A.S.A.D.

Tuesday 7th
To Club for lunch and dinner.

Wednesday 8th
A.S.A.D. Lunched with Mrs Micholls. We went into Christie's to look at *Merlin and Nimue* and the *Garden of Pan*, and then went to see her younger son in hospital at Carlton House Terrace. We looked into the collection of Lady Waterford's drawings at the Amateur Art Exhibition, and then I came home. Club for dinner.

Thursday 9th

Club for lunch. In with boys.

Friday 10th

A.S.A.D. Mother and I lunched with the Fishers. Herbert and I walked to his office and then I went on to take Colonel Micholls some chocolate.

Saturday 11th

Club for lunch. I saw the American troops go down Piccadilly. All the voluntary workers at the Club were dismissed today without any reason. Viv came in for a moment and said he would ring up later. I went to Auntie Stella's and read her the last act of *L' L'Élévation n* and part of the second and had tea.

Sunday 12th

Took Graham to Sissie's. Viv came to tea with us in the nursery. Peggy and Myra to supper.

Monday 13th

To the Grove and then fetched my things from the Australia Club. Took the M.S. of *L'Élévation* to Southampton Street to be typed. Tea with Amy. To see Visetti about some songs to be translated. Dolly Hambourg and the little girls to tea.

Tuesday 14th

I took Nanny and the children to Kings Cross and saw them off to Whaplode. Tea with Nina.

Wednesday 15th

I sold flags at Harrods for Aunt Cissie all morning for the Comfort for the Troops Fund and she gave me lunch.

Thursday 16th

To take Colonel Micholls some chocolate and get books for Clare from the London Library. Christine Ratcliff came for the night. Dined with Molly Wells.

Friday 17th

I lunched with Mrs Micholls. Tea with Mrs Morse. Motored Papa and Clare to Thaxted. I went to stay with the Hopkins'.

Saturday 18th

I took Amy and Everard to *Dear Brutus* for which Barrie had given me a box. I went round afterwards to See Mr du Maurier and gave him *L'Élévation* to look at as Auntie Stella wished.

Sunday 19th

Stayed in bed till lunch. Amy and I for a little walk. Jacomb-Hoods to supper. Raid.

Monday 20th

To P. G. to pick up letters and then to see Marjorie Miles in a nursing home. Amy and I lunched at a pot-house in Wardour Street called Quo Vadis and then to the International.

Tuesday 21st

To P. G. & some shopping. Lunch with Amy and said good-bye. To Selfridges and then to see Marjorie again. Mother, Clare and Papa back also Christine for the night. Kitty came in after supper.

Wednesday 22nd

A.S.A. Depot. Lunch with Denis and Diana. To Lady Ridley's Hospital where I picked up Mrs Micholls and we went to the International together.

Thursday 23rd

To the Grove to tidy. A.S.A. Depot. Tea with Mrs Sims. Uncle Phil sent a carriage and picked up Cherry and we dined with him at the Berkeley. Also Captain Doyley (?) and Col Maude and we all went to *Belinda* by A. A. Milne and laughed. Irene Vanbrugh was very clever.

Friday 24th

A.S.A. Depot. To the Grove to tidy.

Saturday 25th

To the Grove to tidy. Went to see Marjorie. Dined with Uncle Phil.

Sunday 26th

Finished with the Grove.

Monday 27th

At the Grove again. A.S.A. Depot.

Tuesday 28th

To Cranleigh by the 3.45. A car met me and took me to Little Woodlands, Elmhurst, which Molly and Randall Wells have taken for the present. Sir Charles Friswell, their landlord whom I met at Sapphire Lodge came to dinner.

Wednesday 29th

Randall and I walked to Holmberg Hill.

May-June

I have no very accurate record of the very happy fortnight I spent with them. There was tennis at the weekend at the Friswells'. Mr Pease came on Monday night. Randall and I had one or two long walks and Sir Charles came up two or three times after dinner. Enid Erskine came on Saturday June 8 and she and I came up together on Monday 10th with four huge bundles of flowers. The decree in my divorce was made Absolute on June 3rd.

Stanley Baldwin, his wife, and daughter.

May 30th - June 10th
[Editors' note: See previous entry.]

Tuesday 11th
Shopped. Had tea with Gwen at Stewart's.

Wednesday 12th
Went with Gwen from Cox's on business of hers and then to the Hotel Cecil to find out some things about Jim from the Air Ministry. He is a 2nd Lt. Equipment Officer at Regents' Park getting 17/8 a day - probably more, and has not given me anything since March or tried to get the Govt. allowance for the children. I came back to lunch and rang up George Lewis and his secretary told me I must find out some other things, so I went back to the Cecil and everyone was very kind to me. I had tea with Sissie.

Thursday 13th
I spent from 9.30 – 11.30 seeing house agents, trying to get a resident caretaker and going over the Grove. Then I went to Holls, the R.A.F. bankers and got an application form for the allowance to officers' children and took it to Ely Place. George wanted to see me and appeared to be surprised that I hadn't had any money for so long or the Govt. grants – this comes of not complaining. He said he would try to hurry things on a bit. Then I went into St Paul's for a few moments and then by train to Victoria and had lunch and a long talk with Aunt Cissie. Then I went to another home agent and finding a lady who was going to look at the Grove. I asked her to look at 20 and went with her. I don't think she liked it. Then we went to tea with Mrs Micholls whom I found very happy with both boys home at the same time. Then I went to Amy and we had a high tea of eggs, potatoes and bacon, cucumber salad and strawberries and went by bus to the Shaftesbury Theatre to see *Don Giovanni*. It was a delightful performance and I was very happy. We came back on a bus, a most heavenly evening with a clear blue sky and late sunset and

a new moon. I found Christine here when I got back. She had come unexpectedly to stay the night. Mother and Papa came back from Denis and Diana and Denis had told Mother that Equipment Officer is one of the not coveted funk holes in the army. Also Amy told me that Jim had been teaching at a girls' school in Wimbledon. The ladies who kept it knew Mr Jacomb-Hood and they asked him whether Jim was the Mr McInnes whose wife had divorced him and he had to say yes, so they couldn't keep him.

Friday 14th
To the Grove. Lunched with Stella Speyer. Adila Fachiri, Jelly, Mrs Sloop, Elizabeth Lewis, and two Belgian ladies. I had tea with Lady Wemyss and came back on a bus in pelting rain. Clare and Christine and I to a party at Myra's where Jelly Aranyi, Mr Gooley, Fachiri, Mrs Lubbock and Myra played Brahms piano quintet, Ravel trio, Brahms on 2 pianos, César Franck orchestra variations (with Mr Bernard at the other piano). Lots of people were there including Mrs Stoop, Mrs Bigham, Mr Bigham, Mr Howard and Ruth, Babs Hannay, Mr Gleadowe, Captain Deniston, Peggy Ritchie, Reine and Guillaume Ormond, Mr and Mrs Ralph Hawtrey. We came back late with the Ormonds and the Gleadowe party. Christine stops for the weekend.

[Editors' note: The dates are misaligned, skipping Saturday 15th, and instead listing Saturday the 16th.]

Saturday 16th
At the Grove all morning. Joan Willis came for the weekend.

Sunday 17th
Christine, Joan, Miss Evans, a Miss Christison and a Mr Whall, organist at Strand and clarinet player rehearsed the Brahms clarinet quintet. Cousin Stan and Betty came to listen. They played again in the afternoon, repeating the Brahms and then doing a Mozart clarinet quintet. The audience was Mrs Ritchie

and Peggy, Madame Ormond and Reine, Uncle Stan, Mr Sargent, a Miss Smith and a Miss Buchanan, Winnie, the Mr Whall's brother who does stained glass, Mrs Newmarch and later Mr Howard who took Clare back to Tottenridge, and a cousin of his.

Monday 18th

To the Grove. Christine and Joan went. I took Mother to the Australian War Photographs at the Grafton Galleries and then to the Orpen Show. R.A.C. with a friend of his called Mitchell and went to *Nurse Benson*.

[Editors' note: There are no entries for June 19 – June 28]

Saturday 29th

I lunched with Winston at the R.A.C. Aunt Marion rang up and asked me to dinner. We had poisoned fish and went to the *Lilac Domino* and I felt so ill that she brought me home.

Sunday 30th

Sewed. Uncle Phil to lunch. Dr Mills brought a Mr Matsukata to tea. Dined with Uncle Phil.

Monday July 1st

To Queen Victoria St to order some Musical Glass for Winston's wedding present and got tickets for *Figaro* on Wednesday. Tea with Stella.

Tuesday July 2nd

Sewed. Mother and I to Kitty Somervell's dance performance. To see Visetti. I went to the *Seraglio* in Mr Pease's box. He brought me home, calling at the Fachiri's to pick up Clare on the way.

Wednesday 3rd

To the Grove. To *Figaro* with Mr Plank in the afternoon. He came back to tea and I showed him some Eph letters. To the Craies' in evening.

Thursday 4th

To the Grove. Sold my engagement ring. Lunch with Alice MacPherson. To the Annual Shakespeare lecture of the British Academy. Sir Walter Raleigh spoke this year, his subject was "Shakespeare and England." Home with Mother and Papa.

Friday 5^h

To the Grove to show it to Mrs Pollock. Changed some music at Chester's for Mother. To see Gwen at the Grosvenor Hotel after dinner.

Saturday 6th

Did a lot of shopping and business in Kensington. To Horseferry Road and then the Grove. Had high tea at the Craies' and Sissie, Miss Milne, Zoe and I went to *Carmen* at Drury Lane.

Sunday 7th

Sewed and tidied. Mr Davidson to tea and Christine to supper.

Monday 8th

Business. Lunched with Enid and met a pretty Miss (Harrington) Mann. Packed. Went to *Aida* to her pit, a very good performance and home on a bus.

Tuesday 9th

Met children at Victoria at 11.18 and saw Maam for a minute. Nanny went off for her holiday and I took the boys to Paddington and we went to Stourport by the 1.30 and drove out to the Old Hill, Aunt Cissie's "Rest House" where she is letting us be for a month. Miss Maddison who runs it gave us high tea.

Wednesday 10th

The boys and I went down to the Severn where they paddled. After lunch to Dick Brook.

Thursday 11th

Took boys on farm for butter. To the Hall to see Mrs Wallers. We walked towards the Burl before tea and made a round.

Friday 12th

We walked to the church and it rained a good deal.

Saturday 13th

With Miss Maddison to a cottage near Dick Brook for eggs. The boys and I found a paddling place with stepping stones further down the brook and came home through a wood.

Sunday 14th

Very wet. We only got out a little.

Monday 15th

We played in Mr Pratt's barn all morning. We go to the Hall nearly every afternoon to play on the sea-saw, but to-day we went a message for Miss Maddison.

131

Tuesday 16th
We played in the barn again and I gave the boys their first French lesson.

Wednesday 17th
The boys and I walked to Dunley by a cart-track and went on to look at Dunley Hall and then back by a field path to the church and home by the lane past Smith's cottage.

Thursday 18th
Probably explored down to where Dick Brook joins the Severn – a lovely walk.

Friday 19th
I shall never know what I did today.

Saturday 20th
We drove to Wilden after lunch and saw Maam, Aunt Louie and Aunt Edith.

Sunday 21st
We walked all round by the pools.

Monday 22nd
Very wet. We played in the barn a little.

Tuesday 23rd
To Wilden in the afternoon. Clear after a thunderstorm.

Wednesday 24th
We explored a lovely wet walk all along Dick Brook up to the church and left a message at the Rectory.

Thursday 25th
Betty came over and fetched the children and then we all went for a walk. Betty to tea and games.

Friday 26th

We went for a walk with Di and Betty. Mr Proctor the Rector came to tea and then we went over to the Hall to fetch the children's raincoats and found people there, including Christopher Warren.

Saturday 27th

Mr Benson was at the Hall for the week and we saw him.

Sunday 28th

We had a lovely walk.

Monday 29th

To Wilden in the afternoon.

Tuesday 30th

Very hot and fine. Lily to tea.

Wednesday 31st

Very hot again. Miss Baldwin (Rector's niece) to tea.

Thursday, August 1st
We all went to tea at the Hall.

Friday 2nd
Weather broke. Children to tea at the Hall.

Saturday 3rd
Heavy close day and rain. To Wilden – Uncle Fred was there whom I hadn't seen for 20 years.

Sunday 4th
A glorious morning of haze and sunshine. I took the boys to the Intercession Service.

Monday 5th
With children watched sheep dipping.

Tuesday 6th
Kitty Somervell came.

Wednesday 7th
I came up by the 7.55 leaving Kitty with the boys. Diana to lunch. I took her to the Grove to choose things for her new nursery. We have no maids as Alice's husband came back on leave while Gertrude was on her holiday. I dined with Uncle Phil and Mr Coudert at the Bath Club.

Thursday 8th
To the Grove to meet Bowler's men and saw all the pictures taken at the Garden Studio. Lunched with Uncle Phil and Mr Coudert at the Bath Club. The rest of the party was Mr Laughlin (1st sec. of the American Embassy) Mr Hurst, Mr Freshfield, Mr Malkin (English) and an American Mr A. M. Patterson, who is on the War Industries Board. Uncle Phil and I went to the International at the Grosvenor Galleries and had tea at the Carlton. He and Mr

Coudert dined at P. G. and also Herbert and Lettice. Mr Coudert and I had a walk afterwards and then he brought me home.

Friday 9th
Shopping and business. I dined with Uncle Phil and Mr Coudert as guests of Mr Patterson. The other guests were Mr Somers (War Industries Board) and Mr Anderson an international lawyer (both Americans).

Saturday 10th
I wrote letters for Uncle Phil and then he and I and Mr Coudert lunched at the Wellington Club. We walked up to the BathClub afterwards and then Mr Coudert and I went to a cable office and then he took me to Horseferry Road in a taxi and then home. We all dined together at the Rendezvous and also a very dull man called Inigo Thomas and went to Arnold Bennett's new dull play *The Title*. Mr Coudert and I walked home.

Sunday 11th
Tea with Amy.

Monday 12th
Did housework and cooking with Mother. Christine went.

Tuesday 13th
To Kensington. To Horseferry Road and sold some things at the stores.

Wednesday 14th
To the Grove. Mother and I there again after lunch to tidy. To Horseferry Road and the stores. Mother and Papa to dine with Diana.

Thursday 15th

To Horseferry Road and then to meet Clare at Paddington. Uncle Phil and Mr Coudert came round after tea to say good-bye as Mr Coudert goes to America to-night.

Friday 16th

To the Grove. Lunch with Maisie.

Saturday 17th

I met Hubert Somervell (who had just been torpedoed) in the High Street and we went together to Paddington to meet Kitty and the boys. Kitty came back to lunch. The boys got very dirty and mischievous in the garden.

Sunday 18th

Took boys to St Pauls and back by tram and train.

Monday 19th

Took boys to St Pancreas and we went to Elstree where they are to spend a few days with the Somervells. I missed the train back and had to spend 2 hours on Elstree platform.

Tuesday 20th

Colin's 4th birthday. I tidied things at the Grove.

Wednesday 21st

Superintended furniture moving at the Grove all morning. Captain Thirkell turned up about 3 o'clock and we went to Horseferry Road to report and had tea at the R.A.C. He is staying here for the present.

Thursday 22nd

With Captain Thirkell to the Grove and then into town. Lunched with Maisie at "Quo Vadis" and then we all went back and sat in her garden. Captain Thirkell took me out to dinner at the R.A.C.

Friday 23rd

Tidied furniture here all morning. Lunched with Winston. Mrs Harvey to tea. Dined at R.A.C.

Saturday 24th

Tidied things again. Winston came to lunch and we went back to town with him and had tea at the R.A.C.

Sunday 25th

Tidied books. We went to Richmond in a taxi and came back to tea.

Monday 26th – 31st

I can't remember all the things we did this week. George Thirkell asked me to marry him the night after he came here and we are both perfectly happy. We went to one of the overseas dances at Lady Mond's on Friday and to the *Lilac Domino* at the Empire one night and were together the whole time.

Sunday September 1st

We went to tea with Uncle Edward.

Monday 2nd

We had lunch with Winston and did lots of shopping and all went to the *Tales of Hoffman* at the Kings Theatre.

Tuesday 3rd

We did shopping and errands for people in France all day.

Wednesday 4th

I saw George off at Victoria by the 7.50. Tidied things all morning. Went to bed after lunch and didn't get up till supper time. Mr Cockerell to supper.

Thursday 5th

Shopped. Tidied things. Dined with Amy and Everard. A Mr Price there.

Friday 6th

Nanny came back. Shopped. Had early supper with Amy and we went to *Don Giovanni* at the Kings Theatre.

Saturday 7th

Tidied all day.

Sunday 8th

In bed most of the day. Feeling ill.

Monday 9th

Better. To Southsea by the 1.36. Gwen met me and took me to the flat where she has Pat, Michael and Eyleen MacGregor with the baby. I went round to see the Carrs and Stella, Winston, Cedric (brother) Mr and Mrs Carr, Mr Sutton (Mrs Carr's brother) and Col. Walstab, a friend of Win's.

Tuesday 10th

Gwen and I had morning tea with Winston, Mr Sutton, Mr Walker (the best-man) and Col Walstab. After lunch Win fetched me in a car and we went to the church. Stella looked very sweet and afterwards I went into the vestry. The reception was at someone else's house and then Win and Stella went off to Salcombe spending the night at Exeter. Mr Sutton came back to tea with me and Gwen's nice friend Lieutenant Blunt came to tea and stayed to supper.

Wednesday 11th

Mr Sutton took me and Gwen out to morning tea and Mr Walker and Mr Cedric Carr joined us and the bridesmaid Miss Hill. Gwen then took Mike and the baby out. Mr Blunt after supper.

Thursday 12th

Very well. I had tea with Mrs Carr. Gwen and I went to the Hippodrome and were quite amused by a woman Mary Sherrard.

Friday 13th

Shopped with Gwen. We went to Fort Blockhouse by the 4.25 boat and Lt Blunt gave us tea. He is a cousin of Wilfrid Blunt. Boxing finals were going on and we watched from his window and he came back to supper.

Saturday 14th

Came up by the 9.25. Wrote letters and tidied. Babs Hannay to lunch. Dined with Uncle Phil.

Sunday 15th

Took Graham to call on Amy. In with children.

Monday 16th

Shopped. Slept. Dined with Uncle Phil.

Tuesday 17th

To lunch with Maisie and stayed on to tea.

Wednesday 18th

Tidied. Shopped. Took boys to tea with Henry and dined at Hopkins'.

Thursday 19th

Took boys to Somervells' and then in Gardens.

Friday 20th

By 10.50 to Boxmoor and spent the day with Diana.

Saturday 21st

Tried to go to L.S.Q. concert but found a queue half way down Bond Street and came back. Clare had a party for David Howard consisting of Ruth, David, Jerry and Mr Plank to dinner and afterwards Amy and Everard, Kitty, Mrs Ritchie and Peggy Joan Willis, Miss Gunn, Captain James (a friend of David's) Vally, Riette and Mr Crofts, Mr Gleadowe, Babs Hannay. Half way through the evening David put his knee out. He went round to Dr Mills who set it and said he mustn't move, so we set him up in Papa's room and Captain James in Mary's room and Babs with Mother while Ruth and Jerry went to the Gunns'.

Sunday 22nd

David in bed all day. Mr and Mrs Somervell came in the morning also Ruth and Gerry. Captain James and Babs left. Mr and Mrs Howard to tea and supper. Mr Murray, Lady Mary, Rosalind, Mr Toynbee and Agnes called. I sat with David after supper.

Monday 23rd

Wrote letters. With Maisie to the pit to see the *Luck of the Navy*. Mother, Papa, Clare and I dined at the Mount Carmel Restaurant. David was taken to Millbank.

Tuesday 24th

Kitty came to tea with the children and I had tea with Mrs Micholls. Cousin Stan to supper.

Wednesday 25th

To Aeolian Hall for Clare. Got a mackintosh for Colin at Selfridge's and tried to see Mr Baldwin (Mr Cordert's friend) at a Canadian Hospital but he was out.

Thursday 26th

In all day.

Friday 27th

Henry came round to tell me Jim was back. I went to the Air Board after lunch but could learn nothing. Cousin Stan to supper and stay the night. The boys had tea with Amy at Hills and I joined them.

Saturday 28th

I went down to Surbiton and spent the day with Aunt Eva (Mrs Mowbray Gray, Winston's godmother).

Sunday 29th

Took Graham to call on Mrs Cobden-Sanderson and Buff. Pouring rain. In with boys.

Monday 30th

Very wet. To Millbank Hospital to see David Howard and then to tea with Queenie.

Tuesday, October 1st

Shopped for Mother. Aunt Eva came to lunch and I went with her afterwards to do some shopping. Christine after dinner.

Wednesday 2nd

Lunched with Mrs Morris.

Thursday 3rd

Took boys out. Amy and Everard to dinner.

Friday 4th

Lunched with Lucy. To visit Major Crofts at Lady Ridley's Hospital. Stella looked in after tea and Sissie came and she and I went to Quo Vadis in Warlow Street and dined with Mr Plank who took us to the Coliseum to see the Russian dancers in *Carnaval*.

Saturday 5th

To visit Mr Baldwin at the Canadian Hospital. I dined with the Somervells and we had games afterwards.

Sunday 6th

I lunched with Mrs Middleton and Mrs Stillman. Tea with Lady Ritchie and Mrs Flower drove me home. Oliver to tea.

Monday 7th

Nanny went and I took the boys out. Sally came in the afternoon. Denis and Diana to supper.

Tuesday 8th

I had lunch with Aunt Cissie. With Mother to take some odds and ends to Mrs Taylor for her shop in Beauchamp Place and then we had chocolate at Debny's. Jim had called while I was out.

Wednesday 9th

Very well. I had tea with Diana and took her some baby things.

Thursday 10th
I went to see Henry about Jim. Bought woollies for the boys. After lunch I walked to Kensington with the boys and then went to the Lyceum and got tickets for Saturday. Put boys to bed.

Friday 11th
To South Kensington Preparatory School and saw the Headmaster Mr Barton and looked over the school. Called on Henry to give him a message for Graham Peel who is in town. I went down to Surbiton and spent the day with Aunt Eva. To an Overseas Dance in the evening, one of Enid Erskine's. I met a Mr Huntington, attache at the American Embassy at Pelengrad on his way to Washington. He and an older man both of whom knew the Couderts found a taxi for me.

Saturday 12th
Shopped. Lunched with Amy and found Everard in bed with flu. Amy and I went to *The Female Hun* at the Lyceum. I went on to the L.S.Q. concert afterwards and heard the Brahms' clarinet quintet. Dined with Margaret.

Sunday 13th
Christine brought her quartet here to rehearse *Selg isn Derr Mann* with Dorothy Silk a Mrs Gough (?) and Dr Harris (piano). It was unusually bad. Took the boys to see Sissie and Uncle Edward and then to tea with Mrs Mills. Mr Bradley to supper.

Monday 14th
Mr Sutton came to tea. Had lunch with Papa at Lyons and looked at a cookery school.

[Editors' note: There is no entry for Tuesday, October 15, 1918. Every date is off beginning with Tuesday, October 16th as listed,

and every day of the month thereafter, until it is corrected with the double entry of the 25th.]

Tuesday 16th

To look at a cookery school in Buckingham Palace Road. Called on Visetti who wanted to see me about some hare-brained schemes. Called on Mr Wilkinson to ask about his school. Met Mother and Christine at the Pioneer Club where Christine gave us dinner and we went to a Promenade Concert to hear Myra play the Franck *Symphonic Variations*. Met Arnold Bax whom I hadn't seen for a long time.

Wednesday 17th

To the bank. To Mr New, Mother's dentist. Bought cakes for children. Sheila, Patrick, and Moira with nurses came to see.

Thursday 18th

To see Mrs Harvey and Mrs Halsey. Took boys out.

Friday 19th

To dentist. To Gloucester Road Cookery School for my first lesson. Dined with Lilian.

Saturday 20th

In all day working and knitting.

Sunday 21st

I had tea with Betty Gall and dined with Maisie. Hugh and Mimi there and a padre called Davidson.

Monday 22nd

Cooking. To see Visetti. Tea with Dorothy Longman and then to Grosvenor Square to see Molly Wells.

Tuesday 23rd

Cooking all day.

Wednesday 24th

Cooking. Mother and I to a terrible concert at Leighton Home where Buff's Miss Finch made her appearance. We left early by the backstairs. Mr Patterson to tea.

Thursday 25th

Cooking. Took children to Mr New. He cleaned Graham's teeth and is to do a stopping. He found nothing to do for Colin. Mother to R'dean.

Friday 25th

Cooking. Lunched with Sissie and Major Blackwood an Australian padre at the Church Imperial Club, Victoria Street. Stella brought Pat to tea. I dined with Amy.

Saturday 26th

To lunch with Aunt Eva. Enid and I went for a walk. I dined with Auntie Stella at the Savoy and found her so nervy that I stayed the night.

Sunday 27th

Came back early and took Graham to see Sissie. In with children. Val Worthington to tea and stopped to supper. Kitty to supper.

Monday 28th

Cooking. Lunched with Val at his hotel, the Curzon. Met Mother at Victoria and helped her home with her luggage.

Tuesday 29th

Cooked all day and had lunch with Lady Mary. Stella Speyer to tea.

Wednesday 30th

Cooked. Took Graham to dentist.

Thursday 31st

Cooked. Arranged about marriage license. Children had tea with Pat eech and I went on to fetch them. Mel to supper and Mr and Mrs Benson came in afterwards.

J. W. Mackail, Angela's father.

Friday Nov. 1st

Cooked and cleaned gas oven. Mr Walker, Win's best man came to tea and played with the boys and then I dined with him and we went to *Soldier Boy*.

Saturday, 2nd

Shopped. Slept all afternoon. Mrs Fisher to tea. Val to supper.

Sunday 3rd

In all day. It rained. Mrs Newmarch and a Miss Colman to tea. Also Oliver Gotch.

Monday 4th

Cooking.

Tuesday 5th

Cooked all day. Children began colds. Dined with Val and went to the Russian ballet at the Coliseum.

Wednesday 6th

Cooked. To the dentist. Boys in bed all day.

Thursday 7th

Cooked. In with boys who are still in bed.

Friday 8th

Cooked. Boys indoors. Mother, Papa, Ers and I to *Trelawny of the Wells* at the Kings Theatre.

Saturday 9th

Saw a Lord Mayor's Show in the crowd. Amy to tea. Boys out for a little. Dined with Val and we went to the Coliseum for *Carnaval*.

Sunday 10th

In with children.

Monday 11th

The Armistice was signed at 5 o'clock this morning and hostilities ceased on all fronts at 11 o'clock which was announced to London by maroons like an air raid. I tried to get into town after lunch but was turned back at Hyde Park Corner. Dined with Val.

Tuesday, 12th

Mother and I went and sat on German guns in the Mall to watch the King and Queen go to St Pauls. Cooking.

Wednesday 13th

Cooking. To the dentist. Lady Jekyll to supper.

Thursday 14th

Cooking. In with children. Sally went away for a fortnight to be married.

Friday, 15th

In all morning. Mother sent me to bed. Adele Saffery came in and Mrs Morse.

Saturday 16th

In bed all day.

Sunday 17th

In bed.

Monday 18th

In bed.

Tuesday 19th

In bed. Got up after lunch.

Wednesday 20th

Took children out a little.

Thursday 21st

Took boys out.

Friday 22nd

Took boys out. Diana Grove to tea.

Saturday 23rd

Took boys out. Met Colonel and Mrs Clogstoun, Christine to stay.

Sunday 24th

Amy took the boys out. Christine's quartet rehearsed.

Monday 25th

To the Private View of the war pictures at Burlington House, including the Society of Australian Artists.

Tuesday 26th

Took boys out. Sapper Sams from George's Corps called in the morning. Captain Forbes, a delightful padre came to lunch and stayed to tea. Amy took the boys out to tea with her and I fetched them.

Wednesday 27th

Took boys to tea with Maisie. Val fetched me and we dined at Prince's and went to the Coliseum.

Thursday 28th

Lunched at Mrs Wood's Club. In with boys. Sally came back. Clare, Kitty and I dined at Quo Vadis and went to the Coliseum for *Carnaval*.

Friday 29th

Shopped all afternoon. Tea with Mrs Collier. Amy and Everard to dinner.

Saturday 30th

Mr Robinson one of George's subalterns to lunch. Christine gave her first string quartet concert at Leighton House. I brought Mr James and Mr Ker back to tea. Dined with Amy and Everard and we went to *Carnaval*.

Sunday, December 1st

Rained. Graham to tea with Mollie Poynter. I fetched him and he had a throat and shivered and was put to bed.

Monday 2nd

Graham in bed all day. Clare and I to a lecture by Sir O. Lodge at Pamela's.

Tuesday

Graham in all day. Denis, Diana and Val to supper.

Wednesday

Graham sat up to tea. Amy telephoned that George was back from Mainz so I rushed round to see him and ...

[Editors note: Last entry 1918]

George came over on Dec. 10th and we were married on the 13th. Win came up on the 12th and spent the night here and he and Mother and Papa and Clare came to the registrar's office with us. We went to Ely Place to sign our wills and had lunch at Paddington. Mother and the boys and Clare saw us off. We stayed at Oxford from the 13th to the 17th at the Eastgate Hotel where we were starved. George gave me a gold wristwatch. I sold my old wedding ring for £1 and bought George a cane. We came home on the 19th and began interviewing people about possible jobs in England for George. Finally he got his leave extended to January 10th.

Wednesday January 1st

In all day.

[Editors' note: Although the family remained in England for some time, the next we hear is Trooper to the Southern Cross.]

PART II

A READER'S GUIDE TO THE

DIARY

THE ANGELA THIRKELL SOCIETY
SUSAN VERELL AND BARBARA HOULTON

GUIDE INTRODUCTION

The diary and the guide contain miniature portraits of the people, places, events, and the arts involved in Angela's life, beginning when she was Angela McInnes in January 1915 and ending after she had become Angela Thirkell, with the final entry "1919 Wednesday January 1 – In all day."

Almost every entry in the guide contains information from multiple sources. The bibliography provides these sources. The internet was also a valuable tool for confirming information.

Speaking of tools, this guide is a tool to enhance the experience of reading Angela's words. Readers can quickly access the details discovered during the editors' research using the index and the guide, which is a dictionary of people, places, art, music, and the theater, divided into categories. In addition, the index provides an alphabetical listing.

Some entries appear more than once in this guide, as it was appropriate for these entries to appear in various sub-sections. Some of the names in the guide do not appear in the diary but are included as family members of entries and add background information.

All explanatory entries come from multiple sources; if a single source is used, it is footnoted. Otherwise, consider the entries conglomerates from the references. This guide, like the diary and introduction, is published under the non-profit auspices of the Angela Thirkell Society of North America.

SECTION I – GUIDE TO PEOPLE

Angela mentioned a great many people. Seeing friends and acquaintances at lunch, tea, and dinner, proved daily how social Angela was. Her diary probably helped her keep up with her busy life.

Some people will remain forever unknown, but Angela Thirkell first described some in her autobiography, *Three Houses*. Of those people Angela met in Rottingdean and London as a child, most often they were friends of her grandparents, Georgiana and Edward Burne-Jones. Four generations of friendships were created as Colin and Graham played with the children of Angela's multi-generational friends. Angela's mother, Margaret Mackail, shared her friends with Angela. Family friends and relatives came to Jim McInnes's recitals; Angela's sister, Clare, and Angela's husband, Jim, were friends. Even unknown people are mentioned in the guide, with any known information accompanying their listings.

The names in parentheses after the initial listings are the names that Angela used in the diary. Each entry is listed in the following order:

1. Last name.
2. First names and known middle names.
3. Names used in the diary are in parentheses.
4. Maiden names and other family information are in the description.
5. Indented entries, when provided, are family members.

For example, "Ridsdale, Sir Aurelian and Susan (Aurelian and Susan)." Angela states, "Aurelian and Susan called." The definition explains that her maiden name was Sterling. Families

154

are indented.   Primary names within categories are in alphabetical order, except for the Wyndhams, who are organized by families.   For titles, the usage is not traditional.   Titled individuals could have multiple names during their lifetimes.   In addition, Angela may not have used a title when one existed.

As much information as possible was provided.   People with German names during World War I sometimes used the German and sometimes an Anglicized version.   References show both Holst and von Holst for the same person, even though Angela consistently used von Holst in the diary.

Unanswered questions limit some definitions.   Taking Henry James as an example, Angela attended his memorial service on March 3, 1916.   Her family knew the author Henry James as described. Research shows that Henry James, the author, died in London on February 28, 1916; Angela attended his memorial service a few days later.   After Henry James's death, Mr James, Mrs James, the James children, and even Captain James appeared.   However, no information was discovered about those people.

ANGELA'S FAMILY

> "I went to P. G. and Mother, Clare and I joined Papa at Treviglio where we dined and went to *More* at the Ambassadors. Slept at P. G." November 24, 1915

Edward Burne-Jones was a famous pre-Raphaelite artist with a large circle of friends and patrons. He married Georgiana MacDonald, one of the MacDonald sisters famous for marrying well and producing renowned offspring. Her immediate family remained close to most of her relatives over the years. Sir Edward Burne-Jones died in 1898 when Angela was eight years old. His wife (Maam or Ma'am in the diary) left their home in London, the Grange, and moved full-time to their country home, North End House in Rottingdean (R'Dean). Edward and Georgiana had two children who lived to adulthood, Philip (Uncle Phil) and Margaret. Margaret Burne-Jones (Mother) married John Mackail (Papa); they had three children: Angela, Denis, and Clare.

Angela married James Campbell McInnes (Jim) in 1911, and Denis married Diana Granet in 1917. Angela and Denis were not close. However, Angela does see Diana and Denis occasionally during the years of the diary. Angela's and Denis's sister Clare never married.

ANGELA'S IMMEDIATE FAMILY

Burne-Jones, Sir Edward (E. B. J.) – he was Angela's grandfather but was mentioned only once by Angela when she saw his work at an exhibit at the Tate Gallery, yet, his presence was felt. Some people mentioned by Angela knew her and her family because of their longtime patronage of Edward Burne-Jones. Because he was an only child, the Aunties mentioned were his wife's relatives or the well-to-do landed gentry who were his patrons and associates. References appeared listing him as Sir Edward Coley Burne Jones, his name without the hyphen.

He added the hyphen himself, saying, "Who will ever remember the name of an artist named Edward Jones?" He received the baronetcy, which passed to his son Philip, in honor of his work, stating that he only did so because Phil would inherit it.[3] He left a large estate with Georgiana, Philip, John Mackail, and Alfred Baldwin as trustees and with Philip and Margaret as the ultimate beneficiaries after Georgiana died. This estate likely provided the funds for some of the expenses Angela and her family incurred. Although he was not living in 1915, his influence was felt in Angela's life.

Burne-Jones, Georgiana Macdonald (Maam, Ma'am) – she was Angela's grandmother and wife of Edward Burne-Jones. Angela saw her grandmother in London and visited her in Rottingdean and Wilden.

Burne-Jones, Sir Philip (Uncle Phil) – he was Angela's Uncle Phil, her mother's brother, and a constant in Angela's life. Philip's godfathers were Dante Gabriel Rossetti, John Ruskin, and Henry James. (Strickland)[4] He never married, although he was fascinated early with Mrs. Patrick Campbell and later with Mary Wyndham. However, these romances did not work out, and he remained a confirmed bachelor.

Mackail, Margaret Burne-Jones (Mother) – she was Angela's mother. Daughter of Edward Burne-Jones and Georgiana MacDonald. It was her influence that provided musical education for Angela and Clare.

---

[3] MacCarthy, Fiona, *The Last Pre-Raphaelite: Edward Burne-Jones and the Victorian Imagination,* London: Faber and Faber Ltd., 2011.

[4] Strickland, Margot, *Angela Thirkell: Portrait of a Lady Novelist*, The Angela Thirkell Society of North America, 1977.

Mackail, John (Papa) – he was Angela's father, known as Jack to his friends. He was one of the trustees of the Sir Edward Burne-Jones estate. Mackail wrote many books, including translations. He also wrote the biography of William Morris and other works associated with Morris and his philosophy. His book on Latin literature went through 30 editions. In his translation of Maurice Maeterlinck's play, *Pelleas and Melisande*, Mrs. Patrick Campbell (Auntie Stella) was cast as Melisande, and Burne-Jones settings from King Arthur were used for the production. This collaborative effort occurred in 1898 and was an example of the closeness of family and friends. He was also referred to once as Ba (grandfather) when he attended the funeral of his granddaughter, Mary.

Mackail, Clare (Clare) – she was Angela's younger sister. She never married. Both Angela and Clare had been trained in music, a tradition carried on by their mother, who had a musical background encouraged by her mother, Georgiana Burne-Jones. Clare was very active in sports – rowing, tennis, hiking, but she was of fragile health. She met Jim McInnes before Angela did. Clare continued her friendship with him until his breakup with Angela.

Mackail, Denis George (Denis) – he was Angela's younger brother. Angela did not attend his wedding, as she was ill, and he did not attend her funeral, as he had a dentist appointment. He was also an author, worked in the theater, and remained active in the arts, although he was not a painter.

Mackail, Diana (Diana) – she was Angela's sister-in-law, née Diana Granet. She married Denis in 1917. Denis explained that her father was not wealthy when he married her but acquired assets along the way, resulting in "two Rolls-Royces and a country house." They seemed cordial and connected with the rest of the family. The name, Di, referred to the daughter of Stanley Baldwin, also named Diana.

158

McInnes, Colin Campbell (Colin) - he was Angela's second child, considered a baby through most of the diary. He was born in 1914.

McInnes, Graham Campbell (Graham) – he was Angela's oldest child and was born in 1912. He was old enough to have playmates and be considered for school. He was named after his godfather Graham Peel and his father, James Campbell McInnes.

McInnes, Mary Campbell (Mary) – she was Angela's third child who died as an infant. She was born just before Angela's separation from Jim. Angela did not attend her funeral, a common practice in England at the time for bereaved mothers. Her wooden grave markings were at Angela's insistence, as she did not want tombstones.

McInnes, James Campbell (Jim) – he was Angela's first husband. A singer known as Jim to his family, he sang under the name Campbell McInnes or J. Campbell McInnes.

Spencer, Dr John Heatley and Margaret (Peggy and Dr Spencer, Dr Spencer) – she was Jim's youngest sister. He had received a scholarship to attend the Charing Cross Hospital Medical School in 1900, and he was the son of Dr and Mrs William I. Spencer of Napier, New Zealand. Dr Heatley Spencer and Peggy married on August 25, 1915, at St. John's Church in Chelsea. Angela attended their wedding.

ANGELA'S OTHER RELATIVES

"We lunched with Uncle Phil at the Bath Club. Cousin Stan and Oliver came too." September 6, 1915

These well-known families were the Baldwins, the Poynters, and the Kiplings, and they were related to Angela through her grandmother Georgiana Burne-Jones.

THE BALDWINS

"Cousin Stan and Betty came to listen." June 17, 1918

Louisa and Alfred's son was Stanley Baldwin (Cousin Stan), who became Prime Minister in 1935. Angela frequently dined at the Baldwins, but there was no record of which Baldwins were there.

Baldwin, Louisa (Aunt Louie) – she was the mother of Stanley Baldwin. Louisa was Angela's grandmother Georgiana's half-sister. Louisa's husband was the industrialist Alfred Baldwin, who died in 1908. He had been one of the executors of Sir Edward Burne-Jones's estate. Angela saw Aunt Louie and Aunt Edith in 1918 while she visited her grandmother.

Baldwin, Stanley and Lucy (Cousin Stan,–Aunt Cissie) – Stanley married Lucy Ridsdale in 1892. He was a member of Parliament beginning in 1908. By 1917 he was Financial Secretary to the Treasury, becoming Prime Minister after the diary years. His mother was Angela's grandmother's sister Louisa. Rudyard Kipling was his first cousin and close friend. Stanley and Lucy had seven children, with three mentioned by Angela. He was referred to one as Uncle Stan.

> **Baldwin, Diana (Di)** – she was the daughter of Lucy and Stanley Baldwin. She was distinguished from the wife of Denis, who is always called Diana.

> **Lady Esther Louisa Baldwin (Betty)** – she was the daughter of Cousin Stanley and Lucy Baldwin.

> **Baldwin, Oliver (Oliver)** - he was the son of Lucy and Stanley Baldwin. Born in 1899. He grew up to become a socialist politician at odds with his conservative father.

Ridsdale, Sir Aurelian and Susan (Aurelian and Susan) – his sister was Stanley's wife, Lucy Ridsdale Baldwin. She was the

160

former Susan Stirling, and he was a leading member of the British Red Cross Society. Philip Burne-Jones individually painted both Aurelian and Susan. Esther was their daughter.

> **Ridsdale, Esther (Esther)** – she was the niece of Lucy Ridsdale Baldwin, daughter of Sir Aurelian and Susan Ridsdale, and a playmate of Angela's son Graham.

THE POYNTERS

> "We dined with the Poynters and Hugh came back to dinner in his A.S.C. clothes." July 9, 1915

Poynter, Sir Edward (Uncle Edward) – Edward was married to Angela's grandmother Georgiana Burne-Jones's half-sister, née Agnes MacDonald, who died in 1906. He was a painter, designer, and draftsman who served as president of the Royal Academy and was the first baronet Poynter. They had two children, Ambrose and Hugh. The family is noted once as The Poynters.

> **Poynter, Sir Ambrose and Cherry (Cherry and Ambrose)**– he was the son of Edward and Agnes Poynter and a calligrapher, artist, and architect. He designed the Torre Monumental in Retiro, Buenos Aires.

> **Poynter, Sir Hugh Edward (Hugh)** – he was the son of Edward and Agnes Poynter and third baronet Poynter. He was fluent in five languages and used his language skills successfully in business.

> **Poynter, Mollie (Mollie Poynter)** – she is seen twice in the diary: once with Hugh and Uncle Edward and once she had tea with Graham, but nothing else is known about her. She was not the sibling of Hugh and Ambrose, nor a daughter of either Hugh or Ambrose, as both were childless.

THE KIPLINGS

"We motored over to Burwash to see the Kiplings."

May 24, 1915

Rudyard Kipling was 25 years old than Angela. He was her first cousin once removed, as was Stanley Baldwin. Kipling was a famous author and was awarded the Nobel Prize for Literature in 1907.

By the end of 1915, his family had experienced devastating losses. In 1899, Kipling's daughter Josephine developed pneumonia and died. Kipling's son, John, was killed in action during World War I in September 1915, at the age of 18. A third child, Elsie, married George Bambridge but had no children. The home of Rudyard Kipling was called Bateman's and was located in Burwash in East Sussex. Angela mentioned the family only once: "We motored over to Burwash to see the Kiplings," was the extent of her comments. Angela did not say if they were at home.

OTHER MACDONALD RELATIVES

"We drove to Wilden after lunch and saw Maam Aunt Louie and Aunt Edith." July 20, 1918.

Macdonald, Edith (Aunt Edith) – she was Angela's great aunt, Georgiana Burne-Jones's sister. Edith Macdonald never married. Angela saw her, along with Aunt Louie Baldwin, in 1918 while visiting her grandmother.

Macdonald, The Reverend Frederick (Uncle Fred) – he was the brother of Angela's grandmother, Georgiana Burne-Jones and Angela's great uncle. Angela only wrote of him once: "Uncle Fred was there whom I hadn't seen for 20 years."

FAMILY FRIENDS

> We lunched with the Lewises, who sent us home in the car. March 13, 1916

Sir Edward Burne-Jones was devoted to his art and was also a businessman. The Arts & Crafts movement was both creative and profitable. Time not devoted to painting and stained glass was spent at country weekends and city parties with his patrons. As a result, Angela's mother and her Uncle Phil developed friendships with the children of these patrons. These friendships continued with Angela and ultimately with Graham and Colin's playmates.

Although Sir Edward Burne-Jones died in 1896, the relationships he built continued throughout Angela's life. The entries below were mentioned by Angela and illustrated the multi-generational connections.

This listing also contains people who were primarily friends of Angela's parents. Their great friend W. Graham Robertson started a social club called the Loony Club. Members included President Robertson and the Mackails, Henry Justice Ford, and the Speeds.

Multigenerational friends, the Wyndham family, and Auntie Stella are presented in separate categories.

Alma-Tadema, Laurence (Laurence Tadema) – she was the similarly named daughter of artist Lawrence Alma-Tadema, a Pre-Raphaelite artist and close friend of Edward Burne-Jones. She was a writer with a strong interest in Poland, and Jim performed Polish songs for her. She was also a friend of Clare's.

Ashbridge, John and Sylvia Moore (Mr and Mrs Ashbridge) – he was a solicitor; she had her portrait painted by Pre-Raphaelite artist Thomas Frederick Mason Sheard. Their son Sir

Noel Ashbridge, born in 1889, was an engineer who played a vital role in the early technical development of the British Broadcasting Corporation. Angela and Jim saw the Ashbridges at the Cooks during a weekend visit and in London.

Benson, Robin and Evelyn (Mr and Mrs Benson) – he was a merchant banker and art collector. They had a home at Buckhurst Park, Withyham, in East Sussex, which they rented on a 25-year lease from Gilbert Sackville, Earl De La Warr. Robin Benson worked to make the memorial service at Westminster Abbey for Edward Burne-Jones possible. Their son Guy was the second husband of Violet Manners Charteris (Lady Elcho during the diary years). Angela and Jim saw the Bensons at a country weekend and continued to see them in town.

Cobden-Sanderson, Thomas James and Annie (Cobden-Sandersons, Mrs Cobden-Sanderson) – he was an artist, bookbinder, and friend of William Morris. He coined the words "Arts and Crafts." He later founded the Dover Press. He was the godfather of Bertrand Russell. She, also a friend of Morris before her marriage, was a socialist, suffragette, and vegetarian. She spent six months in jail in 1906 after her arrest for demonstrating at the House of Commons and refusing to pay a fine of ten pounds. They had two children, Richard (Dicky) and Stella (married name Speyer).

> **Cobden-Sanderson, Richard and Dorothea (Dicky C-S, Mrs Dicky Cobden-Sanderson)** – he was a printer and designer like his father. Dicky and Dorothea divorced in 1921, and she married Ferdinand (Ferdy) Speyer, Stella Cobden-Sanderson Speyer's ex-husband.

> **Speyer, Ferdinand and Stella (Stella & Mr Speyer, Stella Speyer)** – Stella Cobden-Sanderson married Ferdinand (Ferdy) Speyer in 1910. He fell in love with Stella's brother Dicky's wife, Dorothea. Both couples

divorced in 1921. Ferdy Speyer and Dorothea married. Stella never remarried.

Speyer, Lady (Lady Speyer) – she was the mother of Ferdinand Speyer. Their wealthy banking family supported music and the arts. Lady Speyer sponsored Jim's singing for the soldiers.

Collier, John and Ethel (Mr Collier, Mrs Collier, Lady Collier) – she was the daughter of biologist and anthropologist Thomas Huxley. He was an artist. His painting of Angela wearing a large, red-feathered hat was done in 1914. John Collier was married first to Ethel's sister Marion Huxley who died in 1887. He married Ethel in 1889; the wedding took place in Norway because until the Deceased Wife's Sister's Marriage Act was passed in 1907, such a marriage was illegal in England. Their son Laurence was a friend of Angela's yet not a suitor.[5] Angela went to a Private View of Mr Collier's pictures at the Leicester Galleries. Her parents were friends of the Colliers.

Crawshay-Williams, Joyce (Joyce Crawshay-Williams) – she was the daughter of John Collier and his first wife the former Marion Huxley . Joyce was an illustrator and painter of miniature portraits. She visited Angela for tea.

Colvin, Sir Sidney and Fanny (the Colvins) – he was a curator as well as a literary and art critic. Through his friend Edward Burne-Jones, Colvin was a member of the circle of Dante Gabriel Rossetti from 1868 to 1872. As member of the Society of Dilettanti since 1871, he acted as its honorary secretary from 1891 to 1896. He was a great friend of Robert Louis Stevenson.

---

[5] Hall, Anne, *Angela Thirkell: A Writer's Life*, London: Unicorn Publishing Group, LLP, 2021.

Stevenson dedicated *Travels with a Donkey in the Cévennes* to Colvin, who became his literary adviser. Angela and Jim saw the Colvins occasionally, and they attended a lecture he gave on "*Condensation and Suggestions in Poetry.*"

Craies, William Feilden and Euterpe (the Craies, Mrs Craies) – they lived in Kensington. He was a barrister and lecturer on criminal law. Edward Burne-Jones had regularly attended gatherings at the home of Euterpe's father, Constantine Alexander Ionides. Her sister was Zoe Ionides Manuel. Her aunt was Maisie Woolner. Sabina (Sissie) was their daughter. They were seen frequently by the Mackail and McInnes families.

> **Craies, Sabina (Sissie)** – she was a constant companion of her mother Euterpe.

De Morgan, William and Evelyn (Mr and Mrs De Morgan) – he was a potter, designer, novelist, and life-long friend of William Morris and died on January 17, 1917. Before she married, Evelyn Pickering's paintings were displayed alongside Edward Burne-Jones's at the inaugural exhibit at the Grosvenor Gallery in 1877. Jim attended his memorial service in 1917 and possibly sang there.

Denroche-Smith, Thomas (Mr Denroche-Smith) – he was a judge who came to tea several times and had retired from Bengal civil service. His son, Lieutenant Archibald John Denroche-Smith, was the first British casualty during World War I and died on September 13, 1914.

Fisher, Mr and Mrs Alexander (Mr Alexander Fisher, Mrs Fisher) – he was an Arts and Crafts artist and silversmith who studied at the Limoges school of enameling. He published a book in 1909 entitled *The Art of Enameling Upon Metal: with a short appendix concerning miniature painting on enamel.* Mr Fisher taught Madeline Wyndham how to enamel. The Fishers were friends of Angela's parents. Angela wrote that she did not care for his enamels, but she entertained the Fishers occasionally for tea or dinner.

Ford, Henry Justice (Henry) – he was an artist and illustrator, a friend of Angela's parents and Jim. He played a significant role in Angela's life and was always called just Henry. His identity was confirmed in Margaret Mackail's diary. He was closely associated with Graham Robertson, Angela's parents, and other members of the Looney Club.

Ford, Mr and Mrs Walter (Mr and Mrs Walter Ford) – he was a friend of Angela's parents and a professor of singing at the Royal College of Music. His brother is illustrator Henry Justice Ford.

Gaskell, May (Mrs Gaskell) – she was a family friend which started with her close friendship with Edward Burne-Jones. Angela went to see her at Pembroke Gardens.

Gillick, Ernest George and Mary (the Gillicks, Mrs Gillick) – he was a sculptor, and Mary Tutin Gillick was an artist and a sculptor. Angela visited or had tea with them on several occasions.

Gladstone, Maud (Mrs Henry Gladstone) – she was married to Sir Henry Neville Gladstone, the 1st Baron Gladstone of Hawarden. She was Maud Ernestine Rendel before she married. They had no children, and the barony became extinct. Sir Henry was the third son of Prime Minister William Ewart Gladstone. Prime Minister Gladstone was a friend of Edward Burne-Jones, who attended Gladstone's state funeral in 1898. Mrs Gladstone had tea with Angela. Miss Gladstone is mentioned by Angela and may be a niece of Mrs Gladstone.

Gleadowe, Reginald (Mr Gleadowe) – he was a designer who taught at Winchester College and was Slade Professor of Fine

Arts at Oxford. During War I, he worked for the Admiralty. He was a friend of Clare's.

Hallé, Charles (Charlie Hallé) – he was an artist friend of Edward Burne-Jones and partner with him at the New Gallery, one of the sites of the Pre-Raphaelite Movement. Angela saw him once at P. G. for tea.

Hopkins, Everard and Amy (Mr and Mrs Hopkins) – Everard, brother of poet Gerald Manley Hopkins, was a watercolorist and illustrator. Amy was one of Margaret Mackail's closest friends. Parents of Gerry.

> **Hopkins, Gerry (Gerry)** – he was the son of Everard and Amy, served with great distinction in World War I and was awarded the Military Cross. Angela went to see him when he was home on leave, and they socialized when he was in London.

Hunt, Gladys Holman (Gladys Holman Hunt) – she was the daughter of Pre-Raphaelite painter William Holman Hunt. Angela saw her once in 1917.

Jacomb-Hood, George Percy and Henrietta (Mr and Mrs Jacomb-Hood, the Jacomb-Hoods) – he was a founding member of the Society of Portrait Painters and a friend and neighbor of John Singer Sargent. He played a part in getting Jim McInnes fired from a teaching position after his divorce. She was Henrietta Kemble de Hochepied-Larpent.

Jekyll, Herbert and Agnes (the Jekylls, Lady Jekyll) – he was the brother of garden designer, writer, and artist Gertrude Jekyll. Agnes was an artist, writer, and philanthropist. Her father was William Graham, one of Edward Burne-Jones's best patrons and supporters. She was named Dame Commander of the Order of the British Empire (DBE) in 1918 for her public works. Both Angela and her mother remained friends of theirs for years.

Lewis, Elizabeth (Lady Lewis) – she was the second wife of Sir George Henry Lewis, the first Baronet of Portland Place, who died in 1911. Sargent painted her. The family was intensely interested in Burne-Jones paintings and remained associated with Angela and her mother.

Lewis, Sir George and Marie Anna (the Lewises, George Lewis) – George James Graham Lewis was the second Baronet of Portland Place and a solicitor who Angela consulted about her separation from Jim. Their son was George James Ernest Lewis. Angela stayed at the Lewis home in Broadway in 1917. He was the son of George Henry Lewis and the sister of Katherine Elizabeth Lewis.

> **Lewis, George (Georgie)** – George James Ernest Lewis was the son of George and Marie Anna Lewis. He was born in 1910 and would become the third baronet. He visited with Angela and her children.

Lewis, Katherine Elizabeth (Katie) – she was the daughter of Sir George Henry and Elizabeth Lewis (Lady Lewis) and sister of Angela's lawyer, Sir George Lewis, second baronet. As a child, she was a favorite of Edward Burne-Jones. His letters to Katie started when she was four years old. She often visited Angela with Lady Lewis.

MacLagan, Eric and Helen (the MacLagans, Mrs Eric MacLagan) – he was an art historian. He worked at the Victoria and Albert Museum as an assistant in the textile department and head of the department of architecture and sculpture.

Manuel, Zoe and Stephen (Zoe Manuel and Mr Manuel) – her father was Constantine Alexander Ionides, an art collector famous for his bequest of 82 oil paintings to the Victoria and Albert Museum. He was a friend of Edward Burne-Jones. Her aunt, Aglaia Ionides Coranio, left Zoe a drawing of Fanny Cornforth by Rossetti and *The Days of Creation* by Edward

Burne-Jones. Her sister is Angela's friend Euterpe Craies, and her aunt is Maisie Woolner. The Manuels visit the Mackails and Angela.

Marillier, Christabel and Henry (Christabel and Mr Marillier) – the Marilliers were friends of Angela's parents. He was a journalist, critic, and art historian. They married in 1906. She is the daughter of the artist, Arthur Hopkins. She was the composer of "The Rose and the Ring." In 1899 Henry Marillier wrote *Dante Gabriel Rossetti: An Illustrated Memorial of His Art and Life.* They raised Betty, a daughter from Henry's first marriage.

> **Marillier, Betty (Betty Marillier)** – the daughter of Henry Marillier and his first wife. Betty visited Angela with Christabel

Markham, Violet (Lady Markham) – she was a social reformer who did not favor women being given the vote. Although she married Lieutenant-Colonel James Carruthers in 1915, she continued to use her maiden name. She hosted dances during the war, and Angela frequently attended her dances in 1918.

Mellor, Sir John and Mabel (Mr and Mrs Mellor) – he was Solicitor to the Treasury, King's Proctor, and Procurator General between 1909 and 1923 and an outstanding amateur artist specializing in caricatures. Their children were John Serocold Paget Mellor and Mary Hope Mellor Simonds. Angela and Jim visit them for a country weekend and in London.

> **Simonds, Mary (Mrs Simmonds)** – she was the daughter of Sir John Paget and Mabel Richardson Pearce Serocold Mellor. Angela saw her once for tea.

Murray, Gilbert and Lady Mary (Mr Murray, Lady Mary) – she was the daughter of George Howard, 9th Earl of Carlisle, a life-long close friend of Edward Burne-Jones. Castle Howard passed on her mother's death to Mary, but she let her brother Geoffrey have it. Gilbert Murray was a classical scholar. Their daughters were Rosalind (Toynbee) and Agnes (Murray). Another person named Mr Murray is in the diary, whom Angela met in 1918.

Murray, Agnes Elizabeth (Agnes) – she was Rosalind's younger sister. She called on Angela with her sister. There was also another person named Agnes mentioned by Angela.

Toynbee, Arnold J. and Rosalind (Mr Toynbee, Rosalind Toynbee) – he was a historian, author of numerous books, and a professor of international history at the London School of Economics and King's College London. She was a writer and received high praise for her first novel, *The Leading Note;* it was published in 1910 before she was 20. She was the daughter of Gilbert and Mary Murray.

Rawlinson, May (Mrs Rawlinson) – she was a friend of Angela's mother. She gave Angela a ticket to a charity ball, Angela's first ball. Angela was 18 at the time. William George Rawlinson, her husband, was a wealthy collector.

Robertson, W. Graham (Graham Robertson) – he was an author, artist, collector, and long-time family friend who encouraged Angela when she became a writer. He lived at Sandhills, his Surrey home. Sargent painted him in 1894, and that portrait is at the Tate. He was the founder and self-appointed president of the Loony Club. Angela's parents, Henry Justice Ford, and the Speeds were also members.

Speed, Harold and Clara (the Speeds) – he was a painter in oil and watercolor of portraits, figures, and historical subjects. Angela went to a showing of his work. He also wrote instructional books for artists. They were Angela's parents' family friends and Loony Club members.

Stillman, Maria Spartali (Mrs Stillman) – she was a model for Edward Burne-Jones and a watercolor artist. She was the widow of American journalist W. J. Stillman. She was a devoted mother to her two stepdaughters, Lisa Stillman and Bella Stillman Middleton.

> **Middleton, Bella (Mrs Middleton)** – her stepmother, Maria Spartali Stillman, was an artist and a model for Edward Burne-Jones. Her daughter was Angela's friend Peggy. Peggy's husband, the museum director and archeologist John Henry Middleton, died in 1896.

> > **Middleton, Peggy (Peggy)** – she was the daughter of Bella Stillman Middleton and John Henry Middleton. She was born in 1893 and was a friend of Angela's.

Von Glehn, Wilfred Gabriel and Jane (Mr von Glehn, the von Glehns) – he was an artist and close friend of John Singer Sargent. They met while both were studying at Ecole des Beaux-Arts in Paris and worked together afterward. In 1917 he dropped the Germanic von from his name, becoming **De Glehn**, although Angela referred to him by his former name. They were friends of Angela's parents.

Wells, Randall and Molly (Molly and Randall Wells) – he was an Arts & Crafts architect, craftsman, and inventor. Wells and his client, Major Noble's wife Molly (née Mary Ethel Waters), set up a craft workshop at 94 Horseferry Road in London called St Veronica's, specializing in interior design, bookbinding, calligraphy, and other crafts. The Nobles separated in 1912.

They were divorced in 1916, and Wells and Molly married in 1917. Angela saw them in 1918.

Whitelegge, Lady Fanny and Sir Arthur (Lady Whitelegge, the Whitelegges) – she was a friend of Angela's mother and the daughter of John Callcott Horsley, R.A, and the sister of Sir Victor Horsley. She played the piano and violin. He was a doctor and one of the first doctors to study factory conditions, particularly concerning occupational risks and diseases, from a medical viewpoint. They were friends of both Angela and Jim McInnes.

> **Whitelegge, Christopher (Christopher)** – he was the son of Lady Fanny and Sir Arthur Whitelegge. He was a friend of Angela's.

Woolner, Mary (Maisie) – Edward Burrne-Jones completed a drawing of Maisie at age 18. Her father was Lucas Alexander Ionides, and his brother Constantine was the father of Angela's friends Zoe Manueland Euterpe Craies. Her first husband was named Dowson. She divorced him and helped Angela through her separation and divorce from Jim. She was a friend of both Angela and her mother.

MRS PATRICK CAMPBELL (AUNTIE STELLA)

"To Club for lunch. Tea Auntie Stella." April 2, 1918

It was common for some children to address their elders as aunt or uncle even when they were not related. Auntie Stella (Mrs Patrick Campbell) was one of those people. The Mackails first met her when they moved to Kensington Square, 27 Young Street. She was already a famous actress by that time. Known on stage as Mrs Pat, she had a persona with a flamboyant style, and many books have been written about her. Born in 1865, she married Patrick Campbell in 1884. They had a son and a daughter; the son died in the Boer War in 1900. The daughter, also named Stella, provided hand-me-down clothes for Angela, as described in *Three Houses*.

In 1914, Mrs Pat played Eliza Doolittle in *Pygmalion*. This role was written for her by George Bernard Shaw. Stella's daughter Stella named her child Pat after his uncle and grandfather. Auntie Stella's portrait by Philip Burne-Jones was entitled "The Vampire" and is described in the portraits category of the guide.

Campbell, Beatrice Stella (Auntie Stella) – an actress best known for her appearances in Shakespearean plays. Mrs Pat was her stage name. In 1914, she married George Cornwallis-West, her second husband. She was his second wife; his first wife was Winston Churchill's mother, Jenny Jerome. Her daughter was Stella Patrick Campbell and she married Mervyn Howard Beech. At Auntie Stella's request, Angela translated the play *Elevation* by Henri Bernstein. The play was performed after Angela left England; naturally, Auntie Stella was the star.

> **Beech, Stella and Pat (Stella Beech and Pat)** – she was the daughter of Auntie Stella Campbell. Her son Pat was a friend of Graham McInnes. Stella Beech also became an actress.

ANGELA'S FRIENDS

"I dined with the Ritchies) and Clare and Peggy acted."
January 19, 1915.

Buchan, Susan (Susan)– née Susan Grosvenor, she was a life-long friend of Angela's who was married to author John Buchan. She was also an author, writing under the name Susan Tweedsmuir. She became a baroness in 1935. They lived on Portland Place.

Costeker, Margaret (Margaret Costeker) – she was the wife of Major John Henry Costeker, who was killed at Gallipoli on April 25, 1915. She later married General Sir Frederick Poole, a friend of her deceased first husband.

Gotch, Audrey (Audrey Gotch, Audrey Hobson) – she was the sister of Oliver Gotch. Angela attended her wedding in 1916 when Audrey married Mr Hobson.

> **Gotch, Oliver Hornsley (Oliver)**– he was an Impressionist and modern artist born in 1889. He was also a doctor, serving as a naval doctor in World War I. Brother of Angela's friend Audrey.

Ritchie, Margaret (Peggy, once as Peggie) – she was a nurse during World War I and was honored for her service. She became a doctor after the war. She was also a great friend of Clare's, who called her Pegs.

> **Ritchie, Mrs (Mrs. Ritchie)** – she was Angela's friend Peggy's mother and often visited Angela with her daughter. Not to be confused with Lady Ritchie.

UNCLE PHIL'S FRIENDS

"We had dinner with Uncle Phil and Mr Haselden at the Hyde Park Grill Room. Back to Uncle Phil afterwards and Mr Benson came in." December 18, 1915

It is easy to assume that many of the people mentioned by Angela were also known by her Uncle Philip Burne-Jones, as he and Angela saw each other so frequently. Three people were spoken of by Angela as friends of Uncle Phil and are only present with him. He also knew Americans, provided in a separate list.

Beddington, Frances (Mrs Claude Beddington) – she was the former Frances Ethel Homan-Mulock; her husband was Colonel Claude Beddington, who fought in the Boer War, World War I, and died in action during World War II. Their daughter, Sheila Beddington Wingfield, born in 1906, became Viscountess Powerscourt in 1932.

Haselden, William Kerridgean (Mr Haselden) – he was a cartoonist and caricaturist. He contributed to *Punch,* and during World War I, he wrote a satirical comic strip called the adventures of "Big and Little Willie." He dined with his friend Philip Burne-Jones and Angela on two occasions.

Warter, Mrs. de Grey (Mrs de Grey Warter) – she was the former Vera Estelle Raubenheimer. She was born in South Africa in 1892. Her marriage to Captain Henry de Grey Warter was her first of three marriages. Captain de Grey Warter died in 1917.

AMERICANS AND OTHER FOREIGNERS

"Lunched with Uncle Phil and Mr Coudert at the Bath Club. The rest of the party was Mr Laughlin (1st sec. of the American Embassy) Mr Hurst, Mr Freshfield, Mr Malkin (English) and an American Mr A. M. Patterson, who is on the War Industries Board." August 8, 1918

FROM THE UNITED STATES

Many Americans were in London during World War I; Angela met many of them through her Uncle Philip Burne-Jones. She met many Canadians at the Canadian Club, but she did not name them specifically. She also met Australians who were friends of George Thirkell, listed separately.

Coudert, Charles and Amalie (Mr and Mrs Coudert, the Couderts) – Charles duPont Coudert and Amalie Küssner Coudert were both Americans. He was a wealthy international lawyer, and she was an artist best known for her portrait miniatures of prominent American and European figures of the late 19th and early 20th centuries. Although they had a home in New York City, they spent most of their time in Europe.

Cunard, Lady (Mrs Cunard) – she was the wife of Sir Bache Cunard, the 3rd Baronet. He was the grandson of the founder of the Cunard line and did not live in London. She was the former Maud Alice Burke, known as Emerald; she was an American and a London socialite. Her salon became a popular meeting place for musicians, painters, sculptors, poets, and writers, as well as for politicians, soldiers, and aristocrats. Angela attended a dance at her house with Captain Butler and Uncle Phil.

Laughlin, Irwin B. (Mr Laughlin) – he was first secretary at the American Embassy. In addition to his diplomatic service in London he worked in Japan, Siam, Greece, and Spain. He was a friend of Philip Burne-Jones.

177

Merriman, Roger and Dorothea (Mr and Mrs Merriman and the Merrimans) – he was a professor at Harvard. They were friends of the Hills and their guests at High Head Castle.

Plank, George Wolfe (Mr Plank) – he was an American artist and illustrator. He had a long-time association with *Vogue* magazine, resulting in years of Art Deco-style covers. He was a friend of Uncle Phil's and became a friend of Angela's.

Worthington, Valentine (Val Worthington) – he was an American who was a barrister in London at Essex Court, Temple. He also practiced law in New York. He was a friend of Angela's who saw her socially right before her wedding to George Thirkell.

Angela met several Americans through Uncle Phil's friends, the Couderts:

 - Mr Anderson, an international lawyer
 - Mr Huntington, an attaché at the American Embassy
 - Mr Somers and Mr A. M. Patterson from the War Industries Board

FROM JAPAN

Matsukata, Kōjirō (Mr Matsukata) – he was a Japanese businessman and art collector who lived in London from 1916 until 1918; he was a good friend of Claude Monet. Educated at Rutgers University, he became president of Kawasaki Shipbuilding Company in 1896 and was head of Kawasaki Dockyards from 1916 through 1923, the group's leading company. Dr Mills brought him to tea with Angela.

FROM NORWAY

Rachlew, Norwegian Commander (Norwegian Commander Rachlew) – he was a naval attaché from Norway. Angela showed him the Grove, but there is no evidence that he rented it.

COUNTRY ACQUAINTANCES

"After lunch we walked in the garden and then went on to Old Buckhurst and spent the night with the Colefaxes." May 25, 1915

Weekends and more extended stays in the country were part of Angela's life. She had many friends she often saw in London and at their country estates, such as the Cooks. The families listed below saw or hosted Angela in the country, but there is no record of Angela meeting them in London, although they could have met there.

Colefax, Sir Arthur and Lady Sybil (the Colefaxes) – they lived in Chelsea and at Old Buckhurst in Sussex. He was a patent lawyer, and she was a notable interior decorator. Angela stayed at their country home in 1915.

Conybeare, Charles and Florence (Mr and Mrs Conybeare) – he was a wealthy barrister, and she was a suffragette.

THE MACKAILS' LANDLORDS

> "Lunched with Lady Ritchie. Mrs Warre-Cornish there. I walked by Lady Ritchie's bath chair to Miss Ritchie's new rooms in Radcliffe Gardens and then Miss Ritchie and I went on to the von Glehn's where there was music."
> November 9, 1917

When the young Mackails first married, they moved to 27 Young Street in Kensington Square. Thackeray's old house was on the square, and Lady Ritchie was the Mackails' landlady. Lady Ritchie and Margaret Mackail both named their sons Denis. Even after the Mackails moved to Pembroke Gardens, the families stayed in close touch.

Ritchie, Anne (Lady Ritchie) – she was the daughter of William Makepeace Thackeray and also a writer. Her husband was Sir Richmond Ritchie, who died in 1912. He was also her second cousin.

   Ritchie, Hester (Miss Ritchie) – she was the daughter of Lady Anne. She was an author.

Warre-Cornish, Blanche (Mrs Warre-Cornish) – she was a writer, a cousin of William Thackery, and mother of writer Mary McCarthy. Lady Ritchie was married to Mrs Warre-Cornish's brother, Sir Richmond Ritchie. Mrs Warre-Cornish once gave the following advice to an assistant "In all disagreeable circumstances, remember the three things which I always say to myself: I am an Englishwoman; I was born in wedlock; I am on dry land."

EXPANDING THE MIND

> "To the Annual Shakespeare lecture of the British Academy. Sir Walter Raleigh spoke this year, his subject was Shakespeare and England." July 4, 1918

Angela did more than just socialize. She attended lectures regularly. Sometimes the speakers were well known to her, as when she went to hear her father lecture on Shakespeare, and some were engaging presentations on topics of interest.

Colvin, Sir Sidney (the Colvins, Colvin) - he was a curator, literary and art critic and past president of the English Association of the Burlington Gardens Theater. Through Edward Burne-Jones, Colvin entered the circle of Dante Gabriel Rossetti from 1868 to 1872. Angela went to hear a Colvin lecture.

Ker, William Paton (W.P. Ker) – he was a literary scholar, essayist, and friend of Angela's parents. Angela and Jim went to a lecture by Ker at Bedford College.

Lankester, Ray (Ray Lankester) – he was a zoologist and evolutionary biologist who also served as the third director of the Natural History Museum. Angela attended one of his lectures.

Lodge, Sir Oliver (Sir O. Lodge) – he was a British physicist and writer involved in developing and holding essential patents for radio. Angela and Clare attended a lecture by him at right before Angela's wedding in 1918.

Raleigh, Professor Sir Walter Alexander (Sir Walter Raleigh) – he was an English scholar, poet, and author, born in London in 1861. Angela went with her parents to hear Sir Walter Raleigh's lecture on Shakespeare and England.

MUSICAL ASSOCIATES

"Mr von Holst dined here and talked business with Jim."
March 4, 1915

"Jim's recital at the Aeolian Hall went very well and we
made nearly £100." April 29, 1915

The above two quotes were the only mention of music supporting
the McInnes family. Although Angela's brother, Denis discussed
money freely,[6] Angela does not take his approach.

Many of the Mackail family friends were musicians, and there
was no clear distinction between professional and amateur.

JIM'S TEACHERS

Many people were musically influential in the singing career of
Jim McInnes. He had attended the Royal College of Music, and
the musicians he met there remained influential after he had left
school to study in Europe. One of his mentors was William
Shakespeare. In addition, Professor Albert Visetti appeared in the
diary multiple times, but always during 1918 and not in
connection with Jim.

It is unknown if Jim studied singing with Mr Beigel, but Angela
had lessons with him. Jim thought Angela should have singing
lessons, but she appeared unpleased with the lessons or the
concept. They also saw Mr Beigel socially.

---

[6] Mackail, Denis, *Life with Topsy*, London: William Heinemann, Ltd., 1942.

MUSICAL ASSOCIATES AND FRIENDS

> "Miss Smith to dine and afterwards she and Mr O'Connor-Morris played the César Franck violin sonata and some Bach." December 10, 1915

> "We went into the O'Connor-Morris 's after dinner. Jim sang, and Miss Smith, Mrs Salmond, and our host played." January 3, 1916

He often sang with a piano accompanist but occasionally performed with other musicians. Angela sometimes was his accompanist.

Some people were more managers or conductors than musicians. Others were composers, such as Ralph Vaughan Williams and Graham Peel, and Jim sang their works and visited with their families. Jim performed and socialized with other musicians, some of whom continued to see Angela socially and for concerts after her separation from Jim, and others of whom disappeared from her life after the marriage ended.

Barter, William Arnold (Arnold Barter) – served as conductor of the Bristol choir and Bristol Philharmonic Society. When Jim sang, Barter often conducted.

Bax, Arnold (Arnold Bax) – he was a composer, poet, and author of orchestral music. Family friend and admirer of Angela. His best-known work is the symphonic poem "Tintagel."

Beigel, Victor (Beigel, Mr Beigel) – he was a Hungarian pianist and music teacher of international repute. Angela took lessons from him. He also taught Gervase Henry Elwes.

Bird, Henry Richard (Mr Bird, Henry Bird) – he was an organist and accompanist. Angela attended Henry Bird's memorial concert in 1916.

Borwick, Leonard (Mr Borwick) - he was a concert pianist. He was born in 1868 and toured the USA before 1915. He was still giving recitals in 1921. He died in 1925.

Boult, Adrian Cedric (Adrian Boult) – he was a conductor for the Royal Opera House. He was declared medically unfit to serve in World War I but was able to work at the War Office as a translator. In 1918 he conducted the London Symphony Orchestra in a series of concerts. He married Ann Wilson, the first wife of famous tenor Steuart Wilson, in 1931.

Broadwood, Lucy (Lucy) – she was a great friend of Jim McInnes and a friend of Angela's and her parents. She was a trained classical musician and singer. Her letters and diary have served as source information. Angela met Jim at Lucy's house.

Butt, Clara (Clara Butt) – she was an English contralto and one of the most popular singers in England from the 1890s through to the 1920s. During World War I, Butt organized and sang in many concerts for service charities, and for this was appointed (DBE) in the 1920 civilian war honors. Angela and Jim went to hear her at Albert Hall.

D'Aranyi, Jelly (Jelly) – she was a Hungarian violinist who performed with her sister Adila. Ralph Vaughan Williams' *Violin Concerto* was dedicated to her. She also frequently performed with Myra Hess.

Davies, Fanny (Miss Davies, Fanny Davies) – she was one of the most renowned pianists from Britain, and she was the first pianist to give a piano recital in Westminster Abbey.

Elwes, Gervase Henry and Lady Winefride (the Elwes') – he was influential in developing early 1900s English music and was a tenor who performed with the London String Quartet (L.S.Q.). She was an author and daughter of the 8th Earl of Denbigh, Rudolph William Basil Feilding.

Evans, Irene Grace (Miss Evans) – she was a musician specializing in the pianoforte. She received a scholarship at Trinity College of Music and played with Christine Ratcliff.

Fachiri, Alexander and Adila (Mr Fachiri, Adila von Aranyi, Adila Fachiri) – she was Hungarian violist Adila D'Arányi and sister to Jelly Aranyi. Adila and Alexander married in 1915, and Angela attended their wedding.

Ford, Mr and Mrs Walter (Mr and Mrs Walter Ford) – he was a friend of Angela's parents and a professor of singing at the Royal College of Music. His brother was illustrator Henry Justice Ford.

Guilhermina, Suggia (Suggia) – she was a Portuguese cellist living in London. In 1914 she formed a trio with the violinist Jelly d'Arányi and the pianist Fanny Davies.

Hale, Alfred (Mr Alfred Hale) – he was an amateur music composer and watercolorist. Being independently wealthy, he committed himself full-time to his interests. He wrote about his experiences during World War I in *The Ordeal of Alfred M. Hale: The Memoirs of a Soldier Servant.*

Hambourg, Mark and Dolly (Mr Mark Hambourg, Mrs Dolly Hambourg, the Hambourgs) – he was a concert pianist and author. She was a violinist and the former Dorothea Francis Muir Mackenzie. She saw Angela in both London and Rottingdean. Their children, Sonia and Nadine, were friends with Angela's son Graham.

> **Hambourg, Sonia and Nadine (Sonia and Nadine Hambourg)** – they were daughters of Dolly and Mark Hambourg. They were friends of Graham McInnes and attended his birthday party.

186

Hawtrey, Sir Ralph and Hortense (the Hawtreys, Mr and Mrs Ralph Hawtrey, Hortense von Aranyi Hawtrey) – she was the former Hortense Emilia Sophie D'Arányi. He was a respected economist and author. She was a Hungarian pianist and sister to Adila and Jelly; all three sisters were musicians and friends of Angela's.

Hess, Myra (Myra) – a renowned pianist. She toured Europe and the USA and later became Dame Myra. She was a close friend to Clare, Angela's sister, considering her a kindred spirit.[7]

Hess, Theodora (Miss Theodora Hess) – she was a music enthusiast and performer who was married to Edwin Fisher. They lived on Cheyne Walk in Chelsea. Her husband's sister, Adeline Marie Fisher, was the wife of Ralph Vaughan Williams.

Kelly, Cuthbert (Mr Kelly) – he was choir director for the Oxford House Musical and Dramatic Association in Benthal Green. Concerts were held every Saturday night in the association's Excelsior Hall from November through April.

Kimpton, Gwynne (Miss Gwynne Kimpton) – she was a teacher at the Royal Academy of Music and was the founder/organizer of musical groups and events. She co-founded the Bromley Symphony Orchestra and was the founder of the 88-member Women's Symphony Orchestra. Jim sang for her.

Lasker, Vally (Miss Lasker, Vally) – she was a musician, educator, and close friend of Angela's sister Clare.

Longman, Robert and Dorothy (Bobby Longman and Dorothy Longman) – Angela's friend Dorothy Marriott Fletcher married Bobby Longman and had a baby between 1915 and

---

[7] McGee, Tim, *Barely Clare: The Little-Known Life of Clare Mackail*, The Angela Thirkell Society of North America, 2020.

1918. Bobby was a publisher. Dorothy was an accomplished violinist. She was introduced to her future husband in about 1912 by composer Ralph Vaughan Williams.

Fletcher, Mrs. Jane (Mrs Fletcher) – she was the mother of Angela's friend Dorothy (Dorothy Longman).

Maitland, John Alexander Fuller (Fuller Maitland) – he was an influential British music critic and scholar at *The Times* from 1889 to 1911. He attended Mr von Glehen's birthday celebration.

Mangeot, Andre and Olive (Mr Mangoet, Madame Mangeot) – he was a violinist and impresario.

O'Connor-Morris, Geoffrey and Gildea (Mr O'Connor-Morris, Mrs O'Connor-Morris, the O'Connor-Morrises) – he was a famous church organist in London from 1910 through 1918. In 1918 he became a conductor of Carl Rosa Opera Company.

Ormond, Guillaume (Guillaume Ormond) – he was a cathedral organist and nephew of John Singer Sargent.

Passmore, Walter and Agnes (the Passmores, Mr Passmore) – he was an actor, singer, and composer; she was the former Agnes Fraser and an actress and singer. They married in 1902, had four children, and raised Doris, Mirette, and Walter Passmore from his first marriage.

Passmore, Doris or Mirette (Miss Passmore) – they were the daughters from Walter Passmore's first marriage. She saw Angela one evening after dinner. As she was referred to as Miss Passmore, it was unclear which daughter she was.

188

Passmore, Nancie or Isobel (Miss Passmore) – they were the daughters from Walter and Agnes Passmore's marriage. She came to tea with Graham McInnes. However, as she was referred to as Miss Passmore, it is unclear which daughter she was.

Peel, Graham (Graham Peel, Mr Graham) – he was a close friend of Jim's and a friend of Angela's. The McInnes's son Graham was named for Graham Peel. Peel was also Graham's godfather. Before his marriage to Angela, James McInnes had lived with Graham Peel, a wealthy composer and musician.

> **Dixon, Percy and Katharine (Mr and Mrs Dixon)** – she was Graham Peel's sister.

> **Peel, Elizabeth (Mrs Peel)** – she was Graham Peel's mother. Her maiden name was Graham. He husband was Gerald Peel.

> **Peel, Mr and Mrs John Graham (the John Peels)** – John was a brother of Graham Peel. His wife was the former Dorothy Mary Grace Morant.

> **Peel, Mr and Mrs Robert Graham (the Bob Peels)** – Bob was a brother of Graham Peel. Bob's wife was the former Evelyn Septima Beechy Kingsford.

Pinwell, Constance (Miss Pinwell) – she was a violinist who performed in a trio with Fanny Davies on pianoforte and Arthur Williams on cello. In the diary she performs with Miss Davies.

Ranalow, Frederick and Lilian (the Ranalows, Lilian Ranalow, Mr and Mrs Ranalow) – he was an opera singer and actor. She was the former Lilian Mary Oates.

> **Ranalow, Patrick (Patrick)** – son of Frederick Ranalow. He was killed in Germany during World War II.

Ranalow, Sheila (Sheila) – daughter of Frederick Ranalow.

Ranee of Sarawak (the Ranee of Sarawak, the Ranee) – she was Margaret, Lady Brooke, a writer and composer of music, including the national anthem of Sarawak where she was queen.

Ratcliff, Christine (Miss Ratcliff, Christine Ratcliff) – she was a violinist, founder of the Birmingham Society of Artists (1914), and the founder of a string quartet in London during the time of the diary. She was a student at Morley College in 1916. She was a helpful friend of Angela and Angela's mother.

St John Hornby, Charles Harold and Cicely (the Hornbys, the St John Hornbys, Mrs Hornby, Cicely Hornby) – a founding partner of W.H. Smith. He was High Sheriff of London from 1906-1907. Married to Cicely Rachel Emily Barclay. They lived at Shelley House in Chelsea. They hosted three performances by Jim McInnes.

Salmond, Mrs Norman (Mrs Norman Salmond, Mrs Salmond) – a pianist. After her husband died in 1914, she focused on her son Felix's future as a cellist. She was the former Adelaide Manzocchi.

Shakespeare, William (Mr Shakespeare) – he was a singing teacher who gave lessons in St John's Woods. He taught James McInnes and Lucy Broadwood. He was a professor at the Royal College of Music.

Silk, Dorothy (Dorothy Silk) – she was working as a housemaid in Birmingham during the war when the music editor and choral conductor William G. Whittaker encouraged Gustav Holst to work with her. She was a soprano and made her London debut at Queen's Hall.

Somervell, Arthur and Edith (the Somervells, Mr and Mrs Somervell) – he was a composer and music educator who served as a professor at the Royal College of Music and later as Inspector of Music at the Board of Education. Their daughter Kitty was a friend of Angela's. Angela also saw the other Somervell children, Hubert, Antonia, and Ronnie.

> **Somervell, Antonia (Antonia Somervell)** – she was the daughter of Arthur and Edith Somervell. Angela had supper with her.

> **Somervell, Hubert Arthur (Hubert Somervell)** – he was a soldier during World War I and the son of Arthur and Edith Somervell. He helped Graham McInnes with his toy plane.

> **Somervell, Katherine (Kitty Somervell)** – she was the daughter of Arthur and Edith and a dancer with Sergei Diaghilev's Ballets Russes. She later married David Howard and was the mother of writer Jane Howard.

> **Somervell, Ronnie (Ronnie Somervell)** – he was the brother of Kitty Somervell. He helped Angela and Graham with a toy airplane.

Visetti, Albert (Visetti) – he was a professor of singing at the Royal College of Music. He also wrote and translated, working with Angela in 1918. He was the stepfather of novelist Radclyffe Hall.

von Holst also Holst, Gustav Theodore (Mr von Holst) – he was a music composer and teacher. He was mentioned frequently in Tim McGee's book, *Barely Clare*. He dropped the von in his name and became known as Gustav Holst, but Angela always called him Mr von Holst. He was a lifelong friend of Ralph Vaughan Williams.

Walker, Ernest (Dr Walker) – was the music director at Balliol College at Oxford and arranged Sunday evening chamber music concerts there. Jim performed and Angela attended a concert. Graham Peel studied under Dr Walker.

Warwick-Evans, Dorothy (Mrs Warwick-Evans) – Her husband, Charles Warwick-Evans, studied for six years at the Royal College of Music and became principal cello in the Beecham Opera Company, then leading cello in the Queen's Hall Orchestra. He resigned that post to devote himself to his creation, the London String Quartet. She was the former Dorothy Gladys Elliott.

Williams, Ralph Vaughan and Adeline (RVW, Mr Williams, Mrs Williams) – he was among the best-known British symphonists, and his works included operas, ballets, chamber music, and secular and religious vocal pieces, and orchestral compositions, including nine symphonies. She was the former Adeline Marie Fisher and the sister of Edwin Fisher, the husband of Theodora Hess.

Willis, Joan (Joan Willis, Joan) – she was a friend of Christine Ratcliff, a cello player in Ratcliff's Birmingham Society of Artists, and she also played with Ratcliff in London.

Wilson, Ann (Mrs Steuart Wilson) – she was the first wife of famous tenor Steuart Wilson, a champion of music by English composers of his generation. His first professional performance was with Ralph Vaughan Williams. In 1931 she divorced Wilson and married conductor Adrian Boult. She was the former Ann Bowles.

Wood, Muriel (Lady Wood) – Her husband, Sir Henry Wood, was a conductor best known for his association with London's annual promenade concerts, known as the Proms. Her maiden name was Muriel Ellen Greatrex.

PEOPLE WHO RENTED THE GROVE

"I came up for a few days to arrange about letting the Grove to a Mrs Wright Boycott for several months at 6 guineas a week." August 1917 (date unknown)

Angela and Jim began renting The Grove shortly before Colin was born. Angela handled the sub-letting of the house after her separation from Jim.

Pollock, Mary (Lady Pollock, Mrs Pollock) – she was the wife of Sir Adrian Pollock. They rented The Grove from Angela. He was a solicitor and the Remembrancer of the City of London, the liaison between the City of London and the crown. She was the former Mary Gully.

Wright-Boycott (Mrs Wright Boycott) – she was the wife of Thomas Wright-Boycott, a brigadier general who served during World War I. She rented The Grove from Angela.

UPPER ARISTOCRACY AND A FEW SERVANTS

"Princess Louise was very nice to us both." December 7, 1915

The quote was from an entry when Jim had just performed. The aristocracy were music supporters, and the people listed here mainly were either sponsors or attendees of performances by Jim McInnes. At the other end of the spectrum are women who worked for the McInnes family and testified at their divorce hearing. Nurses, parlor maids, and cooks were seldom mentioned by name by Angela.

Queen Alexandra (Queen Alexandra) – she was the wife of Edward VII.

Campbell, Queenie (Nurse Campbell, Queenie) – she was engaged to take care of Angela after Mary's birth. She testified at Angela's divorce hearing and came to tea.

Cowley, Lily (Lily Cowley) – she was an under nursery attendant who came to work with the McInnes children in January of 1917. She was named in the divorce proceedings and testified for Angela at her divorce hearing.

Jackson, Sally (Sally Jackson) – she was a cook who went to work for the McInnes family in 1915. She testified for Angela at her divorce hearing.

Parson, Barbara (Nanny)[8] – she was the nanny to Graham, Colin, and Mary McInnes. She lived in Whaplode and took baby

---

[8] Angela Thirkell Society (UK) (Eds.), *Letter to a Nanny: How Georgiana Burne-Jones's family was held together in a crisis*, FeedARead Publishing, 2022.

Mary home with her while Angela stayed at Clouds and Stanway after her separation from Jim. Nanny attended Mary's funeral.

Princess Louise, Duchess of Argyll (Princess Louise) – she was one of Victoria and Albert's daughters and a strong supporter of the arts, higher education, and feminist causes.

St Maur, Susan (the Duchess of Somerset) – she was a Scottish writer and philanthropist who wrote under the pen name Mrs Algernon St Maur.

Princess Victoria (Princess Victoria) – she was the daughter of Edward VII and Queen Alexandra.

Wellington, the Duke and Duchess of (the Duchess of Wellington, the Duke and Duchess) – they were the fourth duke, Arthur Charles Wellesley, and his wife, née Kathleen Williams. He was the first duke's grandson.

Westminster, the Duchess of (the Duchess of Westminster) – she was the former Constance Edwina Cornwallis-West and the wife of one of the wealthiest men in the world, the second Duke of Westminster, Hugh Arthur Grosvenor. Her husband's stepfather was George Wyndham.

GEORGE THIRKELL FAMILY AND FRIENDS

"A Mr Thirkell who we met at the Lombards came over a good deal and brought friends." August 18, 1917

As the family of George Thirkell was mostly in Australia, only a few names were mentioned by Angela. However, his brother Winston was in England and became a friend of Angela's. In addition, George had friends in England whom he had met through his military service. Angela married George Thirkell on December 13, 1918.

Blackwood, Donald (Major Blackwood) – he was a chaplain in the Australian Armed Forces from 1912 to 1920.

Carr, Cedric Errol (Mr Cedric Carr, Cedric) – he was Angela's sister-in-law Stella Thirkell's older brother.

Carr, John Thomas and Henrietta (Mr and Mrs Carr) – they were Stella Thirkell's parents and attended her wedding to George's brother, Winston. She was the former Henrietta Sutton.

Elsum, Mr – he was a friend of George Thirkell's who joined George occasionally when he accompanied Angela.

Gray, Evangeline (Aunt Eva) – she was George's brother Winston Thirkell's godmother and met Angela around the time of his wedding. Her husband, Mowbray Gray, died in 1917. He married Helen Evangeline (Eva) Roberts around 1880 in Hobart. Their property was sold in 1882 when they moved to England. The property totaled two hundred and ten square miles, and included in the sale were 3,200 sheep, 1700 head of cattle, and about 25 horses.

Sams, Sapper (Sapper Sams) – A friend of George Thirkell who called on Angela. The term, sapper, was used to designate a military engineering position, later thought to be equivalent of a Private, but a generic term in earlier times.[9]

Thirkell, George (George Thirkell, Captain Thirkell, George, Thirk) – he was Angela's second husband, providing her with the name she carried for the rest of her life. Originally from Tasmania, he was promoted due to his role in the war and left the service a captain. By May of 1918, there were two Captain Thirkells in Angela's life, Win and George. He must have been charming, as he captivated Lady Elizabeth Bowes-Lyon, who later married the future King of England, George VI.

Thirkell, Winston and Stella (Win or Captain Thirkell and Stella) – Robert Mowbray Winston Thirkell was the brother of George Thirkell. He married Stella Marguerite Carr in 1918. Angela attended the wedding and participated in wedding social functions.

---

[9] McInnes, Graham, *The Road to Gundagai*, London: The Hogarth Press, 1985. First published Hamish Hamilton, Ltd, 1965.

WYNDHAM FAMILY

" …brought Graham up to P. G. with me and June 13th took him to Stanway where we spent a very happy month." June 1917

At the beginning of Angela's writing, the Wyndham patriarch Percy Wyndham was dead. Still, his wife, the beloved Aunt Madeline, and their children remained important figures in the life of Angela and her family. Their children in order were Mary (1862), George (1863), Guy (1865), Madeline (1869), and Pamela (1871). They were older than Angela and were friends with her parents before becoming her friends.

The Burne-Jones family and the Wyndham family were linked in friendship for three generations, beginning with Percy Wyndham's patronage of and friendship with Edward Burne-Jones. During Angela's difficult time following her separation from Jim McInnes, she found refuge at Clouds, the home of Aunt Madeline. She also stayed at Stanway House, where Aunt Madeline's daughter Mary, the Countess of Wemyss, lived.

The Wyndham family is large and complicated. One of the confusing points about the family was that when John Singer Sargent painted the Wyndham sisters, Mary Constance Wyndham Charteris was known as Lady Elcho. By 1915, this title had passed on to her daughter-in-law, Violet Catherine Benson Charteris, the wife of Hugo Francis Charteris. Mary was called Lady Wemyss by Angela.

Speaking of Lady Wemyss, she made a list of all the casualties among her family members and closest friends shortly after World War I. That number totaled 25 lives lost, including her sons Hugo and Yvo and nephews Edward Tennant, George Wyndham, and Percy Wyndham.

Many books have been written about this large, complicated, and well-to-do family. The traditional three names weren't enough; Aunt Madeline had five names when she married Percy. Women often married and remarried, and as titles changed, names changed. Angela called two Wyndham ladies aunts because they were close friends of her mother, Margaret. These were Aunt Madeline and Aunt Minnie, but other Wyndham family members were close friends of Angela's, particularly Pamela) and Sibell. The names are presented below in generational order.

THE MATRIARCH, MADELINE

Wyndham, Madeline Caroline Frances Eden (Aunt Madeline) – her maiden name was Campbell; she was the daughter of Sir Guy Campbell, 1st Baronet, and his wife Pamela FitzGerald, the daughter of Lord Edward FitzGerald. She married Percy Wyndham, a British soldier, politician, collector, and intellectual, who built their home called Clouds at East Knoyle, Wiltshire. He died in 1911. They had three daughters, captured by John Singer Sargent in his painting *The Wyndham Sisters: Lady Elcho, Mrs. Adeane–, and Mrs. Tennant*. She had two sons, Guy Wyndham and George Wyndham.

CHILDREN, THEIR SPOUSES, AND THEIR CHILDREN

MARY WYNDHAM

Charteris, Mary Constance, Countess of Wemyss and March (Lord and Lady Wemyss) – her maiden name was Mary Wyndham. She was known as Lady Elcho upon marriage in 18883 to Hugo Charteris, Lord Elcho, until 1914, when the title passed to her daughter-in-law. Her husband would later inherit the titles of 11th Earl of Wemyss and 7th Earl of March. By 1912, her husband lived with his mistress, Lady Angela Forbes, in East Lothian, while Mary lived at Stanway in Gloucestershire; Angela visited Mary there. Lord and Lady Wemyss had seven children. One son, Colin, died in childhood. Two of their sons died during

World War I, Hugo Francis Charteris and Yvo Alan Charteris. Hugo's wife, Violet Catherine Benson Charteris, was known as Lady Elcho during the time of Angela's diary. Other children included Guy Lawrence Charteris, who married Frances Lucy Tennant in 1912; Lady Cynthia Mary Evelyn Charteris Asquith, who married Herbert Asquith in 1910; Lady Mary Pamela Madeline Sibell Charteris, who married Algernon Walker Strickland in 1915; Lady Irene Corona Charteris, known as Bibs, and children Cynthia and Colin were not mentioned in the diary. Both Ego and Yvo were killed in World War I. Mary's children mentioned in the diary are listed below.

> **Charteris, Guy Lawrence and Frances Lucy (Guy and his wife)** – her maiden name was Tennant, and she was the sister of Pamela's first husband. They had one son, Hugo Francis Guy, and three daughters, Anne Geraldine Mary, Frances Laura, and Mary Rose. Frances Laura became the Duchess of Marlborough.

> **Charteris, Hugo Francis and Violet Catherine (Lord and Lady Elcho)** – he was killed in April 1916 in Egypt. Her maiden name was Manners, and her half-sister was author Diana Manners Cooper. They had two sons, Francis David Charteris, who became the 12th Earl of Wemyss on his father's death, and Lt. Col. Martin Michael Charles Charteris.

> **Charteris, Lady Irene (Bibs)** – she was the youngest daughter of the Countess and 11th Earl and Countess of Wemyss. She was born in 1902.

> **Strickland, Lady Mary Pamela Sibell Charteris (Mary)** – she is mentioned by Angela with her sister Bibs. Mary was born in 1885. Mary was purported to be

the child of Wilfrid Blunt.[10] She married Algernon Walker Strickland in December 1915.

GEORGE WYNDHAM

Wyndham, George – he married Sibell Mary, Countess Grosvenor, in 1887. She was the daughter of Richard Lumley, 9th Earl of Scarbrough, and the widow of Victor Grosvenor, Earl Grosvenor, son of the 1st Duke of Westminster. Her son, Hugh Richard Arthur Grosvenor, succeeded as 2nd Duke of Westminster in 1899. Toward the end of George's life, the couple settled at Clouds in Wiltshire. George's only child, Percy Lyulph, known as Perf, was killed in 1914. In Perf's will, he left Clouds to his nephew, Dick Wyndham. George Wyndham died suddenly in June 1913 in Paris at age 49.

GUY WYNDHAM

Wyndham, Lt Col Guy Percy and Edwina (Aunt Minnie) – Aunt Minnie's maiden name was Edwina Johanna FitzPatrick Brooke. They lived at Charford Manor, which they loaned to Angela in 1915. They had three children: George, who died in World War I; Guy Richard Charles, known as Dick; and Olivia Madeline Grace Mary, also in the diary. When Dick was a teenager, he inherited Clouds from his uncle George.

Children of Guy Wyndham mentioned by Angela:

> **Wyndham, Guy Richard Charles (Dick)** – he was born in 1896. Ownership of Clouds passed to him when his uncle was killed in World War I. He also fought in World War I. He visited Angela when he was on leave.

---

[10]Renton, Clauda, *Those Wild Wynhams: Three Sisters at the Heart of Power*, New York: Alfred A. Knopf, 2018.

Wyndham, Olivia Madeline Grace Mary (Olivia) – she was the daughter of Guy Percy and Edwina Wyndham. She was born in 1897. Angela saw her in town and at Clouds.

MADELINE WYNDHAM (daughter)

Adeane, Madeline Pamela Constance Blanche Wyndham – she was not mentioned in Angela's diary. She married John Henry Adeane in 1888. She was known as Mananai. Her daughter, Sibell (Kay-Shuttleworth) , was mentioned often by Angela. Mananai and her husband had seven children: Sibell Eleanor Maud Adeane Kay-Shuttleworth, Pamela Marie Adeane, Madeline Mabel Ambrose Adeane Wigan, Lettice Elizabeth Evelyn Adeane, Charles Percy George Guy Adeane (who died in infancy), Helena Olivia Adeane, and Robert Philip Wyndham Adeane.

Mananai Adeane's daughter Sibell and her relatives:

Kay-Shuttleworth, Sibell Eleanor Maud Adeane (Sibell Shuttleworth) – she was a close friend of Angela's. Her husband, Edward James Kay-Shuttleworth, the third Baron Shuttleworth, died in July of 1917 in an accident as he was returning to military duty in Witham in Essex.

Kay-Shuttleworth, Lawrence (Lawrence Shuttleworth) – he was the brother of Edward James Kay-Shuttleworth. Like his brother, he was killed in 1917.

Hills, Eustace Gilbert and Nina (the Hills, Eustace and Nina Hills) – the former Nina Louise Kay-Shuttleworth was the sister of Lawrence Kay-Shuttleworth. Sibell was her sister-in-law. Eustace Hills's brother was the astronomer Edmond Herbert Grove Hills. They hosted Angela and Jim at High Head Castle and saw Angela in London.

PAMELA WYNDHAM

Glenconner, Pamela Adelaide Genevieve (Pamela Glenconner, Pamela) – in 1895, Pamela Wyndham married Edward Tennant, who became 1st Baron Glenconner in 1906; he died in 1920. In 1922, she married Edward Grey, 1st Viscount Grey of Fallodon. She was an English writer. Lord Grey is mentioned by Angela and listed below. Pamela and Edward Tennant had six children. Edward Wyndham Tennant, known as Bim, died fighting in World War I. Another son, Hester, died in 1916 when he was less than a year old. Her sons David and Stephen Tennant both appear in the diary. She also had a son named Christopher, known as Kit, and a daughter named Clarissa, known as Clare. Pamela's children, Clarissa (Clare), Edward (Bim), and Christopher (Kit), do not appear in the diary. Bim died on September 22, 1916, at age 19, in the war.

Children of Pamela mentioned by Angela:

> **Tennant, David Pax Francis (David)** – he was the son of Pamela Wyndham and Edward Priaulx Tennant (Baron Glenconner) . He was born in 1902. He sang for Angela.

> **Tennant, Stephen (Stephen)** – he was the son of Pamela Wyndham and Edward Priaulx Tennant (Baron Glenconner). He came with his mother to tea with Angela.

SECOND SPOUSES

Grace, Lady Wemyss (Grace Lady Wemyss) – she was the second wife of Mary Wyndham's father-in-law, Francis Charteris, the 10th Earl of Wemyss.

Grey, Sir Edward, First Viscount Grey of Falloden (Sir Edward Grey) – he was Pamela's second husband. When Angela wrote of him, he and Pamela were not married. He was Secretary of State for Foreign Affairs from 1905-1916. He became Lord Temporal of the House of Lords in 1916. He married Pamela Wyndham Glenconner in 1922. It was the second marriage for them both.

STEP-FAMILY OF GEORGE WYNDHAM

George Wyndham's wife had children from a previous marriage. One of his stepsons was the 2nd Duke of Westminster, Hugh Arthur Grosvenor. The Duchess of Westminster was his wife, mentioned in the diary:

> **Grosvenor, Constance Edwina Cornwallis-West (the Duchess of Westminster)** – she was George Wyndham's stepson's wife. George's stepson was the 2nd Duke of Westminster, Hugh Arthur Grosvenor, one of the wealthiest men in the world. The Duchess attended a large tea party with her daughter.

> **Grosvenor, Ursula (Lady Ursula Grosvenor)** – she was George Wyndham's stepson's daughter. She came to tea with her mother, the Duchess of Westminster.

> **Cornwallis-West, Colonel William and Mary (Colonel and Mrs Cornwallis West)** – he was the father of George Wyndham's stepson's wife (Constance Edwina Cornwallis-West) and a solicitor, politician, and honorary colonel. Mary Cornwallis-West's maiden name was FitzPatrick. The Cornwallis-Wests spent summers at

their home, Newlands Manor. They came over from Newlands with the Duchess and Lady Ursula to attend a tea party. Their son George Cornwallis-West married Mrs Patrick Campbell) in 1914.

TWO MORE PEOPLE ON THE FRINGE

Preston, Pamela - in June of 1915, Angela visited Clouds. While there, she wrote of seeing "Pamela Preston" [the quotation marks are Angela's]. In Pamela Tennant's book *Edward Wyndham Tennant: A Memoir by his Mother*, she writes, "I hope Grandmamma and dear Cousin Pamela Preston are well." Unfortunately, the research did not reveal any other information about this relative.

Blunt, Winfrid – he was a poet and a writer. Blunt was purported to be the father of Mary Charteris's child Mary.[11] Blunt also had an affair with William Morris's wife Jane.

---

[11] Renton, Claudia, *Those Wild Wyndhams: Three Sisters at the Heart of Power,* New York: Alfred A. Knopf, 2018.

SISTERS AND AN AUNT

"I went to Adila von Aranyi's wedding to Mr Fachiri."
September 29, 1915

There were more sisters mentioned by Angela than just the Wyndham sisters.

ILBERT SISTERS

Fisher, Herbert and Lettice (Herbert and Lettice) – Lettice Ilbert Fisher was the founder of what is now known as Gingerbread, the National Council for the Unmarried Mother and her Child. She was also an economist and a historian. Her husband served as a Liberal member of Parliament from 1916-1918.

Heseltine, Michael and Olive (Olive and Michael)– Olive Ilbert was an author and critic. She married in 1912. She was the sister of Angela's friends, Lettice Fisher and Joyce Ilbert.

Ilbert, Joyce (Joyce) – she was the unmarried sister of Lettice Fisher and Olive Heseltine. She lived with her parents, Sir Courtenay Peregrine and Jessie Bradley Ilbert. He was Clerk of the House of Commons from 1902 to 1921.

There were two other Ilbert sisters: Jessie, the wife of Sir George Young, and Margaret, who married Sir Arthur William Steuart Cochrane. However, they were not mentioned by Angela.

D'ARÁNYI SISTERS (von Aranyi)

D'Arányi, Jelly (Jelly) – Aranyi de Hunyadvár was a Hungarian violinist who performed with her sister Adila. Ralph Vaughan

Williams' *Violin Concerto* was dedicated to her. She also frequently performed with Myra Hess.

Fachiri, Alexander and Adila (Adila von Arányi, Adila Fachiri, Mr Fachiri, Fachiri) – Adila D'Arányi de Hunyadvár was a Hungarian violist and sister to Jelly and Hortense D'Arányi. She and Alexander Fachiri were married in 1915. He was a barrister. Angela attended their wedding.

Hawtrey, Sir Ralph George and Hortense (the Hawtreys or Mrs Ralph Hawtrey) – he was a respected economist and author. Hortense Emilia Sophie D'Arányi was a Hungarian pianist and sister to Adila and Jelly. All three sisters were musicians and friends of Angela's.

IONIDES SISTERS

Craies, William and Euterpe (Mrs Craies or the Craies) – Euterpe Ionides Craies and her husband lived in Kensington. He was a barrister and lecturer on criminal law. They were friends of the Burne-Jones family. Her sister was Zoe Ionides Manuel.

Manuel, Stephen and Zoe (Zoe Manuel, Zoe, Mr Manuel) – Zoe Ionides married Stephen Manuel in 1911. Her father, Constantine Alexander Ionides, was an art collector famous for his bequest of 82 oil paintings to the Victoria and Albert Museum. He was a friend of Edward Burne-Jones. Her aunt, Aglaia Ionides Coranio, left Zoe a drawing of Fanny Cornforth by Rossetti and The Days of Creation by Edward Burne-Jones. Her sister is Angela's friend Euterpe Craies, and her aunt is Maisie Woolner.

AN IONIDES AUNT

Woolner, Mary (Maisie) – Edward Burne-Jones completed a drawing of Maisie (Mary Aglaia Ionides) at age 18. Her father was Lucas Alexander Ionides, and his brother Constantine

Alexander Ionides, was the father of Angela's friends Zoe Ionides Manuel and Euterpe Ionides Craies. Maisie's first husband was an American named Ben Dowson. She was a friend of Margaret Mackail.

THEATER FRIENDS AND ACQUAINTANCES

"Kitty Somervell to tea." March 16, 1918

Ainley, Henry (Mr Ainley) – he was an actor who starred in a play Angela attended in 1916. She went backstage to see him after a performance, although she thought his play dull. He was a friend of Jim's and gave them seats at the theater several times.

Asche, Oscar (Oscar Ashche) – he was an Australian actor, director, and writer. He was best known for his record-breaking musical, *Chu Chin Chow*, which Angela found dull. He was an innovator in stage lighting and one of the first to use it for dramatic effect.

Barrie, J. M. (Barrie) – he was Angela's godfather. She attended his play, *Dear Brutus,* in 1918. Gerald du Maurier, Daphne Du Maurier's father, starred in that play and acted in *Peter Pan.*

du Maurier, Gerald (Mr du Maurier) – he was an actor and friend of J. M. Barrie. He starred in Barrie's *Dear Brutus.* He and Frank Curzon co-managed the Wyndham Theater from 1910-1925. He became president of the Actor's Orphanage Fund in 1914. He was knighted in 1922. He was the father of author Daphne du Maurier.

Nares, Owen (Mr Nares) – he was an actor friend of Jim. He appeared in silent movies and on the London stage. He gave Jim and Angela a box for an evening for his play *Romance.*

Passmore, Walter and Agnes (Passmores, Mr Passmore) – he was an actor, singer, and composer; she was an actress and singer. They married in 1902.

Playfair, Anne (Mrs Playfair) – Anne Mabel Platts married Sir Nigel Playfair, an actor and a director. She was an actress. Her father-in-law was a famous obstetrician who was the first doctor to recommend bed rest for complicated pregnancies.

Somervell, Katherine (Kitty) – she was the daughter of Arthur and Edith Somervell, and a dancer with Sergei Diaghilev's Ballets Russes. She later married David Howard and was the mother of writer Jane Howard.

Terry, Marion (Marion Terry) – she was an actress whom Angela went to see after a performance. Marion was the younger sister of actress Ellen Terry.

Vanbrugh, Irene (Irene Vanbrugh) – she was a comedic actress. A.A. Milne wrote the title role in the play, *Belinda,* for her. Angela didn't meet her but mentioned her because she starred in a play Angela saw and enjoyed.

WRITERS

"… had a dinner party including Mr Hayward, once sub critic of *The Times* under Fuller Maitland, now at the Manchester Art Gallery." February 1, 1916

Was Angela inspired by her friends who were writers? She didn't say so in her diary, but biographies of Angela Thirkell do acknowledge the role that Graham Robertson played in encouraging Angela to pursue a career in writing. He was known to inspire many of his friends to reach their potential. Angela was fortunate to have him as a friend and a positive voice in her life.

Aubrey-Fletcher, Sir Henry and Mary (Mr and Mrs Henry Fletcher, Mary Fletcher) – Sir Henry Lancelot Aubrey-Fletcher was the 6th baronet. He wrote under the pen name of Henry Wade and was the author of the Inspector Poole mysteries and other novels and short stories. His wife was the former Mary Augusta Chilton.

Birnstingl, Harry (Harry Birnstingl) – he was an architect, supporter of women's suffrage, and a writer. He is best known for an article he wrote in the *Freewoman* about sexuality.

Buchan, Susan (Susan) – née Susan Grosvenor, was a life-long friend of Angela's who was married to author John Buchan. She was also an author, writing under the name Susan Tweedsmuir. She became a baroness in 1935. She and her husband lived in Portland Place.

Charnwood, Dorothea (Lady Charnwood) – Dorothea Mary Roby Thorpe was married to author, academic, Liberal politician, and philanthropist Godfrey Benson. He became Baron Charnwood in 1911. He authored books on Abraham Lincoln and Theodore Roosevelt.

Coke, Lord Henry and Lady Katherine (Lord and Lady Coke– Lord Henry John Coke wrote books about his experiences in Vienna during the revolution of 1848 and in California during the gold rush (published in 1852). He also wrote novels. He and his wife later settled at their family estate, Longford, in Derbyshire. They also lived at St George Hanover Square in London. Lord Coke died in 1916. Lady Coke died in 1920.

Dilke, Ethel (Ethel Dilke) – was a poet and wife of poet Sir Fisher Wentworth Dilke.

Fisher, Mr and Mrs Alexander (Mr Alexander Fisher, Mrs Fisher) – he was an Arts and Crafts artist and silversmith who studied at the Limoges school of enameling. His book, *The Art of Enameling Upon Metal: with a short appendix concerning miniature painting on enamel,* was published in 1909. Mr Fisher taught Madeline Wyndham how to enamel. The Fishers were friends of Angela's parents.

Guedalla, Phillip (Phillip Guedalla) – he was a barrister, historical travel writer, and biographer known for his wit.

Hayward, Lawrence (Lawrence Hayward) – he was an author of the book *Music in Painting* and a critic who worked for Fuller Maitland at *The Times.*

James, Henry (Henry James) – the author was born in New York City on April 15, 1843. He died on February 28, 1916, in Chelsea, London. Angela attended his funeral.

Lang, Mrs Nora (Mrs Andrew Lang) – she was the widow of Scottish poet Andrew Lang, an author, editor, and translator. Nora Allenye Lang was also a translator, collaborator, and writer. Her most well-known book was *The Fairy Books*, a series of 25 collections of folk and fairy tales for children.

Marillier, Christabel and Henry (Christabel and Mr Marillier)– they were friends of Angela's parents. He was a journalist, critic, and art historian. They married in 1906. She is the daughter of the artist, Arthur Hopkins. She was the composer of "The Rose and the Ring." In 1899 Henry Marillier wrote *Dante Gabriel Rossetti: An Illustrated Memorial of His Art and Life*

McLaren, Barbara (Barbara McLaren) – she was an author of *Women of War,* published in 1917. The introduction to her book was written by H. H. Asquith, Prime Minister of England, from 1908 until 1916. Hilda Cook was her friend.

Newmarch, Rosa (Mrs Newmarch) – she was a translator who did work for Angela and saw her socially. Mrs Newmarch was also a poet and wrote books about music.

Pound, Ezra and Dorothy (Mr and Mrs Ezra Pound) – he was the expatriate American poet and critic who often lived in London.

Robertson, W. Graham (Graham Robertson) – he was an author, artist, collector, and long-time family friend who encouraged Angela when she became a writer. He lived at Sandhills, his Surrey home. Sargent painted him in 1894, and that portrait is at the Tate. He was the founder and self-appointed president of the Loony Club. Angela's parents, Henry Justice Ford, and the Speeds were also members.

Speed, Harold and Clara (the Speeds) – he was a painter in oil and watercolor of portraits, figures, and historical subjects. Angela went to a showing of his work. He also wrote instructional books for artists. They were Angela's parents' friends and Loony Club members.

St John Lucas (Mr St John Lucas) – he was a poet known for his anthologies of verse. He was a friend and mentor of Rupert Brooke.

Toynbee, Arnold J. and Rosalind (Mr Toynbee and Rosalind Toynbee) – he was a historian, philosopher of history, author of numerous books, and a research professor of international history at the London School of Economics and King's College London. She was a writer and received high praise for her first novel, *The Leading Note;* it was published in 1910 before she was 20. She was the daughter of Gilbert and Mary Murray.

Verhaeren, Emile (M Verhaeren) – he was a Belgian poet and art critic and was nominated six times for the Nobel Prize.

KNOWN PEOPLE ONLY GLIMPSED

> "Con's little boy. Younger than Graham and a dull little girl Bridget Selincourt with a dull mother." June 4, 1915

Angela's was very social. She had many close friends and also came in contact with people she saw only briefly during these four years. Many of these only glimpsed people were well-known enough to be traceable today.

Brocklehurst, Ellen Catherine (Miss Brocklehurst) – she was born in London in 1899. She married Francis George Harry Hedgeland in 1926. She was the daughter of Samuel Harris George Brocklehurst and Edith Clara Phillips.

Birch-Reynardson, William John and Violet (Mr and Mrs Birch-Rynardson) – he was Justice of the Peace for the county of Oxford. They attended a party to support the people of Belgium. She was the former Violet Maxwell.

Clogstoun, Colonel Henry Oliver and Norah (Colonel and Mrs Clogstoun) – he was an officer with the Royal Engineers served in Cairo and Melbourne before World War I, then he took part in the landing at Gallipoli and various missions in France, working with the Australian military forces. She was the former Norah Stanford MacIlwaine.

Dawkins, Richard MacGillivray (Mr Dawkins) – he was an archaeologist and director of the British School in Athens between 1906 and 1913.

Debenham, Mrs Cicely and Marjorie (Mrs Debenham and Marjorie) – they were the wife and daughter of Sir Ernest Ridley Debenham, the owner of the store Debenhams.

De Selincourt, Bridget (Bridget Selincourt) – Bridget was born in 1910 and the daughter of Janet and Hugh De Selincourt. Hugh

De Selincourt was a journalist and writer. Angela met the child and her mother at the home of Sissie Craies.

Eliot, Charles William (Eliot) – he was the president of Harvard from 1869-1909, serving the longest tenue as president of anyone in the school's history. His niece met Angela at a house party. He was mentioned but did not appear in person.

Fisher-Rowe, Lady (Mrs Fisher-Rowe) – she was the widow of Captain Edward Fisher-Rowe. She was the former Victoria Isabella Liddell.

Grenfell, Francis Wallace (Lord Grenfell) – he was an army officer who retired in 1908 and died in 1925. His second wife was the author Margaret Majendie. He was also an archeologist.

Horsley, Oswald (Oswald Horsley) – he was born in 1893. He was awarded the Military Cross in 1916 and was killed in a flying accident in 1918. His father was Victor Horsley, a pioneer in neurosurgery and a social reformer. His aunt was Fanny, Lady Whitelegge.

Horsley, Pamela (Pamela Horsley) – she was the sister of Oswald Horsley. She and her brother saw Angela at a party. She later married Edward Stanley Gotch Robinson. Her husband was a numismatist specializing in Greek and Roman coins who worked at the British Museum. Pamela was a founder of the Babies Club in Chelsea. The club advocated putting babies whose parents didn't have access to a garden into cages suspended outside open windows to provide what was believed to be vital fresh air for babies. In addition, the club offered free cages to parents.

Huxley, Mrs. Sophy (Mrs Huxley) – she was the wife of the physician Henry Huxley and mother of Anne and Marjorie. She was the former Sophy Stobart.

Huxley, Anne (Anne) – she was the daughter of Henry and Sophy Huxley. Her grandfather was botanist Thomas Henry Huxley. Her first cousin was author Aldous Huxley.

Huxley, Marjorie (Marjorie Huxley) – she was the daughter of Henry and Sophy Huxley. Her grandfather was botanist Thomas Henry Huxley. Her first cousin was author Aldous Huxley.

Ker, William Paton (Mr. W.P. Ker) – he was a literary scholar and essayist.

Lamb, Mrs Mabel and Winifred (Mrs Lamb and Winifred) – Mrs Lamb was active in promoting women's university education and women's suffrage. She was the former Mabel Winkworth. Winifred attended Newnham College, Cambridge, as her mother did, from 1913-1917. She would become a famous archaeologist, art historian, and museum curator.

Lawrence, Charles and Catherine (Sir Charles and Lady Lawrence) – he was 1st Baron Lawrence of Kingsgate. He was a British businessman and railway executive. She was an American and the former Catherine Sumner.

Llewellyn, Samuel Henry and Marion (Mr and Mrs Llewellyn) – he was a Welsh painter and president of the Royal Academy in London in the late 1920s and had been knighted in 1918. She was the former Marion Meater. Their daughter was Gwynedd Marion Llewellyn Meinertzhagen, who was married to the well-known philatelist.

Locker-Lampson, Godfrey (Mr Locker Lampson) – he was a politician (MP), essayist, and aide-de-camp during World War I.

MacLean, Charles Wilberforce and Gladys (the MacLeans, Mrs MacLean) – she was the former Gladys Frances Elaine

Royle. Their son Fitzroy MacLean, born in 1911, was a friend of Ian Fleming's and was widely believed to be the model for his character James Bond. Fitzroy entered into military service during World War II as a private and rose to a brigadier general during the war.

Macmillan, Frederick and Georgiana (Sir Frederick and Lady Macmillan) – she was an American. Sir Frederick's father founded Macmillan Publishing Company.

Mann, Cathleen (Miss (Harrington) Mann) – she was an artist, designer, and the daughter of Harrington Mann, an artist influenced by the works of Sargent and Whistler.

Meinertzhagen, Gwynedd (Mrs Gwynedd Meinertzhagen) , – she was the former Gwynedd Marion Llewellyn and the wife of Louis Ernest Meinertzhagen, an expert on the early stamps of France.

Micholls, Colonel Wilfred Horatio Montefiore (Colonel Micholls) – he served in World War I and received chocolates from Angela on two occasions. His mother Ada Micholls was a close friend of Angela's.

Moens, Miss (Miss Moens) – she was the sister of Seaburne Moens, the headmaster of Rottingdean's Down House School. Seaburne Moens went on to write a history of Rottingdean.

Mond, Violet (Lady Mond) she was the wife of Alfred Mond, first baronet Melchett. He was an industrialist, financier, and politician. She was the former Violet Goetze and a humanitarian and activist. She turned her country home into a sixty-bed convalescent home during World War I. She was also involved in the promotion of infant welfare.

Mudie-Cooke, Henry and Beatrice (the Mudie-Cookes, Mrs Mudie-Cooke) – their daughter Olive was an artist known for paintings of World War I and was an ambulance driver during that war.

Partridge, Bernard (Bernard Partridge) – he was a chief cartoonist of *Punch*. Before his career as a cartoonist, he was an actor. He was knighted in 1925.

Pease, Jack (Mr Pease)– he was the first Baron Gainford and a businessman and politician. A member of Asquith's cabinet between 1910 and 1916, he also served as chairman of the BBC between 1922 and 1926. Angela sat in his box at the theater.

Romily, Nellie (Nellie Romily) – she was the sister of Lady Clementine Churchill and the wife of Bertram Romily. She served as a nurse during World War I and was briefly captured by Germans in Belgium.

Ronaldson, Mrs Thomas Martine (Mrs Ronaldson) – her husband was a portrait artist from Edinburgh who moved to London in 1906.

Slade, Kathleen (Lady Slade) – she was the former Kathleen Scovell and the widow of Sir Cuthbert Slade, fourth baronet.

Spring Rice, Mary (Mary Spring Rice) – she was an Irish nationalist born into an aristocratic Anglo-Irish family in London. In 1913 and 1914, she was actively involved in gunrunning to support an Irish uprising.

Stanford Mrs (Mrs Stanford) – her husband owned St. Aubyn's, a boys' school in Rottingdean. When Angela visited there, she called on Mrs Stanford. Mr Stanford was related to Madeline Wyndham.

Stirling, Charles and Wilhelmina (the Stirlings) – Mrs Stirling, the former Wilhelmina Pickering, was the sister of

Evelyn De Morgan. Wilhelmina was an author of 30 novels and of biographies of her sister and brother-in-law, the De Morgans.

Strachey, Sir Charles and Ada (Mr and Mrs Strachey) – she was the former Ada Margaret Raleigh. They were the parents of songwriter Jack Strachey.

Strachey, Jack (Jack) – he was a future songwriter. He was born in 1894. He accompanied his father, Charles Strachey, to Angela's house.

Thompson, Sir Herbert (Sir Herbert Thompson) – Sir Henry Francis Herbert Thompson was the second baronet and had a career in law and medicine. He was also an Egyptologist. His father, Sir Henry, was a composer and pianist.

Verhaeren, Emile (M Verhaeren) – he was a Belgian poet and art critic, nominated six times for the Nobel Prize.

Walron, Sir William (Mr Walron) – he was a member of the House of Commons from 1880 until 1906. At that time, he became a peer. His son was killed in World War I.

Warre, Marjory (Mrs Felix Warre) – she was the former Marjory Monteith Hamilton. Her husband Felix Warre was a rower for Oxford who won the Silver Goblets at Henley Royal Regatta. He also served in the Royal Garrison Artillery during World War I.

ONE AND DONE AND THE UNKNOWN

"Jim to sing at a hospital for Miss Arkwright." May 7, 1916

Many of these people were involved with Jim's musical performances or might have been guests at dinners or house parties. Often Angela provided only a first or last name. The people in the table below were seen only once.

For some, there was brief information in the entry itself. Some names lend themselves to reasonable assumptions. For example, Mr Russell could be Bertrand Russell, as he was close to Mrs. Patrick Campbell, but this is not confirmed.

Name	Date	Information
Acton, Mr	Apr. 1915	Graham Peel visited him
Algie, Captain	Mar. 1918	Went to Horseferry Road and met Captain Algie
Anderson, Sister	Apr. 1918	To tea
Anran, Mrs	May 1916	To tea
Arkwright, Miss	May 1916	Jim sang at hospital for her.
Baldwin, Miss	July 1918	Mr Proctor's niece (probably distinguishing her from a Baldwin family member)
Baynes, Mrs Cuthbert	July 1915	Met at Mrs. Woods' tea party.
Baddeley, Mr	Nov. 1915	Took train with him
Baldock, Dr	Feb. 1916	Jim's doctor
Barton, Mrs	Oct. 1918	Headmaster at S. Ken. school
Barton, Mrs	Feb. 1918	Gave a dance
Beaumont, Miss	May 1916	To tea
Beir, Mrs	Nov.1916	To tea
Bernard, Mr	July 1916	Played piano at Myra's party
Bigham, Mr	June 1918	Attended party at Myra's
Bigham, Mrs	June 1918	Attended party at Myra's

Name	Date	Information
Bintons, the	Nov. 1915	To tea and dinner
Binyon, Mr and Mrs	Mar. 1915	Came over after dinner
Braithwaite, Miss	May 1916	To Lunch
Brooke, Dr	Aug. 1915	Graham's doctor
Brookes, Mrs Clare	Nov. 1915	Jim sang for her
Buchanan, Miss	June 1918	Came over to hear quartet
Bucy, Mr	Sept. 1915	Dinner with Jim
Buney, Gertie	May 1916	To tea
Campbell, Mrs	June 1916	To tea
Carlile, Mr and Mrs	Feb. 1916	To lunch
Cartmells, Austen	Mar 1917	To tea at their house
Carve, Miss	Sept. 1916	To tea
Chatham, Mr and Mrs	Sept. 1916	To tea
Cockerell, Mr	Sept. 1918	To supper
Colman, Miss	Nov. 1918	To tea
Con's little boy	June 1915	To tea with Graham
Crofts, Major	Oct. 1918	Visited at hospital
Daires, Mrs May	June 1916	To tea
Davidson	Oct. 1918	To tea
Davidson, Padre	Oct. 1918	To dinner
Defaun	June 1916	Composer whose music was played at a party
Deniston, Captain	June 1918	At Myra's party
Dickenson, Miss	Feb. 1918	To dinner
Dickson, Miss	Oct. 1916	To lunch
Don	June 1916	To lunch
Doustes, the	Feb. 1915	Hosts of party for Belgians
Dora	Feb. 1915	With Mrs Little at party
Doyley, Captain	May 1918	Dinner and theater
Dunhill, Aroley	June 1916	To tea

Name	Date	Information
Eady, Miss	Feb. 1915	Came by after dinner
Easton, Miss	Feb. 1915	At party
Edens, Miss	Feb. 1915	Came by after dinner
Edwards, Mr	Mar. 1918	Canadian at dance
Edwards, Nurse	Dec. 1916	Temporary nurse
Ellis, Leroy	May 1915	To tea
Elton, Mr	Oct. 1917	To tea
Elverson, Mrs	Dec. 1916	To tea
Flower, Mrs	Oct. 1918	Drove Angela home
Forbes, Captain	Nov. 1918	Padre; to lunch and tea
Ford, Mrs [not Walter's wife]	April 1916	Sent by Pamela from Wickford
Forster, Nurse	May 1916	employee
Foster, Mrs	May 1916	To lunch
Freshfield, Mr	Aug. 1918	Lunched w Angela & Uncle P
Friswells	May-June 1918	Played tennis at their house
Gall, Betty	Oct. 1918	To tea
Gemmell, Stewart and Marjorie	Feb. 1915	At party
Gladstone, Miss	Sept. 1915	To tea
Gooley, Mr	June 1918	At party at Myra's
Gough, Mrs	Oct. 1918	Musician
Green, Miss	Mar. 1918	To lunch
Gussie	May 1915	To tea
Hamilton, Mrs	Jan. 1916	Went with her to see John Peels
Harris, Dr	Oct. 1918	Played piano
Hayman, Mrs	Dec. 1916	Henry's sister
Hill, Miss	Sept. 1918	Bridesmaid in Win's wedding
Hill, Mr Justice	Nov. 1917	Judge for Angela's divorce
Hogg, Captain	Mar. 1918	To lunch
Holmes, Mr and Mrs	Mar. 1918	Took Angela home from the club

Name	Date	Information
Howarth, Miss	Feb. 1915	Came by after dinner
Hurst, Mr	Aug. 1918	Lunched with others and Uncle Phil
Irvine, Mr and Miss	Jan. 1915	Came by after dinner
James, Mrs	Nov. 1916	To tea
Jenkins, Mr	Dec. 1915	Attended small concert
Jennell, Sylvia	Jan. 1915	To tea
Jennings, Mr	May 1916	To tea
Joy	Mar. 1918	At Uncle Phil's for tea
Kerr, Mr	Feb. 1918	Took Angela to a dance
la Tharque, Mrs	Mar. 1915	Went to the theater
Lake, Miss	April 1916	To lunch
Lawley, Miss	Feb. 1915	To lunch
Leigh, Miss	Mar. 1918	At Uncle Phil's for tea
Limond, Mrs	Jan. 1915	Came by after dinner
Lipscombe, Mr	Mar. 1918	Took Angela home from dance
Little, Mrs	Feb. 1915	At party (with Dorothy)
Locke, Miss	May 1916	To tea
Lubbock, Mrs	June 1918	At party at Myra's
Lushington, Miss	Feb. 1915	Jim sang and stayed w her
MacColl. Miss	Oct. 1917	Angela called on her
MacGregor, Pat, Eyleen and Michael	Sept. 1918	At Southsea for Win's wedding with baby
Malkin, Mr	Aug. 1918	At lunch with Uncle Phil
Matheson, Mr	Nov. 1917	To supper
Mazails, Mrs	Mar. 1916	To tea
Maude, Col	May 1918	Dinner and theater
McKenna, Pamela	Dec. 1917	To lunch
Miles, Mr	July 1915	Agent at Clouds
Milne, Miss	July 1918	Went to theater

Name	Date	Information
Mitchell	June 1918	To theater
Monce, Mrs	June 1916	To tea
Monsell, Sylvia	Dec. 1916	To tea
Morom, Sylvia	Jan. 1918	To tea
Morrison, Mr and Mrs	June 1916	To dinner
Muir, Molly	June 1916	To tea
Naomi	Feb. 1916	Temporary employee
Nesbitt, Mr	Oct. 1915	Gave lecture on ballads
Newbolts	Dec. 1917	Walked w them and Graham
Nichols, Mr	June 1916	To tea
Nielson, Mr	Feb. 1918	New Zealander, came to tea
Norman, Major	Mar. 1918	Brought A home from club
Olivier, Miss	Jan. 1915	To dinner
Paget, Miss	Jan. 1915	To tea
Palgrave, Gwenny and Margaret	June 1916	To tea
Parishes	Feb. 1917	Attended Graham's birthday
Perkins	Feb. 1918	Hosted party
Peta, Mr Raymond	Feb. 1917	A pupil of Jim's
Pitts, Molly	Oct. 1917	Tried to call on her
Batry Pain, Nancy and Eva	Feb. 1915	Attended party for Belgians
Pratt, Mr	July 1918	Barn owner near Dick Brook
Price, Mr	Sept. 1918	To dinner
Proctor, Mr	July 1918	The rector near Dick Brook
Reynolds, Mrs	July 1915	She hosted a party
Richards, Mrs Ernest	July 1915	To tea (with her three children)
Richmond, Lady	Nov. 1915	Margaret Mackail attended her funeral
Rhona	Feb. 1916	To tea with Netta

Name	Date	Information
Robertson, Mrs	Feb. 1915	Came by after dinner
Robinson, Mr	Nov. 1918	Friend of George Thirkell's
Robinson, Miss	June 1916	To tea
Rücker, Mlle	Feb. 1915	To tea
Russell, Mr	Jan. 1918	Met at dance and took her home
Samuel	June 1916	Composer whose music was played at a party
Saunders, Mr	Jan. 1917	Had quartet Jim sang with
Schanter, Irene	Nov. 1915	soloist
Scott, Mrs Douglas	Jan. 1917	To tea
Severn, Lily	Feb. 1915	Came by after dinner
Sherrard, Mary	Sept. 1918	Entertained at Hippodrome
Sichel, Miss	Nov. 1917	Singer
Sims, Mrs	May 1918	To tea
Smith, Mr Pearsall	July 1915	To tea
Smith, Winnie	1917	Met at Pamela G's house
Spender, Mr	Mar. 1915	Came by after dinner
Stockwells	Aug. 1915	Jim went to stay with them
Stuot, Miss	Feb. 1915	Attended party for Belgians
Sullivan, Mrs and Moira	Feb. 1918	Attended Graham's birthday party
Swinburne, Major and Margot	Feb. 1915	To dinner
Talbot, Mr and Mrs Jack	Oct. 1915	Attended small concert
Taparell, Mr	Oct. 1916	To lunch
Thicknesse, Mrs	June 1916	To tea
Thomas, Inigo	Aug. 1918	To dinner
Thompson, Sylvia	Nov. 1917	To tea
Timothy, Miss	Feb. 1915	Came by after dinner

Name	Date	Information
Tor, Mrs	Nov. 1917	Musician
Trollope, Miss	Mar. 1915	To tea
Twisleton, Miss	Mar. 1915	Jim rehearsed with her
Veronica	Nov. 1917	To a party with Ers
Wallers, Mrs	July 1918	Visited at the hall by Dick Brook
Ward, Mr	Feb. 1915	Came by after dinner
Weisse, Miss	Mar. 1915	Jim sang at her school
Whall, Mr	June 1918	Organist at the Strand
Whall, Mr (brother)	June 1918	Made stained glass
Wilkinson, Mr	Oct. 1918	Headmaster at school; Angela called to inquire about
Wingates, Miss	Dec. 1915	To tea
Winn, Miss	Feb. 1915	Came by after dinner

MYSTERIOUS FRIENDS

> "To Henrietta Street to enquire for Douglas who had had
> an operation – took the children." November 8, 1917

Angela knew them so well that they needed only one name in her
writings, as in "Hilda to tea." Guessing their identities was never
an option, no matter how logical the guess was. Unknown people
are listed below, with any information found in the diary.
Perhaps the readers may be able to fill in the blanks. Consider
this an Angela Thirkell Society puzzle.

FIRST NAMES ONLY

Buff – Buff was mentioned with two married ladies and had a
girl named Miss Finch. Angela saw Buff the day after her
divorce hearing, as Angela took Graham to see him.

Douglas – Angela saw Douglas at lunch and dinner. Douglas
was a friend of Graham Peel. He had an operation and was in a
nursing home for his recovery. Angela took the children with her
to see him there.

Ers and Eric – Ers appeared eight times in the diary, both with
and without Eric. It is unclear if Ers was male or female. Eric
didn't appear without Ers in the diary; Ers and Eric attended big
and small parties and dropped by after dinner. Jim sang in
Canterbury for Eric's soldiers.

Gwen – the mystery here is whether Gwen was Gwen Vassall,
who didn't appear until 1918 and quickly became a close friend.

Hay – he performed with Jim as accompanist and was also a
friend. He traveled with Jim and Angela to sing outside of
London.

Hilda – she could be Hilda Cook or someone else. She often appeared in the diary.

Jessie – Jessie lived with Graham Robertson at his home, Sand Hills. She might be Jessie E. Thomas, honorary treasurer of the Loony Club, founded by Graham Robertson in the late 1800s, who was pictured in Anne Hall's biography of Angela Thirkell in a photo of the Loony Club members from 1895. Unfortunately, this connection could not confirmed, so Jessie re mains on the mystery list.

Marion (Aunt) and Sylvia – Aunt Marion and Sylvia appeared to be mother and daughter and often appeared together. Aunt Marion (without Sylvia) played a memorable role when she took Angela to dinner, bad fish was served, and Angela became ill. Unfortunately, the first name of Marion doesn't appear on Angela's family tree or that of the Wyndham family. One fact provided by Angela is that they move around a lot, living in at least three different homes in four years.

Mel – it was unclear if Mel was a man or a woman. Mel is a good citizen, raising money for poor dressmakers by hosting a fashion show and running a slipper shop. Slipper shops were gatherings of volunteers who made items for soldiers during World War I. Mel appeared at tea with Uncle Phil. Angela visited Mel in the hospital, and Mel attended Graham's birthday party. Mel also came to supper one time.

Lyal – it was unclear if Lyal was a man or a woman. This person owned a car, which took Angela and Jim to Kingston. Lyal came to tea and dinner and spent the night and came to tea twice with Mrs Wood. Graham spent the day with Lyal.

Netta – Netta appeared in Angela's writing many times. Angela usually saw her by herself. She kept Angela's children for her once and joined Angela and Graham for lunch. She was a close friend but an unknown.

Sibyl – Angela had many friends with similar names. This person should not be confused with Sibell Kay-Shuttleworth, the granddaughter of Percy and Madeline Wyndham. Angela had tea with this mysterious Sibyl four times and lunch with her once. She might have been Sibyl Colefax, but the connection is not confirmed.

LAST NAMES ONLY

These were people known by their title or by family names. Some befriended Angela in 1918, while others were mentioned throughout the diary.

Allen, Mr – he gave a concert and was a friend of Gerry Hopkins.

Cassels-Brown, Mr (Mr Cassels-Brown) – Mr Cassels-Brown lived in Dorking. He met there with Jim and came up to lunch with Jim and Angela.

Mrs Halsey and Mrs Harvey – these ladies sometimes appeared together but not always.

Mrs Lynn- she took Angela for lunch at her club, joined Angela for tea, and saw her after tea.

Dr Mills – he was Angela's doctor and also treated her children, Graham and Mary. He saw Angela socially for tea. He was David Howard's doctor when he hurt his knee. Dr Mills also testified at Angela's divorce hearing.

Mrs Mills – she came for tea, but was she married to Dr. Mills? He was not at tea with Mrs Mills in the diary.

Mrs Morse – Angela saw Mrs Morse often for tea. Once, she referred to Enid Morse, who may or may not be the same person.

Mr and Mrs Moseley – these people are examples of friends of friends. Angela and Jim saw the Moseleys twice when they visited the Mellors near Manchester, where-Jim was performing.

Mrs Somerville – she came to tea twice with Angela. She should not be confused with members of the Somervell family.

Miss Sparrow – Miss Sparrow came to tea, dinner and dropped in after dinner. She also attended a large party.

FAMILIES

The Carter family – may or may not be a family at all. Angela mentioned numerous Carters. Frank Carter was with the Lewis family on two occasions. Mrs Roland Carter made one appearance. Miss Carter was seen two times. Their relationship with one another was unclear, as was any background information.

The Cook family – Hilda Cook often saw Angela for tea. Was this the same person referred to often simply as Hilda? Other references to the Cook family included Mr Cook, Mr and Mrs Bob Cook, Miss Dora Cook, Mr Leonard Cook, Captain Cook, Miss Cook, Hilda, and the Cooks. The Cooks stayed with Angela for two weeks. Jim sang for Mr Cook in Stratford.

The Dixon families – Graham Peel's sister was Katharine Peel Dixon. She was married to Percy Dixon. Angela refers to them as Mr and Mrs Dixon. Rachel Dixon may be linked to this family. There was another Dixon family, parents of a pupil of Jim's. and Angela go twice to their home near Milford to stay.

The Howard family – This was not the family of Edward Burne-Jones's great friend, George Howard, the 9th Earl of Carlisle and father of Mary Howard Murray. The family Angela wrote about was comprised of Mr Howard, Ruth Howard, Jerry Howard, and David Howard. David was the guest of honor at a party, but he

231

hurt his knee during the festivities and had to go to the hospital. Nothing else was known about them.

The Morris family – This was not the immediate family of William Morris. As with the Howard family, this family wasn't linked to Edward Burne-Jones. They owned a car, something rare, and Mrs Morris drove Angela from the London Symphony Orchestra (L.S.O.). Mr Morris loaned Angela the car once to take the children to a Christmas party. Mrs Morris hosted a working party for making supplies for the war effort. Mrs Morris appeared at an evening event with an unknown Arthur. She and Angela also shared tea and dinner.

The Gibson Family – Mr Gibson and Mrs Gibson appeared in Anglea's diary, as did Dolly Gibson, who could be Mrs. Gibson. Dolly came to tea and stopped by Angela's house after dinner, once accompanied by Mr Gibson and another time with an equally unknown lady, Mrs Patullo.

The James familes – References to Mr James before March 1916 could be Henry James. He was a family friend and might have attended gatherings with Lord and Lady Coke. Angela attended the memorial service for Henry James in March of 1916. Another James family continued to appear in the diary. Angela's boys went to tea with the James children, and the James children attended Graham's birthday party. Mr James came to dinner. Captain James was a friend of Winston Thirkell.

The Powell family – This family lived in Hampstead, and their name was synonymous with puppet shows. Angela went to puppet shows at their house with her parents, with Jim, and a third time by herself.

The Reeves family – Mr, Mrs, Miss, and George Reeves all appeared in Angela's writing, but never at the same event. Mr Reeves and Jim appeared together in a recital in Bath. The name Reeves appeared many times.

The Warren family – Mrs Warren, the Warrens plus Henry, Peter, Dorothy, and Christopher Warren were mentioned by Angela. The Warrens had a car and sent it to meet Angela and Jim. Angela also spent the night with the Warrens. Mrs Warren was seen with Hilda Cook twice.

The Wood family – This family should not be confused with Lady Wood. Mrs Wood belongs to a club where she entertained Angela for lunch. The Woods also had a car, as Mr Wood drove Angela and Jim home. The family lived in Kingston. Mrs Wood was seen mentioned twice with Lyal. Mr Wood and Mr Reeves appeared together twice, but that was probably a different Mr Wood, as those references were about a concert. Angela also went to tea with a Mrs Woods.

FULL NAMES

Johns, Ella (Ella Johns, Ella) –Angela had lunch with Ella Johns as part of a group in 1915 and again with just the two of them in 1917. Nothing more is known about her.

Lankester, Fay Angela saw Miss Lankester one time and saw Fay and Ray Lankester another time. Ray Lankester, the botanist whose lecture Angela attended, never married. Fay could be his sister.

Pearce, Anna – Angela went to Anna Pearce's new house for tea and went to see her new baby. Angela also called on Anna when she wasn't at home, had the Pearces for dinner, and went out to lunch with Anna Pearce.

Massé, Riette – Only once did Angela include her last name in the entry. She is mentioned six times, once with Mrs Newmarch and once with Mr Crofts.

MacPherson, Alice – she appeared four times in the diary, and Angela joined the MacPhersons once for dinner.

Miles, Marjorie – Angela visited Marjorie Miles a few times in a nursing home and had tea with her at 28 Young Street. Angela's parents lived at 27 Young Street before moving to Pembroke Gardens.

Sellar, Marjorie - she appeared as Mrs Craig Sellar. She was seen at tea, at a party, and at the house after dinner

Roos, Major James Claude Vivian – his full name wasn't confirmed in the diary, but he was the only Major Roos in World War I, in a list provided on the British Forces War Records website. In February of 1918, Angela met Major Roos. He was from South Africa. Angela appeared interested in him, seeing him ten times before April 5, 1918. That was the last time she mentioned him as Major Roos when he walked Angela home from a dance.

Saffery, Adele – Angela saw Mrs Saffery and Adele Saffery with a large group of evening visitors and alone for lunch and for tea.

Vassall, Gwen – Gwen was a mystery within a mystery. A close friend of Angela's first seen in 1918, was she the Gwen whose name later appeared alone? She was called Miss Vassall when she first appeared in March 1918. However, the next month she appeared as Gwen Vassall. Gwen was the only name given by the following month, and she was a constant in the diary until September 1918. Then, after often appearing during Winston Thirkell's wedding festivities, she disappeared.

SECTION II – GUIDE TO PLACES

The people were introduced, but the questions remained: Where were they? The following section includes the details of places named by Angela.

Angela visited friends in London and at their country homes. Angela and Jim traveled a great deal. He performed all over Britain, plus they traveled often, when she didn't mention performances. Angela mentioned many places, and not all were located. When there was confusion about a place mentioned, an explanation was included.

HOMES IN LONDON

"Shopped and did some tidying at the Grove for Mrs Wright Boycott." October 15, 1917

44 Belgrave Square – was the Wyndham family home in London. All of Madeline and Percy Wyndham's children were born at this house. Angela went to lunch, tea, and dinner with the Wyndham family here.

The Grange - Edward and Georgiana Burne-Jones lived here before the completion of their country home in Rottingdean. The Grange was one of the family homes described in Angela's book, *Three Houses*. Edward Burne-Jones died here. In 1898, the artist and family friend Charles Fairfax Murray moved into The Grange. By Christmas that year, Georgiana was regarding North End House in Rottingdean as her settled home.

The Grove – Angela and Jim lived in The Grove before their son Colin was born. It was a short distance from the Mackail's home of Pembroke Gardens. Angela supervised the leasing out of The Grove after her separation from Jim.

Pembroke Gardens (P. G) – Angela's parents moved from Young Street to number 6 Pembroke Gardens shortly after the death of Edward Burne-Jones. During the diary years, Angela visited P. G. often and moved with her children here when she separated from Jim.

Portland Place – was the location of the home of John and Susan Buchan. Angela called on them here.

34 Queen Anne's Gate – was the London home of Angela's friend Pamela and her husband Edward Tennant, the first Baron Glenconner. They opened the art gallery part of their home to the public. Angela went here twice to arrange chairs and flowers, possibly for a concert by Jim.

Shelley House – was located on the Chelsea Embankment. The St John Hornby family lived here. Jim sang here three times.

COUNTRY HOMES AND THEIR ENVIRONS

"We went to Carlisle by the 10.0 and were met by a taxi which took us to Highhead Castle, 8 miles out whence the Eustace Hills had asked us." January 1, 1915

Astley Hall - was the country house of the Stanley Baldwins. It was located near Stourport in North Worcestershire. Angela sent her boys to visit here and joined them.

Boxmoor – town and part of Hemel Hempstead in Hertfordshire. Angela visited her sister-in-law Diana here.

Buckhurst Park – was located in Withyham in (East) Sussex; the Benson family rented this estate on a 25-year lease from Gilbert Sackville., Earl De La Warr. Angela and Jim visited at the same time they went to Burwash to see the Kiplings.

Carlisle – was a border city in Cumbria located eight miles south of the Scottish border. Angela took the train here to travel to visit to High Head Castle.

Charford Manor – was the house of Guy Wyndham and his wife. They loaned the house to Angela for two weeks in 1915.

Cholsey – was a village two miles south of Wallingford in South Oxfordshire. Angela took the train here when she visited the country house of the Hills family.

Clouds – was located in East Knoyle in Wiltshire and was designed by Arts and Crafts architect Philip Webb for Percy and Madeline Wyndham. It was first completed in 1886, but an 1889 fire necessitated its rebuilding in 1891. On Percy Wyndham's death in 1911, the Clouds estate was inherited by his son George Wyndham. In 1913, when George Wyndham died, the estate passed to his son Percy Lyulph, ("Perf") Wyndham. In 1914 Perf was killed in World War I, and Clouds was left to Guy Richard

(Dick) Wyndham, the second son of George Wyndham's brother Guy. Angela spent two weeks here after separating from Jim.

Cranleigh – was a village approximately eight miles southeast of Guildford in Surrey. Angela took the train here for her visit with Molly and Randall Wells at Little Woodlands, Elmhurst, which they rented.

Dene – was the country home of the Ridsdale family, located in Rottingdean close to the Burne-Jones home.

Dick Brook – was a small tributary stream of the River Severn that flows through Worcestershire, England. Angela visited here with her children while they stayed at Aunt Cissie's Old Hill close to Stourport.

Eastcote – was a small village in Middlesex, northwest of London. Angela and Jim went here to stay with Douglas.

Elstree – was a large village in Hertfordshire approximately 15 miles northwest of central London. Angela and her sons took the train here when the boys spent a few days with the Somervells.

High Head Castle (Highhead Castle) – was the country home of the Hills family, located in Cumbria, between Carlisle and Penrith. Angela visited High Head in 1915.

Kingston upon Thames – was a town in southwest London ten miles southwest of Charing Cross. Angela's friends, the Wood family, lived here.

Knutsford – was a market town in Cheshire, 14 miles southwest of Manchester. Angela and Jim visited the Mellors here, and Jim sang at one of the Bowdon chamber concerts.

Marden Ash – was the home of Graham Peel in Bournemouth.

North End House – was the country house of Edward Burne-Jones and the home of Angela's grandmother during the time of the diary. In 1880, Burne-Jones had two houses combined to form North End. The house wasn't mentioned by name, but Angela and her family visited here when she wrote of visiting Rottingdean. Angela's book *Three Houses* described her childhood in this house.

Old Buckhurst – was the country house of Sir Arthur and Lady Sybil Colefax and was located in Withyham in East Sussex. Angela stayed with the Colefaxes while visiting the Bensons.

Putney – the University Boat Race started in Putney starting in 1845. It was a district in southwest London. Angela met the Wood family here for lunch, as they lived close by.

Rottingdean (R'dean, Rottingdean) – was a village near Brighton in Sussex. In 1880, the Burne-Joneses bought Prospect House and Aubrey Cottage, combining them to create the family home of North End House. Angela's grandmother (Ma'am or Maam) lived here after Sir Edward Burne-Jones died in 1898. Angela visited her grandmother here. Jim also visited Rottingdean by himself.

Salisbury – was a medieval cathedral city in the county of Wiltshire. Angela and Hilda went here to meet Jim. Angela also went over to Clouds during this time.

Sand Hills (Sand Hills, Sandhills) – was the Surrey home of W. Graham Robertson, a lifelong family friend. He moved from Knightsbridge in London to Sand Hills after his mother died in 1907. Angela visited here to see Graham Robertson and Jessie.

Stanway – was the home of the Wyndhams' oldest daughter Mary, the Countess of Wemyss. It was located in the Cotswolds. Angela and Jim visited here, and Angela spent a month here after separating from Jim.

Stourport – or Stourport-on-Severn was a town in Worcestershire, south of Kidderminster. The Baldwin country house Astley Hall was located close to Stourport. Angela also stayed at Old Hall here. It was close to Dick Brook.

Tewkesbury – was a medieval market town in the north of Gloucestershire. Angela visited here before tea while staying at Stanway.

Thaxted – was a town and civil parish in the Uttlesford district of northwest Essex. Angela went here with her father and Clare.

Theydon – was the village of Theydon Bois in the Epping Forest district of Essex. Angela walked here while staying with the Cook family.

Wilden – was a small village about one mile northeast of Stourport-on-Severn, Worcestershire. Some of Angela's elderly relatives lived here, and Angela visited them.

Wilmslow – was a market town in Cheshire East in Cheshire, England, 11 miles south of Manchester. Angela and Jim took the train here and were met by Mrs Mellor, who brought them to Knutsford.

Wilsford Manor – was the country home of the Wyndhams' daughter Pamela. Angela met both of her husbands while a guest at this house.[12] Angela stayed here in August of 1918.

---

[12] Strickland, Margot, *Angela Thirkell: Portrait of a Lady Novelist,* San Diego: The Angela Thirkell Society of North America, 1977.

ANGELA AND JIM'S TRAVELS

> "A cloudy day, but lovely in the evening and we motored round the Devil's Jumps and back by Tilford and Elsted."
> August 1, 1915

Although many trips outside London involved Jim's performances, the couple also took trips that didn't include mentions of working.

Bateman's – was the home of Rudyard Kipling, located in Burwash, a village in the Rother district of East Sussex.

Bournemouth (B'mouth, Bournemouth) – was the town in southern England where Graham Peel lived. His house was called Marden Ash. Angela and Jim visited together, and Jim visited without Angela.

Buckhurst Park – was located in Withyhamin (East) Sussex, the Benson family rented the estate on a 25-year lease from Gilbert Sackville, Earl De La Warr. Angela and Jim visited at the same time they went to Burwash to see the Kiplings.

Chislehurst – was a suburban district of south-east London. Angela, Jim, and Mr Reeves attended Mr Allen's concert here.

Crowborough – was a town in East Sussex, England, in the Weald at the edge of Ashdown Forest. Angela and Jim stayed at the Beacon Hotel here.

The Devil's Jumps – was a series of three small hills near the village of Churt in southern England. Jim and Angela visited here.

Downton – was a village on the River Avon in southern Wiltshire, England, about six miles southeast of the city of

Salisbury. The parish is on the county boundary with Hampshire. Angela visited here with Jim, her parents, and Hilda

Edinburgh – Angela and Jim traveled here and were joined by Graham Peel. In the diary, she said they were happy here and enjoyed long walks.

Elsted – was a village and Anglican parish in the Chichester district of West Sussex. Angela and Jim visited here briefly.

Exeter – Angela and Jim visited here. Winston and Gwen Thirkell stayed here after their wedding.

Grayshott – was a village in the East Hampshire district of Hampshire. Angela and Jim visited here when they visited Hindhead.

Hindhead - was a village in Surrey. Angela and Jim visited here twice.

Lyndhurst – was a village in the New Forest National Park in Hampshire. Angela and Jim went here with Graham Peel.

Marden Ash – was the home of Graham Peel in Bournemouth. Jim and Angela visited here.

Miz-Maze – was one of England's historic turf mazes, which formed a pattern unlike conventional mazes and was classed as a labyrinth because the path had no junctions or crossings. Angela visited a Miz-Maze three times, once with Jim.

Poole Harbour – was a large natural harbor in Dorset in southern England. Angela, Jim, and Graham Peel visited here.

Romsey – was a historic market town in Hampshire. Romsey Abbey was a 12th-century abbey built in the Norman style, probably by Henry of Blois, upon an earlier Saxon church dating back to the 10th century. Angela and Jim had tea here and visited the abbey.

Seaton – was a seaside town and fishing harbor in East Devon. Angela and Jim visited here and met Graham Peel here.

Shere – was a village between Guildford and Dorking in Surrey. It is considered one of the prettiest villages in England. Jim and Angela had lunch at the Surrey Trust here.

Thursley Pride of the Valley – was a sculpture park in the town of Thursley in Surrey. Angela spent a "heavenly morning" here with Jim.

Tilford – was a village and civil parish at the point where the two branches of the River Wey merged in Surrey. J. M. Barrie lived in Tilford and wrote the prototype for Peter Pan in the countryside there. Angela and Jim visited here briefly.

Woodford – was located approximately 10 miles northeast of Charing Cross in London. William Morris lived in Woodford as a child; his home here was demolished in 1900. Angela and Jim visited here and stayed here in the summer of 1915.

OFF TO CHURCH

"Mother to lunch, and we went to Henry James's memorial service in Chelsea Church." March 3, 1916.

Chelsea Church – was located on Old Church Street in Chelsea. Angela attended a memorial service for Henry James here. James had lived in Cheyne Walk.

St Margaret's Churchyard, Rottingdean – The Burne-Jones family was buried here. Angela's parents and Nanny went to bury baby Mary's ashes at St. Margaret's; the service was held before the stained-glass windows created by Mary's great-grandfather, Sir Edward Burne-Jones.

St Margaret's Westminster – this 12th-century church was on the grounds of Westminster Abbey. Angela went to a wedding and a memorial service here.

St Martin in the Fields – the earliest reference to this church facing Trafalgar Square was in 1222. James Gibbs created its present form in 1710. Jim sang here.

St Paul's Cathedral – Christopher Wren's masterpiece dominated the London skyline for centuries. Angela visited with here with her sons and by herself.

Westminster Abbey – since William the Conqueror's coronation in 1066, all English/British coronations have taken place in this church. Angela went here with her mother to hear a musical performance.

Westminster Cathedral – was the mother church of the Catholic Church in England. Angela and Jim met Lucy Broadwood here.

CLUBS

> "Called on Uncle Phil who had the Couderts with him. He asked Jim and me to lunch with them all at the Bath Club." August 11, 1915

Albemarle Club – by the time Angela lunched here, the club had relocated from Albemarle Street to Ely House on Dover Street. This relocation happened in 1909 as the club sought to distance itself from its association with past club member Oscar Wilde and his trial. Jim became a member of this club in 1915.

Bath Club – was established in 1884 as a gentleman's club and was located at 34 Dover Street in London's West End. The club catered to sporty members and was well-known for its swimming pool. The Bath Club's pool inspired P. G. Wodehouse's fictional Drones Club. Angela's uncle Philip Burne-Jones was a member.

Burlington Fine Arts Club – was a gentlemen's club located on Saville Row. Angela had tea here with Lady Collier.

The Pioneer Club – was a progressive women's club founded in Regent Street, London, in 1892 by the social worker and temperance activist Emily Massingberd. The club moved to 22 Bruton Street, Berkeley Square. Angela's friend Christine was a member. Angela and her mother dined with Christine here.

Royal Automobile Club (R.A.C.) – was located on the site of the old war office and was completed in 1911. The club was established in 1897 for the protection, encouragement, and development of automobiles. Members had the usual club amenities as well as Turkish baths, a swimming pool, and a rifle range. Angela dined here with Major Roos and with Winston Thirkell.

South African Officers Club – was located in Grosvenor Square in London. Angela went here with Major Roos.

Wellington Club – was opened in 1832 and was located in Knightsbridge opposite the Bulgari Hotel. Philip Burne-Jones was a member of the club, and he took Angela there in early June 1916; the club closed permanently later that month.

The word club appeared many times in Angela's diary. She knew which club she was writing about, but today's readers do not. It could often be the Albemarle Club, as Jim had a membership there.

EXPANDING THE MIND LOCATIONS

"To a Private View of Mr Collier's pictures at the Leicester Galleries." July 1, 1915

Bishopsgate Institute – was a center for learning and culture which opened in 1895. Cultural programs, adult education opportunities, a library, and archives were available to the public. Angela ate here with Hilda, but no information was found on the food service at the institute.

British Museum – was the world-famous museum on Great Russell Street and was begun in 1753. Angela and Jim visited here and saw her brother Denis during the visit.

Burlington House – the first Earl of Burlington bought the house in an incomplete state in 1667. It remained a private home until 1854, when the British government purchased it. The Royal Academy took over the main block in 1857 and was joined by other societies during the late 1800s. Angela went to an exhibit here. Burlington House was also the site of a War Hospital Supply Depot.

Christie's – Christie's Auction House held sales during World War I to benefit the war effort. Angela went twice to view the artwork.

Dowdeswell and Dowdeswell – were dealers in old masters' paintings. The business closed in 1917. Angela went to see paintings from Dowdeswell and Dowdeswell at Christie's.

Grafton Galleries – hosted the Royal Society of Portrait Painters exhibit of 46 of Sargent's portraits in June of 1916. Angela also went to a party and saw Australian war photographs. Jim went here to attend an exhibition by the music teacher Mr Shakespeare.

247

Hampton Court – was constructed in 1514 by Cardinal Wolsey. Queen Victoria opened the palace to tourists, and it remains a popular tourist destination. Angela visited here and Richmond with her Uncle Phil.

Imperial War Exhibition – this exhibition opened on January 7, 1918, at Burlington House. Angela went to see it a few days later. The Imperial War Museum sponsored the exhibition. The museum was created in 1917 but didn't open to the public until 1920.

Leicester Galleries – was an art gallery close to Leicester Square, which opened in 1902. Angela went to several exhibits here.

Macmillan's – was a publishing company founded in 1843 and considered one of the Big Five publishers. Angela visited here to see a friend's drawings.

HOSPITALS

Aubrey House – was a private residence in Holland Park loaned by the family of City Financier William Alexander to the War Office in 1916 to be used as an officer's and V.A.D. (Volunteer Aid Detachment) hospital. Jim sang here.

Carlton House Terrace Hospital (Lady Ridley's Hospital) - opened in 1914 as a hospital for officers and expanded in 1917. Located in Lady Ridley's home on Carlton House, St. James, it was staffed by volunteers. It closed in 1919. Angela didn't volunteer here but picked up a friend and visited soldier patients.

Queen Alexandra Military Hospital (Millbank Hospital) – was opened in 1905 and became a military hospital during World War I. It was located in Millbank, close to Tate Britain. David Howard was admitted here after hurting his knee. Angela went to visit him.

St Peter's Hospital – Angela visited her friend Douglas here after he had an operation. She did not name the hospital in her writing, only the street, Henrietta Street. The hospital is in Covent Garden.

Weir Miliary Hospital (Balham) – was an auxiliary hospital during World War I to the First London General Hospital. Clare volunteered here, and Jim performed here for patients.

Entry omission: Angela visited patients at the Canadian Hospital. There was a Canadian Red Cross Hospital close to Hyde Park during World War I. However, it wasn't clear if this was the hospital she visited.

LEISURE

"I went to the Chelsea Flower Show with Nina." May 21, 1915

Barnes – was a district in south London, part of the London Borough of Richmond upon Thames. Angela visited here briefly when she visited Richmond.

Chelsea Flower Show – began in 1912, was held for five days in May, and was sponsored by the Royal Horticultural Society on the grounds of the Royal Hospital Chelsea in Chelsea. Angela attended in 1915.

Lincoln's Inn Fields – was the largest public square in London. It was laid out in the 1630s. Angela went walking here with her Uncle Phil.

Richmond and Richmond Park – was located in southwest London on the Thames River. Although Angela didn't get to Kew Gardens because the train was crowded, she went to Richmond and Richmond Park.

Round Pond – was located in Hyde Park. Angela's sons went ice skating here.

Wimbledon – was a town southwest of London. It contained Wimbledon Commons, one of London's largest areas of common land; Angela visited both the town and the common. Jim sang here to soldiers and taught at a school in Wimbledon after he and Angela separated.

RESTAURANTS AND HOTELS IN LONDON

> "We gave Hilda tea at the club afterwards and then dined at Treviglio. Another beastly raid." October 13, 1915

Angela frequently dined at grill rooms. These rooms were often part of a more formal restaurant and grew in popularity because they did not require patrons to wear formal attire. People leaving their offices or shopping could dine here without needing to return home to dress for the evening. Grill rooms were often located in the basement of restaurants and catered to every taste.

The Gourmet's Guide to London[13] provides all the direct quotations for restaurants and hotels. Because it was published in 1914, it describes the restaurants as Angela was most likely to have experienced them. All quotes below are attributed to this resource.

Bailey's Hotel – was located in Kensington and built between 1874 and 1876. Graham Peel stayed here while visiting London. Angela went there to take him a letter.

Berkeley – the hotel with its ground floor restaurant faced the Ritz across Piccadilly. The Berkeley was "the strong-hold of the country gentleman[14] who "never dined at the Berkeley without coming away a pleased man." Angela dined here with friends and family members and attended a party here.

Driver's Oyster House (Mrs Drivers, Drivers) – appeared to be Mrs Hopkins's favorite restaurant, as she took Angela here

---

[13] Newnham-Davis, Lieutenant-Colonel Nathaniel, *The Gourmet's Guide to London,* New York: Brentano's, 1914. Courtesy of Project Gutenburg.

twice. Located in Glasshouse Street, Driver's was a distributor of oysters for London restaurants and bars and had a restaurant upstairs for the public. Mrs Driver often served as cashier.

Café Royal – was located in Regent Street in London. The reviewer called it "My first love among restaurants." It was an "ideal place for bachelor gourmets...an excellent French restaurant of the second Empire...an ideal place for bachelor gourmets...a favorite of race-horse owners." The restaurant had also been a favorite of Oscar Wilde. Angela dined here with Jim and Graham Peel.

Carlton – was located in Pall Mall. This restaurant had a separate grill room; Angela dined with her Uncle Phil at both. To enter the grill, patrons descended the stairs from the entrance on Piccadilly, where "quite good food was served, including dishes of the day and the usual grill fare." The restaurant's French chef, M. Auguste Escoffier, was well known and highly regarded. He wrote *A Guide to Modern Cookery*.

Hotel Cecil – overlooked the Embankment Gardens and was next to Adelphi Terrace. The hotel was requisitioned for the war effort in 1917 and became the first headquarters of the newly formed the Royal Air Force (R.A.F.) from 1918 to 1919. Angela went here to find information on Jim's salary and his ability to pay child support.

Ciro's – was a fashionable chain of restaurants, with locations in London, Paris, Monte Carlo, and Biarritz. The London restaurant opened in 1915 as a private club because, under club law, it could stay open until 2:00 a.m. It was located in Orange Street close to the National Gallery. Dining and dancing were featured here. Angela and Jim spent an evening here with Uncle Phil in 1916.

Les Gobelins (Gobelins) – was a popular restaurant located next to the New Gallery Cinema in Regent Street.

Harrods – was the world-famous department store on Brompton Road. Mr Harrod opened a store in 1824, moved to its current site in 1851, and rebuilt it after a fire in 1883 burned the store to the ground. Angela had lunch at Harrods and volunteered there with Aunt Cissie (Stanley Baldwin's wife Lucy) and sold flags to benefit a fund for the troops.

The Hyde Park Grill Room –The reviewer wrote extensively about his visit to the hotel and its restaurant, even taking a tour of the facilities after dinner. Still, he did not mention the grill room. Instead, he described the restaurant as having beautiful views of the park and its environs and said it reminded him of the comfortable coloring of the old Savoy dining room. Angela dined here often, and Jim also sang at the hotel.

Pagani's Restaurant – was located on Great Portland Street, served excellent Italian food, and was popular with journalists, painters, and singers. A review stated "The diners who I see at the other tables downstairs at Pagani's all seem to belong to that very pleasant world, artist Bohemia … Great opera singers and musicians who play at the Queen's Hall go to lunch, dine, and sup" at Pagani's. Angela dined here with friends.

Pall Mall Restaurant – was located one door from the Haymarket Theater. The two proprietors were ex-waiters from the Savoy and Carlton restaurants and "see to every detail of the restaurant, kitchen, and cellar with untiring diligence and complete knowledge....Any man who did not wear evening clothes or a dinner jacket in the restaurant would feel himself rather a fish out of water at dinner time." The service was quick and silent, as most patrons went after dinner to the theater. On most of Angela's visits here, she went to the theater with friends after dinner.

Prince's Grill – was located in Piccadilly below the Royal Institute of Painters in Water Colours. This restaurant was known for quicker dining and was popular with ladies, especially shoppers and theatergoers, "a triumph of short dinner over the long one." To enter the grill, patrons descended from an entrance on Piccadilly. "Quite good food was served, including dishes of the day and the usual grill fare." Angela dined here with friends.

Rendezvous Restaurant – was located on Dean Street, and its proprietor, the personality behind the successful restaurant, was a former child runaway from Italy. "Gastronomic scouts soon discovered proprietor Peter Gallina and his little restaurant." Gallina wrote a book, *Eighteen Simple Menus,* with recipes and golden rules for cooks, including "The best cook in the world can not turn third-class materials into a first-class dish." The clientele included every class of Londoners, from princes to art students. Signature dishes were *sole Rendezvous,* a fish dish with a thick white wine sauce, and *souffle Gallina,* with brandied cherries and champagne cognac. Angela dined here with Uncle Phil and friends before attending the theater.

Rumplemayer's Café – was located on St. James Street. The café is mentioned in Virginia Woolf's book *Mrs Dalloway.* Angela and Jim went to tea here.

St Ermin's Hotel (St Ermins) – was located close to St James Park, built as a mansion block, and converted to a hotel in 1899. Jim went here twice about National Service. Later, during World War II, the hotel was a center of spy and espionage activity, but information on government use before that time wasn't available.

The Savoy – was the first purpose-built deluxe hotel in Britain and opened its doors in 1889. The hotel, restaurant, and Savoy Theater were in the Strand in Westminster. The hotel's restaurant was known as the Café Parisian. Servers wore "state livery in the evening in French grey and dark blue, and the restaurant was much patronized by the aristocracy of the theater." Angela dined here with Auntie Stella (Mrs Patrick Campbell).

Scott's Oyster and Supper Rooms (Scotts) – was located in Coventry Street in the West End. The restaurant opened in 1851, moved to Coventry Street in 1891, and moved again to Mount Street in 1967. Angela and Jim went here to lunch.

Simpson's in the Strand – was located close to the Savoy Hotel. Newnham-Davis, said, "Manager Mr N. Wheeler probably knows more about good old English fare than anyone living." P.G. Wodehouse called Simpson's "a restful temple of food." George Thirkell took Angela and Auntie Stella here to dine.

Treviglio Restaurant – was located in Church Street in Soho. This was "(a) little restaurant that might have been lifted bodily from a canal-side in Venice or a small street in Florence." The restaurant was a favorite haunt of Italian journalists in London. Angela ate here more often than at any other restaurant between 1915 and 1918.

Trocadero Restaurant – was a restaurant where patrons went to see and be seen. Located on Shaftesbury Avenue, "its entrance always impressive by its palatial splendor." It was well known for its reasonable and delicious *table d'hôtel* dinners. Once again, there was a restaurant and a grill mentioned in the research. Angela dined here with Jim and referred to the restaurant only as the Trocadero, so which place she went was unclear.

Entry omissions: The Quo Vadis Restaurant opened in 1926 and could not have been the same place Angela referred to. Although Angela wrote that she dined at the Quadrant in Fleet Street, the restaurant was located in Regent Street. There was no information available about Café Brice, Mount Carmel Restaurant, Demaria's, or the B & K Electric.

SHOPPING

"Got a mackintosh for Colin at Selfridge's." September 25, 1918

Bradleys – was a store on Chepstow Place that made gowns, evening dresses, suits, and millinery. The company made military uniforms during World War I. Angela went here and saw clothes on mannequins.

Debenhams – was a retail store that opened in 1778. In 1908, it relocated to Wigmore Street. Angela purchased clothes and a coat for her mother here.

Gramophone Company at Hayes – was located in Middlesex. By the time Angela went with Jim to have his recordings made here, the label had a picture of the dog Nipper listening to His Master's Voice. The Gramophone Company retained rights to the logo even though it became a trademark of the Victor Talking Machine Company in the United States in 1901.

Selfridge's – was the department store that opened in 1909 on Oxford Street. Angela mentioned shopping here twice.

Angela wrote about going to Harrods, but she did not shop there unless she chose not to mention her purchases.

PLACES ASSOCIATED WITH WORLD WAR I

"To visit Major Crofts at Lady Ridley's Hospital."
October 4, 1918

Aubrey House – was a private residence in Holland Park loaned by the family of City Financier William Alexander to the War Office in 1916 to be used as an officer's and V.A.D. (Volunteer Aid Detachment) hospital. Jim sang here.

Burlington House – the first Earl of Burlington bought the house in 1667 before it was completed. It remained a private home until 1854, when the British government purchased it. The Royal Academy took over the main block in 1857 and was joined by other societies during the late 1800s. Angela went to an exhibit here. Burlington House was also the site of the War Hospital Supply Depot (W.H.S.D.).

Cox and Company (Cox's) – was a company affiliated with the military during World War I. Cox and Company handled financial arrangements and services for 250,000 soldiers during the war. The company merged with Lloyd's Bank in 1923. Angela went here with a friend.

Gauche Wood – was the site of a battle in France between the Germans and the South African Brigade. Major Roos's brother died here.

Harrods – was the world-famous department store on Brompton Road. Angela volunteered there with Aunt Cissie (Stanley Baldwin's wife Lucy), selling flags to benefit a fund for the troops.

The Australian Imperial Force's Administrative Headquarters (Horseferry Road) – The headquarters was located on Horseferry Road, and Angela went here to get information about casualties when George Thirkell was on duty.

Hotel Cecil – overlooked the Embankment Gardens and was next to Adelphi Terrace. The hotel was requisitioned for the war effort in 1917 and became the first headquarters of the newly formed the Royal Air Force (R.A.F.) from 1918 to 1919. Angela went here to find information on Jim's salary and his ability to pay child support.

Carlton House Terrace Hospital (Lady Ridley's Hospital) – was opened in 1914 as a hospital for officers and expanded in 1917. It was located in Lady Ridley's home on Carlton House Terrace, St. James and staffed by volunteers. It closed in 1919. Angela didn't volunteer but picked up a friend and visited soldier patients.

Mainz – was a German city on the Rhine River. George Thirkell was stationed there in late 1918, right before he and Angela married.

Millbank Hospital (Queen Alexandra Military Hospital) – was opened in 1905 and became a military hospital during World War I. It was located in Millbank, close to Tate Britain. David Howard was admitted here after hurting his knee. Angela visited him.

St James Hospital (Balham) – St James' Hospital in Balham was an auxiliary hospital during World War I to the First London General Hospital. Clare volunteered here, and Jim performed here for patients.

Serbian Relief Fund Depot – was established in London by an English nurse who escaped Serbia. Angela and Jim worked here to help their friend, Sissie Craies.

Slipper Room – although no record was found of Mel's Slipper Room, lady volunteers made slippers and other supplies for soldiers during World War I at slipper rooms in London, according to the Imperial War Museum records. Angela volunteered at Mel's Slipper Room and saw Mel socially.

South African Officers Club – was located on Grosvenor Square in London. Angela went here with Major Roos.

War Hospital Supply Depots (W.H.S.D.) – Volunteers met at private homes and Burlington House to make items needed for World War I soldiers. Angela frequently volunteered at W.H.S.D., although the location was never given.

AUNT MARION AND SYLVIA'S RESIDENCES

> "We went down to lunch with Aunt Marion and Sylvia who are temporarily in a little house at Sanderstead." September 4, 1915

Although these characters were mysteries, Angela's visits documented their housing choices.

Chorleywood (Chorley Wood) – was a village and a civil parish in the Three Rivers District, Hertfordshire, on the border with Buckinghamshire. Angela visited Aunt Marion and Sylvia here.

Sanderstead – was a village and medieval-founded church parish at the southern end of Croydon in south London. Angela visited Aunt Marion and Sylvia when they lived here.

Slough – was a town in Berkshire halfway between London and Reading. Angela visited Aunt Marion and Sylvia here.

WINSTON THIRKELL PLACES

> "The reception was at someone else's house and then Win and Stella went off to Salcombe spending the night at Exeter." September 10, 1918

George Thirkell's brother Captain Winston Thirkell (Win) became Angela's friend.

Exeter – Angela and Jim visited here. Winston and Stella Thirkell stayed here after their wedding.

Salcombe – was a popular resort town in Devon. Winston and Stella Thirkell went here after their wedding.

Southsea – was a seaside resort and a geographic area of Portsmouth. George's brother Winston Thirkell and Stella were married there in 1918.

Surbiton was a suburban neighborhood in southwest London within the Royal Borough of Kingston upon Thames. George's brother Winston's godmother, Mrs Mowbray Gray (Aunt Eva), lived here, and Angela visited her.

SERVANTS TRAVEL

"I took Nanny and the children to Kings Cross and saw them off to Whaplode." May 14, 1918

Whaplode – was a village in the South Holland district of Lincolnshire, England. It was the home of Nanny Barbara Parson, who took Angela's children to her home to stay with her.

Wickford – was a town and civil parish in the south of Essex. Pamela Glenconner sent two women from Wickford to help Angela.

JIM SANG HERE

> "We went to Eton by the 3-45. I had tea with Dolly
> Binton while Jim rehearsed. The concert was at 6."
> November 13, 1915

James Campbell McInnes supported his family, with the help of
Angela's family, by singing. He visited the places below to sing,
occasionally visiting without Angela, perhaps making
arrangements for performances.

Aeolian Hall – was located on Old Bond Street and began as the
Grosvenor Gallery. It was acquired by the Aeolian Company in
1903 and converted into office space, a showroom for musical
instruments, and a concert hall. Jim performed here several
times.

Apsley House – was the home of the first Duke of Wellington
and his descendants and stood at Hyde Park Corner. Angela and
Jim went to tea here after Jim sang for the fourth Duke and
Duchess of Wellington.

Aubrey House – was a private residence in Holland Park loaned
by the family of City Financier William Alexander to the War
Office in 1916 to be used as an officer's and V.A.D. (Volunteer
Aid Detachment) hospital. Jim sang here for Clare's shell-
shocked officers.

Balham – was also known as St James' Hospital in Balham and
was an auxiliary hospital during World War I to the First London
General Hospital. Clare volunteered here, and Jim performed
here for patients.

Bath – Jim performed here in a concert with Mr Reeves.

Bechstein Hall – was located on Wigmore Street and renamed
Wigmore Hall in 1917. The original name was for the German

piano manufacturer who built it between 1899 and 1901. Jim sang here for Gwynne Kimpton.

Birmingham Town Hall – in Victoria Square, Birmingham, opened in 1834 and is still an active concert hall.

Bradford – was a city in West Yorkshire. Jim went there.

Canterbury – Jim visited here twice to sing for soldiers.

Dorking – was a market town in Surrey about 21 miles south of London. Ralph Vaughan Williams and Graham Peel lived in Dorking. Jim went here to see Mr Cassels-Brown.

Englefield Green – was a village in the Borough of Runnymede, in Surrey, approximately 20 miles west of central London. Angela went here with Jim, who performed at Miss Weisse's school.

Eton – Jim and Irene Schanter performed at a concert here, and Angela visited with Dolly Binton.

Guildford – was a town in Surrey. It was located 28 miles southwest of London. Jim went here alone to sing and with Angela another time.

Harrow – was located in northwest London and was best known for Harrow School, an independent boarding school for boys. The school was founded in 1572. Jim performed at a school in Harrow; whether it was the Harrow School was unclear.

Hyde Park Hotel – was located on Knightsbridge, the hotel was converted from a block of apartments in 1908. Jim sang here.

Kentsford – was a village in Suffolk. Jim went here without Angela.

Kettering – was a market and industrial town in Northamptonshire. Jim sang here.

Kingsley – was a village in Cheshire West and Chester. Jim went here without Angela.

Knutsford – was a market town in Cheshire, 14 miles southwest of Manchester. Angela and Jim visited the Mellors here, and Jim sang at one of the Bowdon chamber concerts.

Leeds – was the largest city in the county of West Yorkshire. Jim went here without Angela.

Manchester – Angela and Jim went here for Jim to perform with Hay in the Gentlemen's Concert. This was a series of concerts begun initially as an amateur gathering of flautists circa 1770. A concert hall was built in 1777 and concerts continued until 1920.

Morley College – was founded in 1889 by artist, social reformer, and suffragette Emma Cons. Morley Memorial College for Working Men and Women was the first institution of its kind to admit both genders on an equal footing. Jim sang here. Mr von Holst conducted.

Northampton – was a market town and civil parish in the East Midlands. Jim went here to sing, and he taught here.

Nuneaton – was a market town in the Borough of Nuneaton and Bedworth in northern Warwickshire. Jim went here to sing.

Oxford – Jim performed here at Balliol College. Angela and George stayed here four days right after their marriage.

Oxford House Musical and Dramatic Association – was established in 1898 to provide musical entertainment for the citizens of Benthal Green. Jim performed here.

The Palladium – Jim sang at the Sunday League Concerts at the Palladium. The Palladium was constructed in 1910 and was a premier venue for variety performances.

People's Palace – was located in the Mile End in the Borough of Tower Hamlets. It opened in 1887. Jim sang here.

Petersfield – was a market town in the East Hampshire district of Hampshire. It was 15 miles north of Portsmouth. Jim went here.

Queen's Hall – was located at Langham Place, opened in 1893, and became London's premier concert hall. Promenade Concerts (the Proms) were held here beginning in 1895. Jim performed here.

Reigate – was a town in Surrey, 19 miles south of central London. Jim went here without Angela.

Repton – was a small town in Derbyshire noted for its abbey, priory, and St Wystan's Church. Jim sang here,

St Martin in the Fields – the earliest reference to this church facing Trafalgar Square was in 1222. James Gibbs created its present form in 1710. Jim sang here.

St Paul's Girls' School – was located in Hammersmith. Jim rehearsed here, and Angela attended the rehearsal. Angela attended school here as a child after winning a scholarship. She wrote for the school newspaper[15].

---

[15] Hall, Anne, *Angela Thirkell: A Writer's Life,* London: Unicorn Publishing Group, LLP, 2021.

Salisbury – was a medieval cathedral city in the county of Wiltshire. Angela and Hilda went here to meet Jim. Angela also went over to Clouds during this stay.

Shelley House – was located on the Chelsea Embankment. The St John Hornby family lived here. Jim sang here three times.

Stratford – Jim sang here for Mr Cook,

Sunderland House – was the home of the Duchess of Marlborough, nee Consuelo Vanderbilt, at the time of the diary. She was separated from her husband, who lived at Blenheim Palace. Jim sang here.

Toynbee Hall – was a charitable institution, founded in 1884, that worked to address the causes and impacts of poverty. Jim sang here.

Wimbledon – was a town southwest of London. It contained Wimbledon Commons, one of the largest areas of common land in London. Angela visited both the town and the common. Jim sang here to soldiers and taught at a school in Wimbledon after his separation from Angela.

Worthing – was a seaside town in West Sussex, at the foot of the South Downs, ten miles west of Brighton. Jim went here for a concert without Angela.

SECTION III –THE MUSIC OF JAMES McINNES

by Aurora Siegl

James McInnes (1874-1945), baritone, was a favorite singer of British society when Angela Mackail married him in 1911. Not all Barsetshire readers know that music was also a skill for Angela. Her grandmother, Georgiana Burne-Jones, provided musical education for Angela's mother, Margaret Mackail. In turn, Margaret provided Clare and Angela with singing and piano lessons. Angela frequently accompanied her husband's singing engagements, although she seldom reported it in the diary entries. He worked with other professional musicians as well.

You will note that Angela frequently used a shortened name of the song title in the diary. Additional biographical data is not generally provided for the composers of various works except for conductors and composers known in the diary and included in other sections.

Jim's specialty was German *lieder* (art songs), and he was known for his beautiful voice and emotional presentation of these works. Because Angela was fluent in German, she helped translate these lieder for her husband. World War I quickly reduced the desire for German music in England, and Angela and Jim were both involved in the effort to change the repertoire. The diary entries highlighted the couples' shared love of classical music.

Jim previously lived with the composer Graham Peel (1877-1937), known mainly for his art songs, folk songs, and ballads. They continued to be friends, and Jim performed Peel's composed works and arrangements. Jim also performed the works of Edward Elgar (1857-1934) and premiered some works of British composers Samuel Coleridge Taylor (1875-1912), George Butterworth (1885-1916) and Ralph Vaughan Williams

(1872-1958). Vaughan Williams even dedicated his song *Boy Johnny* (1902) to "J. Campbell McInnes, Esq." Composer Gustav Holst (1874 – 1934), who was also director of the St Paul's Girls School, sometimes conducted the orchestras where Jim sang.

Jim had an exceptional voice and was also known for his appreciation of language and the words in a song as well as his love of melody. The following letter is from Ralph Vaughan Williams to conductor Arnold Barter in 1913. It shows not only the collaboration between Williams and James McInness, sometimes referred to as Campbell McInnes or J. Campbell McInnes, but the high esteem in which Jim's voice was held.

Letter from Ralph Vaughan Williams to Arnold Barter:[16]

Dec 19th 1913
Hotel-Suisse
Ospedalette – Ligure
Riviera
Italy

Dear Mr Barter

I have had an enthusiastic letter from McInnes, which increases the regret which I feel that I was not able to be present at your performance of the "Sea Symphony." I do thank you and your performers from the bottom of my heart – it is that enthusiasm which makes everything live and which makes you & your people such a vital force in musical life.

---

[16] Letter No. VWL342. Letter from Ralph Vaughan Williams to Arnold Barter, Vaughan Williams Charitable Trust, 1913.

Will you thank your choir & orchestra <u>most heartily</u> from me – I hope they recognise what an <u>encouragement</u> it is to a composer to feel that he has friends, through his music, whom he has never seen.

Yrs sincerely

Ralph Vaughan Williams

The Bristol Philharmonic Society had given a further performance of *A Sea Symphony* following that of April 1911 (the third performance of the work) with Campbell McInnes as soloist. Writing to Ralph Vaughan Williams in 1942, Steuart Wilson observed in connexion with a performance of the *Sea Symphony*, "All the way through ... I was haunted by Jim McInnes' voice – I don't think anyone will ever sing it so well again. "

Steuart Wilson (1889-1966) was himself a famous tenor, also singing the music of his English contemporary composers. He was knighted in 1948.

WORKS MENTIONED IN THE DIARY

The diary entries for the Jim McInnes' performances are included for ease of reference in following the descriptions of the works and their background.

> February 15, 1915 – "The concert was successful and they liked Graham's *Requiem* and the *Youth is Pleasure*."

The two songs mentioned are Graham [Peel's] *Requiem* and [*In*] *Youth is Pleasure*. The lyrics for *Requiem* were by Robert Louis Stevenson. Although a performance of *Verdi's Requiem* was performed, these two pieces are distinguished from one another in the diary. The lyrics for *In Youth is Pleasure* were by R. Wever from circa 1550. Sources debate whether the R. stood for

Robert or Richard. Graham Peel published a book in 1905 called *Camella, A Song Cycle in Miniature. Eight Elizabethan Lyrics,* containing *In Youth is Pleasure.*

Requiem[17]

Under the wide and starry sky,
Dig the grave and let me lie
Glad did I live and gladly die,
And I laid me down with a will.
This be the verse you grave for me:
Here he lies where he longed to be;
Home is the sailor, home from sea,
And the hunter home from the hill.

In Youth is Pleasure[18]

In a harbour grene aslepe whereas I lay,
The byrdes sang swete in the middes of the day,
I dreamed fast of mirth and play:
In youth is pleasure, in youth is pleasure.

Methought I walked still to and fro,
And from her company I could not go,
But when I waked it was not so:
In youth is pleasure, in youth is pleasure.

Therefore my hart is surely pyght
Of her alone to have a sight
Which is my joy and hartes delight:

---

[17] Stevenson, Robert Louis, *Requiem.* Underwoods, London: Chattus and Windus, 1898: Project Gutenberg.

[18] Peel, Graham, In *Youth is Pleasure, Camella, A Song Cycle in Miniature. Eight Elizabethan Lyrics,* London: Boosey & Co.

In youth is pleasure, in youth is pleasure.

March 11, 1915 – "Jim sang the *Winterreise* at Miss Weisse's school."

March 18, 1915 – "After dinner, Pamela brought Sir Edward Grey to have some music, and Papa came in too. Jim sang the *Purcell Hymns*: *Star Vicino* and *Vittoria*: *Where'er you walk* and *si tra i ceppi*: *Silent Noon* and *Bredon*: *The People that walked* and *Nasce al bosco*: *Feldeinsamkeit; Honor and arms.*"

Winterreise, 1828, is a song cycle for voice and piano by Franz Schubert (1797-1828), a setting of 24 poems by Wilhelm Müller (1794-1827). Schubert wrote these somber and passionately tragic songs in the last year of his life.

This included a number of different pieces, described below.

- *Purcell Hymns*, Composer Henry Purcell.
- *Star Vicino*, Composer Anonymous from the 1600s.
- *Vittoria, Mio Core,* Composer Giacomo Carissimi.
- *Where'er you walk*, 1744
    Composer George Frederick Händel (1685-1759).
- *Si tra i ceppi [Yes, Even in Chains]*, ranked as the
- best-known vocal works of George Frederick Händel
    translated from Italian.
- *Silent Noon*, Composer Ralph Vaughan Williams.
- *[In summertime on] Bredon,* Composer Graham Peel, 1911.
- *The People that Walked [in Darkness]*
    Composer George Frederick Händel.
- *Nasce al Bosco [Born in the Woods],*
    Composer George Frederick Händel.
- *Feldeinsamkeit, [In Summer Fields]*

Composer Charles Edward Ives.
— *Honor and Arms*, Composer George Frederick Händel.

> March 27, 1915 – "Jim sang in the *Bavar Cantata,*
> Edward Elgar for Mr von Holst."

The *Bavar Cantata* was a set of six songs for voices and piano (1895) or voices and orchestra (1896). The collection was called *From the Bavarian Highlands*. Gustav Holst, born Gustavus Theodore von Holst, was an English composer, arranger, and teacher. Angela referred to Holst as Mr von Holst or von Holst.

> May 16, 1915 – "Jim sang in the evening in hall including the *Ernste Gesänge*."

[Vier] Ernste Gesänge (1896), a four-song cycle for bass and piano by Johannes Brahms (1833-1897). Three songs dealt with death and the transience of life, while the fourth song emphasized faith, hope, and charity. The translated title from German is *Four Serious Songs*.

> September 18, 1915 –"Jim sang *Ich will den Kreuzstab* at Morley College."

The piece of music that Jim most frequently sang was *Ich will den Kreuzstab gerne tragen*, a solo cantata for bass and accompaniment, composed by Johann Sebastian (J.S.) Bach in 1726. A cantata has several movements and is usually religious. The translated title from German is *I will gladly carry the cross-staff*. Although Jim was a baritone, he sang many works written for bass, which is slightly lower than baritone, and showed his vocal range. Angela frequently refers to this piece as *Kreuzstab*.

The text for *Kreuzstab* was written by Cristoph Birkmann (1703-1771), an ordained minister. While studying theology and mathematics at the University of Leipzig, Birkmann also studied under Bach from 1724 to 1727, during which time he wrote the texts for many of Bach's cantatas, including *Kreuzstab*.

The cantata deals with the bass protagonist who gladly shoulders the cross and lays all of his sorrows at his own grave. One verse tells how Jesus boards a ship and makes a journey toward his heavenly home. The cantata then parallels Jesus' voyage with the suffering and pain of the protagonist as each travel towards death in hopes of a merciful afterlife.

> March 18, 1915 – "After dinner, Pamela brought Sir Edward Grey to have some music, and Papa came in too."

> October 13, 1915 – "We lunched at the Albemarle Club with Mr Reeves and then to the Aeolian Hall where Jim sang the *House of Life* and a Scotch Group at the first Classical Concert. Mr Borwick playing."

House of Life (1904) was composed by Ralph Vaughan Williams (1872-1958). The six songs in this series were based on the poems of Dante Gabriel Rossetti (1828-1882): 1. *Love Sight*, 2. *Silent Noon*, 3. *Love's Minstrels*, 4. *Heart's Haven*, 5. *Death in Love*, 6. *Love's Last Gift*.

As a young boy, Ralph Vaughan Williams was sent to a school in Rottingdean, then a village where Sir Edward Burne-Jones and later Rudyard Kipling lived. These were Angela's grandfather and cousin, respectively. He studied at the Royal College of Music and, in 1890, studied organ with Francis Edward Gladstone, cousin of the Liberal Prime Minister.

Leonard Borwick (1868-1925) was a noted English pianist.

> October 22, 1915 – "To tea with Gwynedd Meinertzhagen. Jim sang *Ich will den Kreuzstab* in my translation with Miss Ratcliff to do the obbligato…. Also he sang

La Procession	César Franck
Le Joli tambour	Graham Peel
D'une prison	Reynaldo Hahn"

Angela translated German for her husband. Obligato means an essential but subservient instrumental part that accompanied the voice (the accompaniment).

- *La Procession Dieu s'avanche à traves les Champsi. La Procession* was a solo song for voice (usually bass) and piano or orchestra composed by César Franck (1822-1890). The text was by poet Auguste Brizeux (1803-1858). The translated title from the French was "*The Procession [God Walks Through the Fields]*."
- *Le Joli tambour*, Graham Peel arranged this French folk song. The translated title is *The Pretty Little Drummer Boy*. The folk song, popular among soldiers, was from the mid-eighteenth century during the reign of King Louis XV (1715-1774). It is sometimes called *Trois Jeunes Tambours*.
- *D'une prison* was composed by Reynaldo Hahn (1874-1947). The title translated from the French was *From a Prison*. The song was based on a poem by Paul Verlaine (1844-1896).

The Procession - God Walks Through the Fields[19]
God is advancing through the fields!
Through the moors, the meadows,
the green thickets of beech trees.
He comes, followed by the people and carried by the priests:
To the canticles of man, birds, mingle your songs!
We stop. The crowd around an ancient oak tree bows,
adoring, under the mystical monstrance:

---

[19] Auguste Brizeux, original lyrics translated from *The Procession - God Walks Through the Fields*.

Sun! shine on him your long setting rays!
To the canticles of man, birds, mingle your songs!
You, flowers, with the incense exhale your aroma!
O celebrate! everything shines, everything prays and everything perfumes! God advances through the fields.

The drumming sounds in French that sound like like "rat a tat a tat" are "ri ran, ran pa ta plan." The lyrics for *Le Joli tambour* in English are:

> *The Pretty Little Drummer Boy*[20]
> A young drummer coming back from war
> Et ri ran, ran pa ta plan.
>
> Repeat the pattern above:
> The younger one has a rose in his mouth…
> The king's daughter was at her window…
> Nice drummer, give me your rose…
> King's daughter, give me your heart…
> Nice drummer, ask my father for it…
> Your Majesty, give me your daughter…
> Nice drummer, you're not rich enough…
> I've got three ships out on the good sea…
> One loaded with gold, the other with jewels…
> And the third one is to take out my sweetheart…
> Nice drummer, tell me who your father is…
> Your Majesty, he's the King of England…
> Nice drummer, I give you my daughter…
> Your Majesty, I thank you for this…
> In my country there are even prettier girls…

---

[20] Palomares, Monique and Yannucci, Lisa, Translation of *Trois Jeunes Tambours*, French folk song.

The lyrics for *D'une prison* were written originally in French by Paul Verlaine; the composer was Reynaldo Hahn.

From a Prison[21]
The sky is above the roof
So blue, so calm!
A tree, above the roof
Cradles his palm
The bell, in the sky that we see
Gently tinkles
A bird on the tree that we see
sings its complaint

My God, my God, life is here
Simple and quiet
This peaceful rumor
Come from the city
What have you done, oh you there
Crying endlessly
Say, what have you done, here you are
From your youth?

December 2, 1915 – "To P. G. after dinner when Jim sang the *Kreuzstab* with Miss Ratcliff's quartet."

This work, a cantata for solo bass, is often performed by Jim and is explained in the September 18, 1915, entry.

December 8, 1915 – "To Bristol… I went to rehearsal with Jim. There was a very good performance of

---

[21] Translation from lyrics by Paul Verlaine, *D'une Prison*.

277

R.V.W.'s *Carols* under Mr Arnold Barter — also *Elijah Part II.* "

R.V.W. was Ralph Vaughan Williams. [*Fantasia on Christmas*] *Carols* (1912), composed by Ralph Vaughan Williams (1872-1958), was a 12-minute piece for baritone, chorus, and orchestra based on English Christmas carols. Jim premiered the piece with the composer conducting in 1912.

The oratorio *Elijah* (1846) by Felix Mendelssohn (1809-1847) was an orchestral piece for choir and solo voices with the title role for a bass-baritone. Mendelssohn composed this oratorio in two versions, English and German. The very first performance of the oratorio *Elijah* was in its English version on August 26, 1846, at Birmingham Town Hall, conducted by the composer himself.

Arnold Barter was the director and often conductor of the Bristol Philharmonic Society. He conducted the contemporary works of British composers like Rallph Vaughan Williams, George Butterworth, and Holst to name a few.

January 2, 1916 – Jim sang *Ich will den Kreuzstab.* "

Kreuzstab, a cantata for solo bass, is often performed by Jim and is explained in the September 18, 1915, entry.

January 13, 1916 – "After dinner Pamela and Sir Edward Grey came, and Jim sang. *I long to Sing the Siege of Troy. Who is Sylvia? Wandrers Nachtlied.* Then *wherever you walk, Largo* (twice). *Ruddier than the cherry.* Then *The People that Walked. Why do the nations?* Then the *Purcell Hymns.*"

The following list provides information about these works:

- *I Long to Sing the Siege of Troy.* This was composed around 1788 by English stage songwriter Charles Dibdin (1745-1814).
- *Who is Sylvia?* (1826) was an art song (lieder) composed by Franz Schubert (1797-1828). The lyrics were from William Shakespeare's (1564-1616) *The Two Gentlemen of Verona.*
- *Wandrers Nachtlied* (1823) set to music as lieder (art songs) by Franz Schubert, poem by Wolfgang Goethe (1749-1832). The title translated from German is *Wanderer's Night Song.*
- *Wherever you Walk – (where'er you walk)* (1744), a song from George Frederick Händel's oratorio *Semele.*
- *Largo –* (1738), from George Frederick Händel's opera *Xerxes,* an aria lauding the shade of a tree.
- *[O] Ruddier than the cherry (1732),* from composer George Frederick Händel's opera *Acis and Galate.*
- *The People that Walked [in Darkness]* (1741), from the oratorio *Messiah* by George Frederick Händel.
- *Why do the Nations?* (1741), from the oratorio *Messiah* by George Frederick Händel.
- *The Purcell Hymns.* Henry Purcell was an English composer. Although he incorporated Italian and French stylistic elements, Purcell's style was a uniquely English form of Baroque music. The individual hymns were not listed.
- February 2, 1916 – "Jim woke up with a throat. However, he managed to get through the Gentleman's Concert at Manchester."

The Gentleman's Concert at Manchester was a series of concerts begun initially as an amateur gathering of flautists circa 1770; a concert hall was built in 1777, and concerts continued until 1920.

June 27, 1916 – "We went to a rehearsal and found it put off. Had tea at the club. Dined with Mr Hudson in Queen

279

> Anne's Gate; a birthday party for Suggia who played. also Tertis, Defaun, Samuel: Cammaerts recited and Jim sang."

Guilhermina Suggia (1880-1950) was the principal cellist in the local orchestra in Portugal at the age of twelve, and she studied with cellist Pablo Casals.

Lionel Tertis (1876-1975) was an internationally celebrated violist. Gustav Holst (1874-1934), Ralph Vaughan Williams (1872-1958), and others composed pieces specifically for Tertis.

Defaun and Samuel are unknown.

Emile Cammaerts (1878-1953) was a noted Belgian playwright, poet, and author who lived in England and wrote mainly in English and French.

> March 26, 1916 – "Jim sang at Toynbee Hall. We gave Hilda tea at the club and then to South Place, where he did the *Senons Songs*."

The *Senons Songs* were composed by Gilles Senons.

> November 4, 1916 – "Jim out with the shooters and played tennis after lunch. He sang about 40 songs after tea."

Mentioning 40 songs hints at the vastness of Jim's repertoire.

> November 5th, 1916 – "We had singing again. We came up with Lord Wemyss and Lady Elcho in the evening."

Lady Elcho later became Countess of Wemyss when her husband became Count. Angela's *Wild Strawberries* was based on her visits with Lady Elcho.

November 6, 1916 – "Sent out more concert notices."

The concert was possibly the upcoming Bach, cantata.

November 11, 1916 – "Jim had a rehearsal of quartet for
Bach cantata at 3."

The cantatas composed by Johann Sebastian Bach, known as
Bach cantatas, were a body of work consisting of over 200
surviving independent works and at least several dozen that were
considered lost.

After November 11, 1916, Angela continued to briefly document
Jim's performances, but her notations became increasingly terse.
Only *I Bear my Cross* and *den Kreustab* were listed. Jim began
to teach weekly in January 1917 at Northampton. Angela did not
see him after May 1, 1917, and the musical emphasis shifts.

SECTION IV – THE THEATER

Angela Thirkell was from a family of artists and writers, with the musical addition provided by James McInnes, her first husband. However, the theater played a significant role in her life. Her brother Denis, better known as an author, first worked as a stage-set designer, notably for Angela's godfather J. M. Barrie's *The Adored One* and George Bernard Shaw's *Pygmalion* before 1915. World War I put a damper on performances in general, as people were not so anxious to attend because of the potential for an air raid.

A significant play, *L'Élévation* was translated by Angela McInnes under the name *Uplifted*. Henri Bernstein, a Parisian, originally wrote *L'Élévation* in 1917. It told a story of a woman and two men, one her husband and one a soldier. The play attracted the attention of Mrs Patrick Campbell, Auntie Stella, who saw the female role as perfect for herself. In 1918, she asked Angela over to read it to her (presumably translating French to English in the process). By May 1918, the diary entry appears, "Took the M.S. of *L'Elevation* to Southampton Street to be typed." She later took it to the theater and "gave him [Mr du Maurier] *L'Elevation* to look at as Auntie Stella wished."

Because of the war, the play was not produced until 1924, with Mrs Patrick Campbell in the starring role. Angela Thirkell was named as a playwright and the play is identified as "Thirkell, Angela, *Uplifted* (Sheffield 23/3/23; Brixton 28/9/23): adapted from *L'Élévation* (1917) by H. Berstein."[22]

---

[22] Nicoll, Allardyce, *English Drama 1900-193: The Beginning of the Modern Period Part 1*, Cambridge University Press, 1973.

THEATERS

"...to the *Lilac Domino* at the Empire one night and were together the whole time." August 26-31, 1918

Alhambra – was a popular theater and music hall at Leicester Square, demolished in 1936. Angela went here with her Uncle Phil.

Ambassadors – was a new theater that opened in 1916. Angela went here twice to see the same play, *More*.

Burlington Gardens Theater – was located on the Burlington Estate in central London. The street Burlington Gardens contained many historic buildings. One of these buildings housed the theater where Angela went to a lecture.

The Coliseum – opened in 1904 and was located in St Martins Lane. The stage was huge: 55 feet wide and 92 feet deep. Angela went to the London Coliseum in 1916 with Jim and in 1918 to see Russian performances.

Royal Theater, Drury Lane (Drury Lane) – faced Catherine Street and backed onto Drury Lane. This theater was the fourth on the site and was built in 1812. Angela sat in the Baldwins' box here in early 1918, shortly after the installation of gas lighting throughout the theater.

Empire Theater – was located in Leicester Square. Angela and George Thirkell went to a play here after they became engaged to be married.

Leighton House – was built for painter Frederic Leighton in Holland Park, London; it was a private home when Angela attended two concerts here. It opened as an art museum in 1929.

Lyceum – was the West End Theater located on Wellington Street with origins back to 1765. Angela attended a play here.

New Gallery Cinema – was initially built in 1888 as an art gallery, it was briefly a restaurant before being converted in 1913 to a cinema. It was located next to Les Gobelins restaurant.

Philharmonic Hall – was located on Great Portland Street; the hall was built in 1907-1908 and was initially called St James Hall. The name change occurred in 1914. It was known for its cinemograph displays. Angela and Jim saw submarine motion pictures here.

Royal Albert Hall (Albert Hall) – was located on the northern end of South Kensington Seating more than 5,000 people, the Royal Albert Hall was opened by Queen Victoria in 1871. Angela sat in the Duchess of Wellington's box to hear Clara Butt.

Scala – was a theater on Charlotte Street that was a cinema from 1911-1918. Angela and Jim went here to see war pictures.

Angela mentioned the Kings Theater in her diary; this theater could be His Majesty's Theater. She also wrote of the Shaftesbury Theater. This theater could be the Prince's Theater on Shaftesbury Avenue. Because these references were unclear, they were not listed here.

VISITS TO THE THEATER

The entries below were in the diary but listing them here provides an opportunity to see the scope of Angela's social life involving the theater. Between June 1917 and May 1918 alone, German bombers attacked London 17 times, and there were also Zeppelin attacks. The theater was a place to escape these concerns. They were given the use of the Duchess of Wellington's box in November 1915, and Jim sang for her benefit at a later date, and they socialized at other times. These visits refer to theater visits only. Although this is all in the diary itself, seeing a list provides evidence of the part the theater played in the life of Jim and Angela and their friends and Angela's life after her divorce.

January 23, 1915 – "Jim and I dined at Treviglio and then met Henry and went to the pit of *Potash and Perlmutter*."

February 25, 1915 – "We dined at chez Treviglio and went to the *Tales of Hoffman*."

April 24, 1915 – "Nanny got back at 6.30 and Jim and I dined at the Pall Mall Restaurant and went to *Oliver Twist.*"

July 29, 1915 – "…went to *Quinneys* for which Mr Ainley had given Jim seats for the second time."

November 20, 1915 – "I heard Clara Butt at the Albert Hall from the Duchess of Wellington box."

November 23, 1915 – "I met Jim and Graham at the club and we had lunch and went to *Romance* for which Mr Nares had given Jim a box."

November 24, 1915 – "Clare and I joined Papa at Treviglio where we dined and went to *More* at the Ambassadors."

April 10, 1916 – "To a pupils' concert at Graham Street. We dined at the Gobelins with Mrs Hopkins, Gerry and Mr Allen and went to *More* at the Ambassadors."

June 30, 1916 – "… we joined the Baldwins at *Fishpingle*, a dull play."

September 16, 1916 – "Dined at the Pall Mall Restaurant and to see Oscar Asche's dull play *Chu Chin Chow*."

December 4, 1917 – "Captain Thirkell called for me and we picked up Mr. Elsum and a Miss Lanch and dined at the Australian Officers' Club in Piccadilly and went to *Chu Chin Chow*."

January 18, 1918 – "Took Graham to the Baldwin's Box for the Drury Lane pantomime, *Aladdin*. We only stopped for two acts and he enjoyed it very much."

April 16, 1918 – "Gerry Howard to spend the night and he and Mother and Papa and Clare went to *The 13th Chair* to see Auntie Stella.

May 18, 1918 – "I took Amy and Everard to *Dear Brutus* for which Barrie had given me a box."

May 23, 1918 – "Also Captain Doyley(?) and Col. Maude and we all went to *Belinda* by A.A. Milne and laughed."

June 13, 1918 – "…went by bus to the Shaftesbury Theatre to see *Don Giovanni*. It was a delightful performance and I was very happy."

June 18, 1918 – "R.A.C. with a friend of his called Mitchell and went to *Nurse Benson*."

June 29, 1918 – "We had poisoned fish and went to the *Lilac Domino* and I felt so ill that she brought me home."

July 1, 1918 – "To Queen Victoria St to order some Musical Glass for Winston's wedding present and got tickets for *Figaro* on Wednesday."

July 2, 1918 – "Brother and I to Kitty Somervell's dance performance. I went to *Seraglio* in Mr Pease's box."

July 3, 1918 – "To *Figaro* with Mr Plank in the afternoon."

July 6, 1918 – "Had high tea at the Craies' and Sissie, Miss Milne, Zoe and I went to *Carmen* at Drury Lane."

July 8, 1918 – "Went to *Aida* to her pit, a very good performance and home on a bus."

August 10, 1918 – "We all dined together at the Rendezvous and also a very dull man called Inigo Thomas and went to Arnold Bennett's new dull play *The Title*."

August 26-31, 1918 – "We went to one of the Overseas dances at Lady Mond's on Friday and to the *Lilac Domino* at the Empire one night and were together the whole time."

September 2, 1918 – "… all went to the *Tales of Hoffman* at the Kings Theatre."

September 6, 1918 – "Had early supper with Amy and we went to *Don Giovanni* at the Kings Theatre."

September 23, 1918 – "With Maisie to the pit to see the *Luck of the Navy*."

October 12, 1918 – "Amy and I went to *The Female Hun* at the Lyceum."

November 1, 1918 – "Win's best man came to tea and played with the boys and then I dined with him and we went to *Soldier Boy*."

November 8, 1918 – "Mother, Papa, Ers and I to *Trelawney of the Wells* at the Kings Theatre."

CARNAVAL

The Coliseum was the theater where Serge Diaghilev presented ballets in London, and Kitty Somervell often performed in them, although not mentioned here.

October 4, 1918 – "...dined with Mr Plank who took us to the Coliseum to see the Russian dancers in *Carnaval*."

November 5, 1918 – "Dined with Val and went to the Russian ballet at the Coliseum."

November 9, 1918 – "Dined with Val and we went to the Coliseum for *Carnaval*."

November 27, 1918 – "Val fetched me and we dined at Prince's and went to the Coliseum."

November 28, 1918 – "Dined with Amy and Everard and we went to *Carnaval*."

November 30, 1918 – "Kitty and I dined at Quo Vadis and went to the Coliseum for *Carnaval*."

SECTION V – GUIDE TO ART

Art, like music and theater, played an important role in Angela's life. Having a famous artist for a grandfather, influenced her throughout her life.

Angela knew famous artists, attended exhibitions featuring their work and saw their artwork in the houses of her family and friends.

PORTRAITS

"To Sargent at 11.0 to sit for a charcoal drawing." December 7, 1915

Although most of these paintings weren't mentioned in the diary, the portrait sitters were. In addition, it should be noted that most of these portraits were painted outside of the years of the diary. More complete descriptions of the models are provided in other sections.

JOHN SINGER SARGENT PAINTINGS

The famous painter, John Singer Sargent, captured the era of Angela's early life with his portraits. He not only painted the three daughters of Madeline and Percy Wyndham and drew a charcoal portrait of Angela, but he also painted many of their friends.

Cazalet, Maud (Mrs Cazalet) – she and two of her sons sat for a portrait by John Singer Sargent. Sargent also painted her husband, William Marshall Cazalet. Mr Cazalet was a friend of Kipling's and an Olympic athlete, competing in 1908. She was the former Maude Lucia Heron-Maxwell.

James, Henry (Henry James) – he was an author born in New York City on April 15, 1843. He died on February 28, 1916, in Chelsea, London. Angela attended his funeral.

Lewis, Elizabeth (Lady Lewis) – she was the second wife of Sir George Henry Lewis, the first baronet of Portland Place, who died in 1911. Sargent also painted her husband.

Ormond, Reine (Reine) – she was a friend of Angela's sister, Clare. She was John Singer Sargent's sister Violet's daughter. Reine was pictured in a number of her uncle's paintings. Her sister Rose-Marie Ormond was also in many Sargent paintings, and he called her "the most charming girl that ever lived."

Ormond, Violet (Lady Ormond) – she was the sister of John Singer Sargent and mother of Reine, Rose-Marie, and Guillaume Ormond. She was the wife of Louis Francis Ormond.

Simonds, Mary (Mrs Simonds) – she was painted by John Singer Sargent in 1911. She was the former Mary Hope Mellor.

Robertson, W. Graham (Graham Robertson) – he was an author, artist, collector, and long-time family friend who encouraged Angela when she became a writer. He lived at Sandhills, his Surrey home. Sargent painted him in 1894, and that portrait is at Tate Britain Gallery.

PHILIP BURNE-JONES PAINTINGS

Angela's Uncle Phil was also an artist. One of his most famous works was his portrait 1917 of his father, Edward Burne-Jones. He also painted other family members and friends.

Campbell, Beatrice Stella (Auntie Stella) – An actress best known for her appearances in Shakespearean plays. She was known as Mrs Pat on the stage. Philip Burne- Jones fell in love with Stella Campbell, and she was the model for his 1897 painting *The Vampire.* The painting inspired Rudyard Kipling to write his poem "The Vampire" and was Philip Burne-Jones's best-known painting.

James, Henry (Henry James) – Philip Burne-Jones painted his godfather in 1894.

Kipling, Rudyard – In1900, Philip Burne-Jones painted his cousin in 1899.

Poynter, Sir Edward (Uncle Edward) – he was married to Angela's grandmother Georgiana Burne-Jones's half-sister Agnes. He was an artist, designer, and draftsman who served as president of the Royal Academy and was a first baronet. The portrait was painted in 1909.

Ridsdale, Sir Aurelian and Susan (Aurelian and Susan) – he was a leading member of the British Red Cross Society, and his sister was Lucy Ridsdale Baldwin (Stanley Baldwin's wife).

EDWARD POYNTER PAINTINGS

Baldwin, Louisa (Aunt Louie) – she was the mother of Stanley Baldwin. Louisa was Angela's grandmother Georgiana's half-sister.

Burne-Jones, Georgiana Macdonald (Maam, Ma'am) – she was Angela's grandmother and wife of Edward Burne-Jones.

Charteris, Mary Constance, Countess of Wemyss and March (Mary Lady Wemyss) – her maiden name was Mary Wyndham. She was known as Lady Elcho upon her marriage in 18883 to Hugo Charteris, Lord Elcho, until 1914, when the title passed to her daughter-in-law.

Markham, Violet (Lady Markham) – she was a social reformer who did not favor women being given the vote.

Poynter, Agnes – Edward Poynter painted a portrait of his wife, the former Agnes MacDonald.

Poynter, Edward – the artist completed a self-portrait in 1877.

TWO MORE ARTISTS' PAINTINGS

Collier, John (Mr Collier) – he painted a portrait of Angela wearing a hat featuring a large red feather. Angela went to a Private View of Mr Collier's pictures at the Leicester Galleries.

Micholls, Ada (Mrs Micholls) – she started a drawing of Angela during a visit. She was an artist trained at the Royal College of Art and the wife of Edward Montefiore Micholls and the mother of Colonel Wilfred Horatio Micholls.

EXHIBITIONS

"To a Private View of Mr Collier's pictures at the Leicester Galleries." July 1, 1915

Collier, John (Mr Collier) – painted a portrait of Angela wearing a hat featuring a large red feather. Angela went to a Private View of Mr Collier's pictures at the Leicester Galleries.

Dowdeswell and Dowdeswell – were dealers in old masters' paintings; the business closed in 1917. Angela visited this business to see pictures.

Dyson, Will (Mr Dyson) – was Australia's first official war artist, his depictions of Australian soldiers on the Western Front focused on the ordinary soldier's loneliness, miserable conditions, suffering, and humor. Angela attended a showing of his work.

Fisher, Mr Alexander (Mr Alexander Fisher) – was an Arts and Crafts artist and silversmith who studied at the Limoges school of enameling. His book, *The Art of Enameling Upon Metal: with a short appendix concerning miniature painting on enamel,* was published in 1909. The Fishers were friends of Angela's parents. Angela went to a display of Mr Fisher's enamels.

Orpen, Sir William Newenham Montague (Orphen) – was one of the most prolific of the official war artists sent to the Western Front. In May 1918, a display of his artwork was featured at Agnew's Gallery in Old Bond Street. Angela went to the exhibition with her mother.

Pennell, Joseph (Pennell) – was an American draftsman, etcher, lithographer, and illustrator for books and magazines. A prolific artist, he spent most of his working life in Europe. Angela went with a friend to see his drawings.

Speed, Harold – was a painter in oil and watercolors, painting portraits, figures, and historical subjects. He also wrote instructional books for artists. Angela went twice to see exhibits of Harold Speed's work.

Waterford, Louisa (Lady Waterford) – studied painting and drawing with John Ruskin and fellow Pre-Raphaelites. She died in 1891. Angela and Mrs Micholls went to an exhibit of Lady Waterford's drawings at the Amateur Art Exhibition.

BIBLIOGRAPHY

Published Sources:

Angela Thirkell Society (UK) (Eds.), *Letter to a Nanny: How Georgiana Burne-Jones's family was held together in a crisis*, FeedARead Publishing, 2022.

Glenconner, Pamela, *Edward Wyndham Tennant: A Memoir by his Mother,* New York: John Lane, 1920.

Hall, Anne, *Angela Thirkell: A Writer's Life,* London: Unicorn Publishing Group, LLP, 2021.

Hibbert, Christopher and Weinreb, Ben, *The London Encyclopaedia,* New York: St. Martin's Press, 1983.

MacCarthy, Fiona, *The Last Pre-Raphaelite: Edward Burne-Jones and the Victorian Imagination,* London: Faber and Faber Ltd., 2011.

Mackail, Denis, *Life with Topsy*, London: William Heinemann, Ltd., 1942.

McGee, Tim, *Barely Clare: The Little-Known Life of Clare Mackail,* Southeastern, PA: The Angela Thirkell Society of North America, 2020.

McInnes, Graham, *The Road to Gundagai*, London: The Hogarth Press, 1985. First published Hamish Hamilton, Ltd, 1965.

Nicoll, Allardyce, *English Drama 1900-1930: The beginning of the Modern Period Part 1*, Cambridge University Press, 1973.

Palomares, Monique and Yannucci, Lisa, Translation of Trois Jeunes Tambours, French folk song, cited July 18, 2022, from https://www.mamalisa.com/?t=es&p=138.

Renton, Claudia, *Those Wild Wyndhams: Three Sisters at the Heart of Power,* New York: Alfred A. Knopf, 2018.

Strickland, Margot, *Angela Thirkell: Portrait of a Lady Novelist,* San Diego: The Angela Thirkell Society of North America, 1977.

Taylor, Ina, *Victorian Sisters: The Remarkable Macdonald Women and the Great Men They Inspired,* Bethesda, MD: Adler & Adler Publishers, Inc., 1987.

Thirkell, Angela, *Three Houses,* Wakefield, RI: Moyer Bell, 1998.

PROJECT GUTTENBERG

Newnham-Davis, Lieutenant-Colonel Nathaniel, *The Gourmet's Guide to London,* New York: Brentano's, 1914. Courtesy of Project Gutenburg, https://www.gutenberg.org/ebooks/53304.

Wever, R., "In Youth is Pleasure". Edited by Sir Arthur Thomas Quiller-Couch. *The Oxford Book of English Verse.* Oxford: Clarendon, 1919: Project Gutenberg. www.gutenberg.org/ebooks/66619.

Stevenson, Robert Louis, "Requiem." *Underwoods*, London: Chattus and Windus, 1898: Project Gutenberg. www.gutenberg.org/ebooks/438.

ACKNOWLEDGMENTS

This book would not have been possible without the contribution by Simon McInnes of family records in his possession. We are all grateful to him for this opportunity and to Toby Crick, Serena Thirkell, and the Estate of Angela Thirkell for permission to print. We want to thank Aurora Siegl for writing the section on Music and her accomplished approach to research. Sir Ralph Cobbe of the Vaughan Williams Charitable Trust gave permission to reprint the Ralph Vaughan Williams letter. We also thank Tim McGee for his trove of pre-Raphaelite knowledge and treasures, and the members of the Edward Burne-Jones Facebook page for their knowledge and assistance. The much-appreciated photos are public domain and available from Wikimedia Commons. For review, Sara Bowen put us on the road to making the reader's road more accessible. Thanks to Penelope Fritzer and John Childrey for their review and comments. Diane Smook continues to provide Anglea Thirkell Society publication covers. Thanks to Sunny Gwaltney, secretary, and Susan Scanlon, treasurer, for this distribution on behalf of the Angela Thirkell Society.

Finally, we would like to thank our readers. Barsetshire fans will make the connection to many places and people in the Thirkell books. Some readers might learn something new about London during World War I.

From the editors, thank you. It has been a lot of work and a lot of fun.

–Susan Verell and Barbara Houlton

INDEX SECTIONS

The index is divided into sections.

- Names of people as referenced, followed by names of people seen once.
- Names of places – streets, villages, theaters, concert venues, or restaurants. Also includes organization names.
- Names of music.
- Name of plays or lectures.

Where the guide differs from the diary in capitalization or imbedded punctuation, the diary takes precedence. As with the diary explanations, references elsewhere or explanations added are in square brackets. When two people always appear together, the names are included together. Otherwise, they are indexed separately. For people whose last name ends in 's," apostrophes are not included in the index. The diary frequently names pieces of music in lower case; the standard today is title case. Finally, the few occurrences of parentheses in the index refer to nicknames or indicators when two people have the same name.

The goal is for the diary reader to be able to find similar references for any individual, place, play, or music.

INDEX

298

299

301

303

Faraday, 49
Feilding, Rudolph William
    Basil, 185
Finch, Miss, 145
Fisher, Alexander, 108
Fisher, Edwin, 187, 192
Fisher, Herbert, 206
Fisher, Lettice Ilbert, 206
Fisher, Mr Alexander, 166,
    212, 292
Fisher, Mrs, 147, 166, 212
Fisher-Rowe, Edward, 216
Fisher-Rowe, Mrs, 44
Fisher-Rowe, Victoria Isabella
    Liddell, 216
Fishers, the, 123
FitzGerald, Edward, 199
FitzGerald, Pamela, 199
Fleming, Ian, 218
Fletcher, Jane, 188
Fletcher, Mary, 3, 211
Fletcher, Mr & Mrs Harry, 9
Fletcher, Mrs, 4, 9, 37, 69, 71,
    89, 97, 99
Fletchers, the, 29, 35
Forbes, Angela, 199
Ford, Henry Justice, 163, 167,
    171, 186, 213, 285
Ford, Mr and Mrs Walter, 9,
    167, 186
Ford, Mr Walter, 18
Fords, Walter, 80
Fowler, Lettice, 24
Fowler, Mrs, 24, 44
Fox, Mrs, 55, 68
Franck, César, 7, 9, 37, 44,
    128, 144, 184, 275
Fred, Uncle [MacDonald], 134
Freshfield, Mr, 177
Friswell, Sir Charles, 125

Gallina, Peter, 254
Gaskell, May, 11, 167
George [Lewis], 127
George [Thirkell, George],
    122, 149, 150, 151
George VI, 197
Gerry, 3, 119
Gerry [Hopkins], 16, 50, 65,
    140
Gertrude, 134
Gibson Family, 232
Gibson, Dolly, 27, 46, 63, 232
Gibson, Mr, 5, 9, 232
Gibson, Mrs, 10, 11, 232
Gibsons, the, 17
Gillick, Ernest George, 167
Gillick, Mary Tutin, 167
Gillick, Mrs, 12, 68, 70
Gillicks, the, 3, 7, 40, 91
Gladstone, Francis Edward,
    274
Gladstone, Henry Neville, 167
Gladstone, Miss, 167
Gladstone, Mrs Henry, 59
Gladstone, Mrs. Henry, 167
Gladstone, William Ewart,
    167
Gleadowe, Mr, 4, 7, 101, 128,
    140
Gleadowe, Reginald, 167
Gleadowe, the, 128
Glenconner, Pamela Adelaide
    Genevieve Wyndham, 104,
    198, 199, 203, 204, 205,
    236, 240, 262, 294
Goethe, Wolfgang, 279
Gotch, Audrey, 64, 175
Gotch, Oliver, 104, 116, 147,
    175

Graham [McInnes], 2, 3, 4, 5,
10, 11, 16, 17, 22, 23, 27,
29, 33, 35, 36, 40, 46, 48,
49, 50, 52, 53, 54, 56, 57,
60, 62, 63, 72, 74, 79, 80,
82, 83, 86, 87, 90, 91, 94,
96, 99, 100, 101, 103, 104,
105, 106, 109, 110, 112,
115, 116, 117, 118, 119,
120, 123, 139, 141, 145,151
Graham [Peel], 8, 13, 14, 15,
17, 19, 20, 23, 25, 35, 41,
48, 49, 60, 61, 73
Graham, William, 168
Graham, Mr, 15, 48, 49
Graham, Mr and Mrs, 67
Gray, Evangeline [Eva, Aunt],
196
Gray, Mowbray, 196, 261
Gray, Mrs Mowbray (Aunt
Eva), 141, 142, 143, 145
Grenfell, Francis Wallace, 216
Grenfell, Lord, 52
Grey, Edward, 203, 204, 278
Grey, Sir Edward, 13, 49, 272,
274
Grosvenor, Constance
Cornwallis-West, 195, 204,
205
Grosvenor, Hugh Arthur, 195,
204
Grosvenor, Hugh Richard
Arthur, 201
Grosvenor, Ursula, 24, 204,
205
Grosvenor, Victor, 201
Guedalla, Phillip, 100, 112,
212
Guilhermina, Suggia, 186
Gunn, Miss, 140

Gunn's, the, 140
Guy [Wyndham], 24, 101,
108, 115
Guy and his wife [Wyndham],
79
Guy, Mr and Mrs, 24
Guy, Mrs [Wyndham], 21, 24
Gwen, 228
Gwen [Vassall], 119, 122,
127, 130, 138, 139
Haas, Madame, 12, 70
Hahn, Reynaldo, 37, 275, 277
Hale, Alfred, 27, 186
Hall, Anne, 229, 294
Hall, Radclyffe, 191
Hallé, Charlie, 29, 168
Halsey, Mrs, 68, 69, 101, 120,
144, 230
Hambourg, Dolly, 81, 111,
123
Hambourg, Dorothea,
Mackenzie, 186
Hambourg, Mark, 186
Hambourg, Mrs, 65, 73
Hambourg, Nadine, 186
Hambourg, Sonia, 186
Hambourg, Sonia and Nadine,
112
Hambourgs, the, 72, 82, 84
Hamilton, Mrs, 68
Hamilton, Mrs John, 119
Händel, George Frederick,
272, 273, 279
Hannay, Babs, 128, 139, 140
Harold, 3
Harold [Speed], 14, 117
Harvey, Mrs, 68, 119, 137,
144, 230
Haselden, Mr, 45, 68
Haselden, William, 176

Haseltine, Olive Ilbert, 206
Hawtrey, Hortense D'Aranyi, 187
Hawtrey, Hortense Emilia Sophie D'Arányi, 187, 207
Hawtrey, Mr and Mrs Ralph, 128
Hawtrey, Mrs Ralph, (Hortense von Aranyi), 27
Hawtrey, Ralph, 187, 207
Hawtreys, the, 39, 46
Hay, 3, 8, 9, 39, 67, 228, 265
Hayward, Lawrence, 211, 212
Hayward, Mr, 52
Hedgeland, Francis George Harry, 215
Henry, 5, 12, 16, 18, 21, 27, 33, 68, 75, 82, 89, 92, 93, 97, 100, 103, 104, 140, 141, 143, 223
Henschel, 9
Herbert [Fisher], 123
Herbert and Lettice [Fisher], 135
Heseltine, Michael, 206
Heseltine, Olive, 68
Heseltines, the, 120
Hess, Myra, 95, 185, 187, 207
Hess, Theodora, 61, 101, 187, 192
Hilda, 3, 8, 9, 11, 12, 13, 14, 15, 16, 17, 18, 19, 21, 22, 24, 25, 26, 29, 30, 35, 36, 37, 39, 40, 44, 45, 50, 56, 58, 59, 64, 65, 69, 70, 91, 92, 228, 229, 231, 239, 242, 247, 251, 267, 280
Hills, 27, 65, 79, 141
Hills, Edmond Herbert Grove, 203

Hills, Eustace, 29, 30, 58, 71, 202
Hills, Eustace Gilbert, 178, 202, 237, 238
Hills, Mr, 2, 3, 4, 5, 10, 13
Hills, Mrs, 2, 20
Hills, Nina and Eustace, 37
Hills, Nina and Mr, 9
Hills, Nina Louise Kay-Shuttleworth, 4, 71, 178, 202, 237, 238, 250
Hills, the, v, 7, 14, 17, 26, 55, 60, 73, 88
Hills, the Eustace, 2, 40
Hobson, Audrey, 95, 96
Holman Hunt, Gladys, 97
Holst, Gustav, 155, 183, 190, 191, 265, 269, 273, 280
Holst, Mr von, 5, 10, 11, 14
Hopkins, Amy, 168, 251, 286, 287, 288
Hopkins, Arthur, 170, 213
Hopkins, Everard, 168, 286, 288
Hopkins, Gerald Manley, 168
Hopkins, Gerry, 39, 61, 100, 101, 168, 230, 286
Hopkins, Mrs, 3, 35, 36, 46, 57, 61, 68, 76, 81, 96
Hopkins, the, 16, 39, 60, 65, 72, 76, 84, 99, 100, 101, 124, 140
Hopkinses, 82, 96, 112
Hornby, Cicely, 112
Hornby, Mrs, 21, 44, 66
Hornbys, the, 20, 40, 51, 83, 112
Horsley, John Callcott, 173
Horsley, Oswald, 216
Horsley, Pamela, 216

307

308

310

244, 245, 246, 247, 249,
250, 252, 253, 254, 255,
256, 257, 258, 261, 263,
264, 265, 266, 267, 268,
269, 270, 272, 273, 274,
277, 278, 279, 280, 281,
282, 283, 284, 285
McInnes, Mary, 158, 159,
194, 244
McInnes, Peggy, 11
McLaren, Barbara, 4, 45, 49,
213
Meinertzhagen, Gwynedd
Marion Llewellyn, 37, 217,
218, 274
Meinertzhagen, Louis Ernest,
218
Meinertzhagen, Mrs, 70
Mel [Mel's Slipper Room], 10,
27, 42, 97, 112, 146, 229,
259
Mellor, John, 170, 238, 265
Mellor, John Serocold Paget,
170
Mellor, Mabel Serocold, 170,
238, 240, 265
Mellor, Mr, 51
Mellor, Mrs, 51, 62, 64, 79,
105
Mendelssohn, 278
Merriman, Dorothea, 178
Merriman, Mr, 2
Merriman, Mr and Mrs, 2
Merriman, Roger, 178
Merrimans, 2
Micholls, Ada, 218, 292, 293
Micholls, Colonel, 123, 124
Micholls, Edward Montefiore,
292
Micholls, Mr, 12

Micholls, Mr and Mrs, 101
Micholls, Mrs, 81, 82, 89, 96,
101, 108, 117, 118, 119,
121, 122, 124, 127, 141
Micholls, Wilfred Horatio
Montefiore, 218, 292
Middleton, Bella Stillman,
172
Middleton, John Henry, 172
Middleton, Mrs, iii, 12, 70,
142
Middleton, Peggy, 12, 49, 172
Middletons, the, 12, 49
Mike [MacGregor], 139
Miles, Marjorie, 110, 115,
124, 234
Millar, Mrs, 103
Millars, the, 4
Mills, Dr, 4, 22, 27, 97, 100,
101, 129, 140, 178, 230
Mills, Mrs, 70, 143, 230
Milne, A. A., 125, 210, 286
Milne, Miss, 287
Mimi, 144
Minnie, Aunt, 101, 115
Mitchell, 286
Moens, Miss, 73, 218
Moens, Seaburne, 218
Moira, 144
Mollie [Poynter], 12
Mond, Alfred, 218
Mond, Lady, 137
Mond, Mrs, 70
Mond, Violet Goetze, 218,
287
Monet, Claude, 178
Moon, Dr, 7
Morris family, 232
Morris, Jane, 205
Morris, Mr, 232

Ormond, Guillaume, 106, 188, 290
Ormond, Guillaume and Reine, 128
Ormond, Madame and Reine, 129
Ormond, Reine, 101, 290
Ormond, Rose-Marie, 290
Ormond, Violet, 290
Ormonds, the, 128
Orpen, Sir William Newenham Montague, 293
Packer, Mrs, 72
Page, Mrs, 42, 58
Pamela [Glenconner], 13, 49, 50, 60, 151, 226, 272, 274, 278
Papa [Mackail, John], 1, 3, 5, 7, 8, 9, 13, 24, 32, 36, 41, 45, 51, 53, 54, 57, 64, 76, 80, 84, 88, 90, 105, 114, 117, 119, 124, 128, 130, 135, 140, 143, 147, 151, 272, 274
Partridge, Bernard, 219
Partridges, [the Bernard], 72
Passmore, Agnes Fraser, 188, 189, 209
Passmore, Doris, 188
Passmore, Isobel, 189
Passmore, Mirette, 188
Passmore, Miss, 4, 35
Passmore, Miss and Mr, 7
Passmore, Mr, 10
Passmore, Nancie, 189
Passmore, Walter, 188, 189, 209
Passmores, the, 3
Pat, 116, 138
Pat [Beech], 145

Patrick, 22, 99, 144
Patrick [Ranalow], 54
Patterson, Mr A. M., 134, 135, 145, 177, 178
Patullo, Mrs, 7, 10, 70
Pearce, Anna, 22, 27, 37, 103, 233
Pearces, 62
Pease, Jack, 125, 130, 219, 287
Peel, Dorothy Morant, 189
Peel, Elizabeth, 189
Peel, Evelyn Kingsford, 189
Peel, Gerald, 189
Peel, Graham, 1, 37, 84, 143, 159, 189, 192, 221, 225, 228, 231, 238, 241, 242, 243, 251, 252, 264, 270, 271, 272, 275, 285
Peel, John, 189
Peel, Katharine, 189
Peel, Mrs, 14, 23
Peel, Mrs Bob, 48
Peel, Robert, 189
Peels, the John, 51
Peggie, 54
Peggy, 36, 52
Peggy [Ritchie], 4, 101, 103, 123, 140
Pennell, Joseph, 57, 293
Perrins, the, 48, 56
Phil, Uncle, 1, 4, 5, 7, 12, 28, 30, 32, 34, 35, 39, 40, 41, 42, 43, 45, 49, 56, 61, 64, 65, 66, 67, 68, 69, 70, 71, 74, 80, 83, 97, 100, 109, 110, 111, 112, 114, 116, 118, 120, 121, 125, 129, 134, 135, 136, 139
Pinwell, Constance, 189

314

Ritchie, Margaret (Peggy), 175
Ritchie, Miss [Hester], 181
Ritchie, Mrs, 97, 140, 175
Ritchie, Mrs and Miss, 9
Ritchie, Mrs and Peggy, 37, 101, 129
Ritchie, Peggie, 116
Ritchie, Peggy, 5, 128
Ritchie, Richmond, 181
Ritchies, the, 4, 103, 105
Robertson, Graham, 39, 54, 163, 167, 171, 211, 213, 229, 239, 290
Robinson, Edward Stanley Gotch, 216
Romberg, 71
Romily, Bertram, 219
Romily, Nellie, 59, 219
Ronaldson, Mrs, 13
Ronaldson, Mrs Thomas Martine, 219
Roos, Major, iii, vii, 112, 113, 114, 118
Roos, Major James Claude Vivian, 234, 245, 257, 259
Roosevelt, Theodore, 211
Rosalind [Toynbee], 8, 140
Rossetti, Dante Gabriel, 71, 157, 165, 169, 170, 182, 207, 213, 274
Rubens, the, 77
Rubens, Walter, 77
Ruskin, John, 157, 293
Russell, Bertrand, 164, 221
Ruth, 105, 122
Ruth [Howard], 140
Sackville, Gilbert, 164, 237
Saffery, Adele, 121, 148, 234
Saffery, Mrs, 11, 97

Sally, 142, 148, 149
Salmond, Mrs Norman, 22, 48, 184, 190
Sams, Sapper, 149, 196
Sargent, 43, 44, 49, 68, 129
Sargent, John Singer, 168, 169, 171, 172, 188, 198, 199, 213, 218, 247, 289, 290
Schanter, Irene, 264
Schubert, 272, 279
Schubert, Franz, 272
Scott, Katie, 60, 72
Selincourt, Bridget and her mother [de Selincourt], 22
Sellar, Marjorie, 12, 13, 234
Sellar, Mrs Craig, 8
Senons, Gilles, 280
Shakespeare, Mr, 3, 10
Shakespeare, William, 183, 190
Shaw, George Bernard, 174, 282
Sheard, Thomas Frederick Mason, 163
Sheila, 22, 62, 96, 99, 144
Sheila [Ranalow], 13, 50, 54
Shuttleworth babies, 66
Shuttleworth, Sibell, 26, 32, 68, 116
Shuttleworth, Sibell [see Kay-Shuttleworth], 66
Sibell [Kay-Shuttleworth], 39
Sibyl, 7, 44, 57, 68, 110, 230
Silk, Dorothy, 143, 190
Simonds, Mary Hope Mellor, 170, 290
Simonds, Mrs, 79
Sissie [Craies, Sissie], 4, 8, 11, 22, 33, 45, 53, 54, 56, 66,

68, 74, 75, 90, 97, 110, 111,
  115, 117, 118, 119, 123,
  127, 130, 142, 143, 145
Sissie, Aunt, 120
Slade, Cuthbert, 219
Slade, Kathleen Scovell, 219
Slade, Lady, 53
Sloop, Mrs, 128
Smith, Miss, 44, 48, 129
Somers, Mr, 135, 178
Somerset, Duchess of, 19
Somervell, Antonia, 25, 101,
  106, 191
Somervell, Arthur, 191, 238
Somervell, Edith, 191, 238
Somervell, Hubert, 136, 191
Somervell, Katherine (Kitty),
  115, 130, 134, 191, 210,
  287, 288
Somervell, Kitty, 191
Somervell, Mr and Mrs, 140
Somervell, Mrs, 101
Somervell, Ronnie, 105, 191
Somervells, the, 117, 118,
  136, 140, 142
Somerville, Mrs, 12, 231
Somerville, Mrs John, 13
Sparrow, Miss, 5, 9, 11, 13,
  86, 231
Speed, Clara, 163, 171, 213
Speed, Harold, 163, 171, 213
Speeds, the, 58, 100, 119
Spencer, Dr Heatley, 31, 33,
  50, 64, 159
Spencer, Peggy McInnes, 33,
  50, 159
Spencer, William I., 159
Spencer-Churchill, Consuelo
  Vanderbilt, 267
Speyer, Ferdinand, 164, 165

Speyer, Lady, 18, 165
Speyer, Stella, 7, 88, 120, 128,
  145, 164, 165
Speyer, Stella and Mr, 11
Speyers, 62
Spring Rice, Mary, 219
St John Hornby, Charles
  Harold, 190, 236
St John Hornby, Cicely
  Barclay, 190, 236
St John Lucas, Mr, 214
St Maur, Susan, 195
Stan, Cousin [Baldwin], 66,
  86, 88, 106, 118, 141
Stan, Cousin and Betty
  [Baldwin], 128
Stan, Cousin and Oliver, 32
Stan, Uncle [Baldwin], 129
Stanford, Mrs, 72, 219
Stella, 111
Stella [Beech], 120, 145
Stella [Thirkell, George], 130,
  138, 139, 142
Stella, Auntie, 118, 119, 120,
  122, 123, 124, 145
Stephen [Glenconner], 104
Stevenson, Miss, 5
Stevenson, Robert Louis, 165,
  270
Stillman, Lisa, 172
Stillman, Maria Spartali, 172
Stillman, Mrs, 42, 102, 142
Stillman, W. J., 172
Stillmans, the, 49
Stirling, Charles, 219
Stirling, Wilhelmina
  Pickering, 219
Stirlings, the, 103
Stoop, Mrs, 128

319

321

Talbot, Mr and Mrs Jack, 37, 226
Taparell, Mr, 76, 226
Thicknesse, Mrs, 71, 226
Thomas, Inigo, 135, 226
Thompson, Sylvia, 98, 226
Timothy, Miss, 9, 226
Tor, Mrs, 99, 227
Trollope, Miss, 13, 227
Twisleton, Miss, 11, 227
Veronica, 101, 227
Wallers, Mrs, 131, 227
Ward, Mr, 7, 227
Warren, Christopher, 133
Weisse, Miss, 12, 227
Whall, Mr, 128, 227
Whall, Mr (brother), 129, 227
Wilkinson, Mr, 144, 227
Wingates, Miss, 43, 227
Winn, Miss, 7, 227

PLACES

A&N [Army and Navy Stores], vi, 97
A.S.C. [Army Service Corps], vii
Academy, the, 17, 19, 88, 122
Adelphi Terrace, 252, 258
Aeolian Hall, 17, 36, 52, 66, 141, 183, 263, 274
Agnew's Gallery, 293
Air Ministry, 127
Albemarle Club, 3, 14, 20, 33, 36, 42, 245, 246, 274
Albert Hall, 41, 185, 284, 285
Alhambra, 65, 283
Amateur Art Exhibition, 122, 293

Ambassadors, 41, 61, 156, 283, 285, 286
Anglo South American Depot, vi, 120, 121, 122, 123, 124, 125
Apsley House, 56, 263
Astley, 76, 77
Astley Hall, 237, 240
Aubrey House, 91, 249, 257, 263
Aurora (painting), 100
Australian Club, 104, 106, 107, 123
Australian Imperial Force's Administrative Headquarters, 257
Australian Officers' Club, 103, 286
B & K Electric, 60, 70, 88, 255
B'Mouth [Bournemouth], vii, 13, 30
Bailey's Hotel, 20, 251
Balham, 18, 22, 76, 249, 258, 263
Balliol, 19, 265
Barnes, 32, 250
Bateman's, 162, 241
Bath, 43, 73, 232, 263
Bath Club, 30, 32, 43, 70, 134, 135, 159, 177, 245
Beacon Hotel, 20
Bechstein Hall, 89, 263
Bedford College, 65
Belgrave Square, 21, 23, 101, 108, 115, 235
Berkeley, 53, 65, 97, 110, 115, 125, 251
Berks and Wilts Downs, 30

323

325

MUSIC

328

PLAYS

Made in United States
North Haven, CT
18 September 2022

24277847R10192